The Values-Driven Organization

Based on significant new research from multiple sources, Richard Barrett creates a compelling narrative about why values-driven organizations are the most successful organizations on the planet. According to Barrett, understanding employees' needs—what people value—is the key to creating a high performing organization. When you support employees in satisfying their needs, they respond with high levels of employee engagement—they willingly bring their commitment and creativity to their work.

This book updates and brings together, in one volume, two of Richard Barrett's previous publications, *Liberating the Corporate Soul* (1998) and *Building a Values-Driven Organisation* (2006), to provide a reference manual for leaders and change agents who wish to create a values-driven organization. The text provides both a leadership approach and a language for organizational transformation and culture change that incorporates concepts such as cultural entropy, values alignment and whole system change.

With an updated set of cultural diagnostic tools and a wide range of new and exciting case studies on culture and leadership development, *The Values-Driven Organization* will be essential reading for students, researchers and practitioners in the fields of organizational change, leadership and ethics.

Richard Barrett is Founder and Chairman of Barrett Values Centre. He is a Visiting Lecturer at the Consulting and Coaching for Change leadership course run jointly by HEC Executive Education in Paris, France and the Saïd Business School, University of Oxford, UK. He is also an Adjunct Professor at Royal Roads University, Canada and is a Visiting Lecturer at Exeter University, UK.

"Richard Barrett has made extraordinary contributions to our understanding of the seemingly nebulous yet critical topics of organizational values and culture. His frameworks for measuring cultural entropy and enabling whole system transformation are elegant, deceptively simple and yet dramatic in their practical implications. Richard's thinking is expansive, his reservoir of knowledge is vast and his connection to timeless wisdom is profound. His work is indispensable to the Conscious Capitalism movement."

Raj Sisodia, Co-founder and Co-Chairman, Conscious Capitalism Inc and Professor of Marketing at Bentley University, USA.

The Values-Driven Organization

Unleashing human potential for performance and profit

Richard Barrett

Routledge
Taylor & Francis Group

LONDON AND NEW YORK

First published 2014
by Routledge
2 Park Square, Milton Park, Abingdon, Oxon OX14 4RN

Simultaneously published in the USA and Canada
by Routledge
711 Third Avenue, New York, NY 10017

Routledge is an imprint of the Taylor & Francis Group, an informa business

British Library Cataloguing in Publication Data
A catalogue record for this book is available from the British Library

Library of Congress Cataloging in Publication Data
The values-driven organization: unleashing human potential for
performance and profit / Richard Barrett.
  pages cm
Includes bibliographical references and index.
1. Corporate culture. 2. Organizational behavior. 3. Values.
4. Management–Social aspects. I. Title.
HD58.7.B3714 2013
658.3'124–dc23   2013003834

ISBN: 978-0-415-81502-4 (hbk)
ISBN: 978-0-415-81503-1 (pbk)
ISBN: 978-0-203-06651-5 (ebk)

Typeset in Times New Roman
by Cenveo Publisher Services

MIX
Paper from
responsible sources
FSC   FSC® C013056
www.fsc.org

Printed and bound in Great Britain by
TJ International Ltd, Padstow, Cornwall

Contents

Figures

Tables

Foreword

Values-driven organizations are the most successful organizations on the planet.

You may think that sounds like a bold claim: It is a bold claim; and, it is true! My promise to you is by the time you get to the end of this book you will not only understand why values-driven organizations are the most successful on the planet, you will also understand what steps you need to take to: (a) create a values-driven organization; and (b) ensure that your organization continues to reap the rewards of being values driven well into the future. Let me explain why I believe values-driven organizations are the most successful organizations on the planet.

The flowering of democracy

At this point in our collective human history we are witnessing an unprecedented shift in human values. Millions of people all over the world are demanding their voices be heard, not just in how our nations are governed, but also in how our organizations are run. They want equality, fairness, openness and transparency; they want to be responsible and accountable for their lives; and, they want to trust and be trusted. They also want to work for organizations that are seen to be ethical and do the right thing in the eyes of society. They want to feel pride in the organization they work for.

More people than ever before want to be involved and consulted in choosing the values that are used in governing their lives. And if you have individuated—reached the stage in your psychological development where you are seeking freedom and independence—you will want to live in a nation and work in an organization that believes in the principles of democracy—in a nation and an organization that embraces equality, accountability, fairness, openness and transparency.

Over the past six years, WorldBlu,[1] an organization that accredits work places that live by democratic principles, has attracted hundreds of organizations to its cause. I am proud to say that my own organization, Barrett Values Centre, made the WorldBlu list of most democratic workplaces at our first attempt in 2012. Some of the more well-known companies that have been accredited by WorldBlu include Zappos.com, HCL Technologies, New Belgium Brewery, DaVita, Great Harvest Bread Company and the WD-40 Company.

Just in case you thought that democratic principles can only be implemented in small companies, the organizations that made the WorldBlu list of democratic workplaces in 2012 ranged in size from five employees to 90,000. In the press release that announced the 2012 list of accredited organizations, Traci Fenton, the founder of WorldBlu, makes the following statement:

> We have evolved from the Industrial Age, a manufacturing-centric period of our history in which the command-and-control model of business arguably worked, to a new, Democratic Age—an age of unprecedented transparency that enables a power-to-the-people ethos unlike anything we've ever before seen. This new, Democratic Age requires that businesses and their leaders embrace an entirely new operating system, one that is based on freedom— not the outdated model of fear and control. When we consciously choose to design our workplaces based on freedom, rather than fear and control, we unleash human greatness, build world-class organizations, and change the world for the better.[2]

Evolution of human consciousness

Wherever you look in the world you can see this evolution of consciousness occurring. Fifty years ago we were content to live and work in hierarchical, authoritarian governance structures. We were thankful to have a job and sufficient income to meet our family's needs. Today, this is not enough.

The unprecedented growth in income and prosperity over the past four decades has created a new global middle class who have met their basic needs and are now looking to satisfy their growth needs. They want freedom and equality and they want to be accountable for their own futures—they want to embrace democratic values in every aspect of their lives.

Organizations that recognize this evolution in consciousness nurture the psychological development of their employees by creating a culture that dispenses with control, hierarchy, status and fear, and promotes freedom, equality, accountability, fairness, openness, transparency and trust.[3] By focusing on the evolution of consciousness of their employees—building their skills, nurturing their talents and supporting them in their individuation (finding their freedom and autonomy) and self-actualization (finding their passion and purpose)—these organizations are attracting the most talented people.

It is becoming increasingly clear, that to succeed in the twenty-first century individually as a professional, or collectively as an organization, you need to differentiate yourself not by what you do, but by *who you are* and *how you do what you do*.

> In this networked global economy, it is getting harder for organisations and individuals to succeed solely on the basis of what they produce or the services they provide. ... If you make something new (or better, faster, and/ or cheaper), the competition quickly comes up with a way to make it still better and deliver it at the same or an even lower price.[4]

Consequently, in the twenty-first century, quality, price, speed and service will no longer be enough to guarantee success: You will also need to operate with integrity, and be 100 per cent focused on building a sustainable future for your employees, your customers, the communities where you are based and for society in general.

I predict that in the twenty-first century, the rat race will be replaced by the values race.

If you want to succeed in business in the era we are now entering, your values must be evidenced in every decision you make and every action you take. Furthermore, your behaviours must align with your values—you must be seen to be walking the talk and operating with integrity. This is important, not just for building societal goodwill, it is also important for building the resilience of your organization.

Resilience and goodwill

In order to be sustainable in the twenty-first century organizations need to strengthen their resilience and increase societal goodwill.

Rosabeth Moss Kanter, professor of Harvard Business School and chair of the Harvard University Advanced Leadership Initiative, believes that a focus on values and culture enables an organization to fulfil these two objectives.[5]

> In the face of turbulence and change, culture and values become the major source of continuity and coherence, of renewal and sustainability. Leaders must be institution-builders who imbue the organisation with meaning that inspires today and endures tomorrow. They must find an underlying purpose and a strong set of values that serve as a basis for longer-term decisions even in the midst of volatility. They must find the common purpose and universal values that unite highly diverse people while still permitting individual identities to be expressed and enhanced. Indeed, emphasizing purpose and values helps leaders support and facilitate self-organizing networks that can respond quickly to change because they share an understanding of the right thing to do.[6]

The reason why leaders and organizations need to embrace and live their most deeply held values is because that is how they generate trust. Trust builds internal cohesion and external goodwill. Only when we build trust can we form meaningful relationships inside our organizations and empathic connections with stakeholders outside our organizations.

In *Trust: The Social Virtues and the Creation of Prosperity*, Francis Fukuyama states:

> One of the most important lessons we can learn from economic life is that a nation's well-being, as well as its ability to compete, is conditioned by a single, pervasive cultural characteristic: the level of trust inherent in a society.[7]

He goes on to say:

> Widespread mistrust in a society … imposes a kind of tax on all forms of economic activity, a tax that high-trust societies do not have to pay.[8]

The tax that Fukuyama refers to, I call "cultural entropy." Cultural entropy[9] is the degree of dysfunction in an organization or any human group structure (community or nation) that is generated by the self-serving, fear-based actions of the leaders. As cultural entropy increases, the level of trust and internal cohesion decreases. To gain trust, the leaders have to operate with authenticity and live with integrity. They have to demonstrate that they care about their people and the common good.

At some point in the distant past, our evolutionary forefathers learned to evaluate each new person they came into contact with as a potential friend or foe. It was programmed into our DNA as a survival mechanism. We still do it today, automatically, without thinking. Consequently, the first thing you want to know, whenever you enter into a relationship with another person or a group, such as an organization, is: Can you trust this person or the leaders of the organization you want to get involved with? You intuitively understand that your future well-being, safety and survival could depend on the judgment you make about this person's character or the character of the leaders of the organization.

When you work in an organization, the level of trust you have in your supervisor, manager or leader not only influences how open, candid and honest you are, it also influences the efficiency and performance of the organization. When you are suspicious of someone, you will not disclose your innermost thoughts. You keep things back; you are tentative with your opinions, and you are guarded in the ideas that you share. You avoid connecting and cooperating with people you do not trust.

In *The Speed of Trust*, Stephen Covey states:

> Trust always affects outcomes—speed and cost. When trust goes up, speed will also go up, and costs will go down. When trust goes down, speed will also go down, and costs go up.[10]

Watson Wyatt, a global, human capital consulting firm, highlighted the financial importance of creating a high trust culture in their 2002 research report on WorkUSA.

> Three-year total returns to shareholders are significantly higher at companies with high trust levels, clear linkages between jobs and objectives, and employees who believe the company manages change well … Only 39 percent of employees in US companies trust their senior leaders. In addition, the percentage of employees who say they have confidence in the job being done by senior management dropped five points between 2000 and 2002 to 45 percent.[11]

Bill George a professor at Harvard Business School, and former chief executive of Medtronic, the world's leading medical technology company, states:

> What concerns me are the many powerful business leaders who bowed to stock market pressure in return for personal gain. They lost sight of their True North and put their companies at risk by focusing on the trappings and spoils of leadership instead of building their organisations for the long term ... The result was a severing of trust with employees, customers, and shareholders ... In business trust is everything.[12]

Leaders build trust when they live authentically in alignment with their most deeply held human values. If you want to succeed in the twenty-first century, you will need to become a trusted member of our global society, and you will need to become a values-driven leader.[13] You will need to do this, not just to gain advantage over your competitors, but to protect the investments you make in your company and build its resilience.

David Gebler, a recognized expert on culture and compliance, believes the cultures created by our leaders can be a significant risk factor to a company's success.[14] The truth of this assertion has been evidenced in recent years by the scandals and subsequent failures of Enron, Tyco International, WorldCom and several other organizations. These scandals, which cost investors billions of dollars and destroyed the pension rights of thousands of people, shook public confidence in the national securities markets. In all these corporate scandals the values of the leaders and the cultures they created were the root cause of these failures.

More recently the lack of moral authority shown by the leaders of HSBC and Barclays Bank has resulted in heavy fines and a shift in customers' business to more ethical banks. Companies who are not paying attention to how they do things are being punished by the authorities and consumers. In the words of Dov Seidman, an authority in the ethical conduct of organizations and author of *How: Why How We Do Anything Means Everything*:

> It is no longer *what* you do that matters most and sets you apart from others, but *how* you do what you do. Sustainable advantage and enduring success—both for companies and the people who work for them—now lie in the realm of how, the new frontier of conduct.[15]

A lapse in moral integrity or a failure to live by acceptable rules of morality can significantly impact your bottom line or even worse, contribute to the failure of your organization.

What this means is that your values are not just the new arena of competitive advantage, they are the *sine qua non* for effective leadership: *Who you are and what you stand for have become just as important as the quality of the products and services that you sell.* As the leader of an organization, you court financial disaster if you and your staff do not operate with the highest levels of ethical integrity. Leaders who do not pay the strictest attention to the values and culture of their organization are a liability.

As the leader and steward of your organization, it will be incumbent on you to display the highest levels of ethical leadership and ensure your leadership team and every employee does the same. Lapses in ethics have cost companies billions of dollars over the past few decades and, in some cases, like Barings Bank, led to the downfall of the company.

Barings was the oldest merchant bank in London until its collapse in 1995. One of the bank's employees, Nick Leeson, lost US$1.3 billion speculating primarily on futures contracts. Because of the absence of oversight and a lack of ethical values, Leeson was able to make seemingly small gambles in the futures arbitrage market at Barings Futures Singapore and cover for his shortfalls by reporting these losses as gains to Barings in London by corrupting the accounts.

He was able to get away with this because Leeson doubled as both the floor manager for Barings' trading on the Singapore International Monetary Exchange (SIMEX) and head of settlement operations. Two different employees would normally have held these positions. In effect, Leeson was able to operate with no supervision from London.

After the collapse, several observers, including Leeson himself, placed much of the blame on the bank's deficient internal auditing and risk management practices. In *Rogue Trader*, Leeson states: "People at the London end of Barings were all so know-all that nobody dared ask a stupid question in case they looked silly in front of everyone else."[16]

An internal memo dated in 1993 had warned the London headquarters about allowing Leeson to be both trader and settlement officer. "We are in danger of setting up a system that will prove disastrous." Nothing was done.

In January 1995, SIMEX expressed concern to the bank about Leeson's dealings, but to no avail as the bank still wired him $1 billon to continue his trading. A report by the Singapore authorities into the collapse regards with disbelief the protestations by Leeson's superiors, all of whom were forced to resign, that they knew nothing of Leeson's corrupt activities. The problem at Barings Bank was a problem of culture. And the problem began at the top.

What the leaders of Barings Bank failed to do was to follow the advice given by Tom Peters and Robert H. Waterman, Jr. in their all-time best seller, *In Search of Excellence: Lessons from America's Best-Run Companies*, published in 1982. Peters and Waterman state: "Clarifying the value system and breathing life into it are the greatest contributions a leader can make."[17] This is just as true and even more important today than when Peters and Waterman wrote these words more than three decades ago!

Navigating complexity and dealing with uncertainty

In addition to the commitment benefits that accrue from *nurturing the individuation and self-actualization of your employees* and *creating internal cohesion and external goodwill*, values-based governance structures help you to clarify your decision-making processes when you encounter complex situations that you have never experienced before. They also help you navigate through uncertainty.

The world is a vastly different place from what it was 50 years ago. Global climate change, terrorism, internal wars and conflicts, international crime, corruption, drug trafficking, pandemics and sovereign debt crises are making the world a much more complex place to do business in than ever it was before.

Every year, almost without exception, every sector of business becomes more complex. Along with this increase in complexity, we are also experiencing an increase in uncertainty. Rapidly emerging economies such as Brazil, Russia, India and China are changing the face of international business. Competition is increasing all over the world and at the same time we are growing more interdependent. Knowing what to do and how to successfully navigate this rapidly changing business and economic landscape has become increasingly difficult and stressful.

We can no longer rely on the beliefs we have accumulated based on our past experiences to make decisions about the future. We are living in a new world. We need a new way of making decisions—a new guidance system that gets to the heart of what it means to preserve human life and increase the well-being of people. We need to let our deeply held human values dictate our decisions.[18]

Business as saviour

The complexity and uncertainty in our modern world are exacerbated by the fact that many of the major issues we are facing are global but the structures we have for dealing with them are national. There is no global governance structure to regulate the world.[19] In the international world of politics there is no consensus on what to do about the global commons. The most powerful nations of the world continue to focus on their own self-interest; they cannot be relied upon to work for the global common good.

I believe we have to turn to business if we want to create a sustainable future for humanity. For me, the following statement by Willis Harman, co-founder of the World Business Academy, rings more true each year:

> Business has become the most powerful institution on the planet. The dominant institution in any society needs to take responsibility for the whole. But business has not had such a tradition. This is a new role, not well understood or accepted. So business has to adopt a tradition it has never had throughout the entire history of capitalism: to share responsibility for the whole. Every decision that is made, every action that is taken, must be viewed in the light of that responsibility.[20]

Our business leaders are not just business leaders, they are also, along with their families, citizens of our global society: They are part of our common humanity. The future our leaders are creating, through the decisions they make today, will be the future their children and their children's children will inherit. To make the *right* decisions, they and every one of us needs to care about our children's and grandchildren's futures. It is time to put intergenerational fairness on everyone's agenda.

> Think of it like this: You are invited to a dinner party along with other people. Half the people don't show up because they were travelling in a car which breaks down. Meanwhile, dinner gets started. The food is delicious. Everyone eats their share, but they are still hungry. They don't know what has happened to the other guests. So they decide to have a good time, enjoy themselves, and finish off all the food. Then the other guests arrive—four hours late. There is no food left. The guests who arrived late are very hungry, but there is nothing left to eat.
>
> Think of the "other guests" as future generations, and think of "food" as the world's natural (mineral and ecological) resources. That will give you an idea about the meaning of intergenerational fairness, or intergenerational equity, as it is sometimes known.[21]

Making decisions that take account of the needs of future generations is not a new idea. In 1987, the Brundtland Report, commissioned by the UN General Assembly, provided long-term development strategies for achieving sustainable ecological development. The Brundtland Commission defined sustainable development in the following manner: "Sustainable development is development that meets the needs of the present without compromising the ability of future generations to meet their own needs." If we go further back in history we find that the Constitution of the Iroquois Nation in North America contained the following clause:

> In all of your deliberations in the Confederate Council, in your efforts at law making, in all your official acts, self interest shall be cast into oblivion. Cast not over your shoulder behind you the warnings of the nephews and nieces should they chide you for any error or wrong you may do, but return to the way of the Great Law which is just and right. Look and listen for the welfare of the whole people and have always in view not only the present but also the coming generations, even those whose faces are yet beneath the surface of the ground – the unborn of the future Nation.[22]

When you expand your sense of identity in this way, by caring about future generations and see yourself as a member of our global society, you will find that your consciousness expands too. You will begin to realize that you can only consider yourself successful if everyone you identify with is successful. To do this you must shift your motivation and focus from "I" to "we".

The shift from "I" to "we"

It is clear to me that our modern society, and the business world in particular, are suffering from too many leaders who are focused on their own self-interest.

We need a new leadership paradigm—a shift in focus from "I" to "we"; from *"what's in it for me"* to *"what's best for the common good"*; and from *"being the best* in *the world"* to *"being the best* for *the world."*[23]

The first shift from "I" to "we" requires our leaders to put the interest of their organization ahead of their own self-interest. In *Good to Great*,[24] Jim Collins calls these people level 5 leaders. What distinguishes them from other leaders is they channel their ego needs away from themselves and into the larger goal of building a great company. It is not that these leaders have no ego or self-interest: Indeed, they are incredibly ambitious, but their ambition is first and foremost for the institution, not themselves. They identify with the organization and every employee. When you identify with something or someone, you care for it, or them.

The failure of business leaders to make this first shift from "I" to "we" is the single most important inhibitor of a company's sustainable performance. Ego-driven leaders may be charismatic, but they are also a tremendous liability to their organizations. Their focus on their own self-interest will always ultimately be at the expense of the success of the organization.

The second shift from "I" to "we" requires business leaders to embrace not just the interests of their organization, but the interests of their partners with whom they have formed strategic business alliances, as well as the interests of the local communities in which they operate. Having partners that support one another builds mutual resilience; caring about the well-being and sustainability of the local communities where you operate builds societal goodwill.

The third shift from "I" to "we" involves not just supporting the interests of your business partners and the local communities in which you operate, but supporting the interests of all your stakeholders—employees, suppliers, customers and shareholders as well as the interests of our global society. Wherever there are people that "touch" your business, you need to show them you care about their needs. This concept of caring about all your stakeholders lies at the heart of the growing interest in conscious capitalism. I will discuss the benefits that come from this approach in more detail in Chapter 2.

Each of these three shifts from "I" to "we" requires the leader and the leadership team to expand their sense of identity to include all the organization's stakeholders. Expanding your sense of identity in this way is synonymous with expanding your level of consciousness.

In the twenty-first century our business leaders will need to be seen to be caring not just for all their stakeholders, but also for the poor, the disadvantaged and the ecology of the environment in which we all live and upon which we depend for our survival. In short, you will need to be seen to be caring not only for everyone who "touches" your company, but for everyone that is part of our global society—for the whole of humanity and our collective life support system.

Our business leaders need to face up to the fact that business has become a wholly owned subsidiary of society, and society has become a wholly owned subsidiary of the environment (the planet Earth). If we lose our environment and our life-support systems, our society will perish. If we lose our society, we will lose our economy, and our businesses will perish too.

Conclusions

At this point in our human history, leading a values-driven life is not just a societal imperative; it is also a personal imperative for millions of people around the world who are currently individuating and moving towards self-actualization. These are not only potentially the most successful people on the planet, they also represent the most intelligent, the most creative, and once they have found an organization where they can find and fulfil their sense of purpose in life, the most enthusiastic and committed employees you can find. These are exactly the people you want in your organization if you are going to increase your ability to survive and thrive.

To be successful in the values race, the values that your organization embraces must not only align with the values your employees live by and aspire to, they must also align with the values of the societies in which you operate.

Do not fall into the trap that so many leaders fall into, believing they are the ones that should choose the organization's values. Everyone in your organization needs to be involved in choosing the organization's espoused values. If you are the leader of your organization you get to have the final choice, but the shortlist of values you choose from should be those that are embraced by the majority of the employee population. Without this participation and interaction with the employees, the values will not be embraced and will not be lived or shared.

The values you choose for your organization must guide all your decision making: Both what you do, and how you do it. They must be embedded in every policy, system and process of your organization, and completely govern how everyone in your organization behaves. They must be built into your incentive and reward structures. You must internalize the values-race by promoting those who exemplify the organization's values.

You cannot become a values-driven organization if you operate with a culture of fear. Fear undermines trust, destroys internal cohesion and prevents people from individuating and self-actualizing. You must eliminate fear from your organization if you want to be a contender in the values race.

Summary

Here are the main points of the Foreword:

1. There are four main reasons why people are paying more attention to values—the flowering of democracy, the evolution of human consciousness, the need to build resilience and goodwill and the need to navigate increased complexity.
2. Because of the increase in global prosperity, millions of people all over the world have been able to meet their basic needs and are now awakening to their higher order needs. They are seeking to live in nations and work in

organizations that embrace democratic principles—values such as freedom (autonomy), equality, accountability, fairness, openness and transparency.

3. In the twenty-first century, the rat race will be replaced by the values race.
4. We need a new leadership paradigm—as shift in focus from "I" to "we"; from *"what's in it for me"* to *"what's best for the common good"*; and from *"being the best* in *the world"* to *"being the best* for *the world."*
5. Business has become a wholly owned subsidiary of society, and society has become a wholly owned subsidiary of the environment (the planet Earth). If we lose our environment and our life-support systems, our society will perish. If we lose our society, we will lose our economy, and our businesses will perish too.

Notes

1   www.worldblu.com/ (last accessed 3 June 2013).
2   Traci Fenton, Inspiring Democracy in the Workplace: From Fear-Based to Freedom-Centered Organizations, *Leader to Leader Magazine*, Spring, 2012.
3   Part 2 of my book, *Love, Fear and the Destiny of Nations: The Impact of the Evolution of Human Consciousness on World Affairs*, describes these seven values in detail. These are the values that are necessary to build a high-trust democracy (see pages 195–302).
4   Dov Seidman, *How: Why How We Do Anything Means Everything* (New York: John Wiley & Sons), 2011, p. xiii.
5   http://blogs.hbr.org/kanter/2010/06/ten-essentials-for-getting-val.html (last accessed 28 March 2013).
6   "Imagining the Future of Leadership," *Harvard Business View Blog*, http://blogs.hbr.org/imagining-the-future-of-leadership/2010/05/adding-values-to-valuations-in.html (last accessed 28 March 2013).
7   Francis Fukuyama, *Trust: The Social Virtues and the Creation of Prosperity* (New York: Free Press Paperbacks), 1995, p. 7.
8   Francis Fukuyama, *Trust: The Social Virtues and the Creation of Prosperity* (New York: Free Press Paperbacks), 1995.
9   For a more detailed explanation of cultural entropy and how to measure it see Chapter 6.
10 Stephen M.R. Covey, *The Speed of Trust: The One Thing That Changes Everything* (New York: Free Press), 2006, p. 13.
11 www.watsonwyatt.com/research/printable.asp?id=w-557 (last accessed 28 March 2013).
12 Bill George, *True North: Discover Your Authentic Leadership* (San Francisco: Jossey-Bass), 2007.
13 Richard Barrett, *The New Leadership Paradigm* (Asheville, NC: Fulfilling Books), 2011.
14 Email exchange between the author and David Gebler, February 2010.
15 Dov Seidman, *How: Why How We Do Anything Means Everything* (New York: John Wiley & Sons), 2011.
16 Nicholas William Leeson, *Rogue Trader* (London: Warner Books), 1996.
17 Tom Peters and Robert H. Waterman, Jr., *In Search of Excellence: Lessons from America's Best-Run Companies* (London: Profile Books), 2004, p. 291. First published by Harper & Row, 1982.

18 The principal differences between belief-based decision making and values-based decision making are explained in the following chapter.

19 Richard Barrett, *Love, Fear and the Destiny of Nations: The Impact of the Evolution of Human Consciousness on World Affairs* (Bath: Fulfilling Books), 2012.

20 Willis Harman, *New Business of Business: Taking Responsibility for a Positive Global Future* (with Maya Porter).

21 Richard Barrett, *The New Leadership Paradigm* (Asheville, NC: Fulfilling Books), 2011, pp. 268–269.

22 www.constitution.org/cons/iroquois.htm (last accessed 19 June 2013).

23 Richard Barrett, *The New Leadership Paradigm* (Asheville, NC: Fulfilling Books), 2011.

24 Jim Collins, *Good to Great* (New York: HarperCollins), 2001.

Preface

The idea for this book came from an interaction with my publisher. In 2011, Routledge, who had recently bought the publishing rights to two of my previous books, *Liberating the Corporate Soul* (1998) and *Building a Values-Driven Organisation* (2006), suggested that I might like to update these titles in new editions. I agreed. However, since *Building a Values-Driven Organisation* was basically an update and expansion of *Liberating the Corporate Soul*, I suggested that we might think about combining the new editions of the two books into one, and updating the material with new research carried out since the publication of *Building a Values-Driven Organisation* in 2006.

As we continued to think about the new book, and a possible title, it became evident to me that this project could be much more than an update of the previous two books: It could become a project to create a basic and enduring text book for leaders, change agents and consultants on how to build a values-driven organization.

I felt inspired by this idea. It was a challenge that would allow me to incorporate a significant amount of relevant new research material on values, leadership and culture, and it would also allow me to incorporate material from my more recent books, *The New Leadership Paradigm* published in 2011, *Love, Fear and the Destiny of Nations (Volume 1)* published in 2012, and *What My Soul Told Me*, also published in 2012. With this thought in mind, I set about writing this book with enthusiasm and excitement.

Four mantras

I realized at the outset of this project that there were several principles I had set out in my earlier books that it would be important to incorporate in this book. These principles or mantras as I am fond of calling them form the philosophical bedrock of all my writings on organizational culture, performance and leadership. The four mantras are:

- Cultural capital is the new frontier of competitive advantage.
- Organizations don't transform, people do.

- Organizational transformation begins with the personal transformation of the leaders.
- Measurement matters: Whatever you measure (focus your attention on a regular basis) tends to improve.

With regard to this latter mantra, my point is that when you measure and map the values of an organization on a regular basis, and *act on the results* you will not only see a shift in values and behaviours, you will also see a shift in the culture of the organization. The shift you will observe will be evolutionary in nature—from a focus on the lower levels of organizational consciousness to a focus on full spectrum organizational consciousness, where all levels of consciousness are fully reflected in how the organization operates.

The same is true of individuals. When people get regular feedback on how they are coming across to others, and how they can improve their performance, they tend to modify their values and behaviours, eventually evolving towards full spectrum personal consciousness.

Full spectrum individuals and organizations are not only the most successful, they are also the most resilient. They are successful because they have developed the ability to respond appropriately to all life situations. The core competence that drives individuals and the leaders of organizations towards full spectrum consciousness is commitment—commitment to becoming all you can become as an individual or as an organization; commitment to personal and organizational fulfilment.

The central questions

The two central questions I want to address in this book are "What is the source of our commitment?" and "How do leaders create the conditions that engender high levels of commitment from their employees?" If you cannot wait to find the answers to these questions, then I suggest you take a peek at Chapter 16. If you can wait, then read on.

Building a high level of commitment is important because it creates employee engagement, and employee engagement raises performance and leads to success. The more engaged people are in their work, the more successful an organization becomes.

Part I of this book presents the evidence to support this statement and sets out four criteria that are necessary to increase employee engagement. The four criteria are:

- values alignment;
- mission alignment;
- personal alignment; and
- structural alignment.

Part II of the book focuses on the diagnostic tools that provide the information you need to work towards meeting the first two of these criteria—the values alignment and mission alignment of employees with their organizations. Part III of the book focuses on the diagnostic tools that provide the information you need to work towards meeting the third criterion—the personal alignment of the leaders, managers and supervisors of the organization. Part IV focuses on the fourth criterion—structural alignment: How to embed the values and behaviours that generate high levels of employee engagement into the cultural fabric of the organization.

Acknowledgements

After 15 years of using the Seven Levels of Consciousness Model and the Cultural Transformation Tools to measure, map and monitor the values of individuals and all forms of group structures (teams, organizations, communities and nations), I am convinced that when leaders are committed to change, the insights the model and tools provide can facilitate deep personal and cultural transformation. I am not alone in this conviction. Since 1997, more than 4,000 consultants and change agents in over 50 countries have learned how to use the models and tools I describe in this book. Many of these consultants have built successful consultancy practices by offering these tools, along with their expertise in change management, to their clients. Many of these change agents have successfully guided their organizations to higher levels of performance using these tools to support the cultural evolution of their organizations.

I am thankful to these consultants and change agents for the wonderful personal relationships we share, and for their constant support and feedback in continuing to develop the tools, as well as their generosity in sharing evolving best practices in cultural transformation, many of which form part of this book.

I am grateful to the wonderful team of people at Barrett Values Centre (BVC) for their commitment to the evolution of human consciousness, and I am indebted to our partner/trainers for spreading the word, helping us to constantly improve our trainings, and providing ongoing support to new users of the model and tools.

In particular I would like to thank the following partner/trainers: MaryJane Bullen, John Cambell, Sally-Anne Cotton, Melissa Dean, Beatrice Dewandre, Lisa Doig, Rita Haque, Tom Hatton, Hector Infer, Adolfo Jarrin, Niran Jiang, Sallie Lee, Sander Mahieu, Ellen Miller, Melanie Moeller, Chris Monk, Karen Muller, Helen Jane Nelson, Else Nollet, Hein Reitsma, Hugo Smith-Meyer, Dirk Spangenberg, Susan Spargo, Johan Spruyt, Takao Suzuki, Guy Tunnicliff, Helen Urwin, Pleuntje Van Meer and Cindy Vanover.

I would also like to thank past and present BVC team members: Mark Brooks, Jessica Brown, Allyn Chambliss, Catherine Clothier, Phil Clothier (CEO), Nathan Egge, Tor Eneroth, Christopher Gomez, Tyler Kim, Hannah Lee, Ella Long, Patrick McGuire, Ed Manning, Ashley Munday, Sara Olsen, Jenny Quinn, Emma Riley, Joan Shafer, Brittney Stauffer and Mark Tucker.

A big word of thanks also to some of our long-term users for their support and encouragement in helping us to fine tune the existing Cultural Transformation Tools, develop new tools and contributing to our research. These people include: Tom Brady, David Carter, Goren Garberg, David Gebler, Peter Paul Gerbrands, Per Hellsten, Annalise Jennings, Mark Lelliott, Judith Mills, Erik Muten, Tom Rausch, Johan Ryd, Sonia Stojanovic, Jim Ware and Cindy Wigglesworth.

Over the years, numerous other leaders, researchers, consultants and internal change agents have been very supportive of our work. These include Giovanna D'Alessio, Ane Araujo, Marcel van der Avert, Don Beck, Susan Beck, Gita Bellin, Tom Boardman, Jan Boethius, Anel Bosman, Hendrik Jan Bot, Caio Brisolla, Mike Brown, Rinaldo Brutico, Mike Budden, Ruth Butikofer, Sylvana Caloni, Martina Cinicola, Tess O'Kane Cope, John Counihan, Keith Cox, Bernardo Teixeira Diniz, Gary Dobkins, Uwie Dwitya, Vania Faria, Traci Fenton, Christine Feuk, Marc Gafni, Gwendoline Gerbrands, Kiran Gulrajani, Chris Hagen, Debbie Henderson, Vincent Ho, Elske Hooglugt, Gabriella Infer, Llewellyn de Jager, Bjarni Jónsson, Lena Langlet, Heinrich Langner, Hervé Lefèvre, John McFarlane, John Mackey, Rob Mallick, Odino Marcondes, Ted Marusarz, Sylvana Mello, Peter Merry, Beth Michaels, Michelle Miller, Karen Muller, Ahmad el Nashar, Marianna van Niekerk, Dov Seidman, John Smith, Marcello Palazzi, Lui Pangiarella, Adam Perry, Mark Rock-Perring, Niven Postma, Michael Rennie, Lelani Robertson, Arsenio Rogriguez, Rosanna Roos, Rich Ruhmann, Angela Ryan, Marie Ryd, Martin Sande, Shubhro Sen, Yevgeny Sinyakov, Raj Sisodia, Patrik Somers, Hubert St. Onge, Takao Suzuki, Robert Taen, Marilyn Taylor, Steve Trevino, Daniel Truran, Sharon Venn, Eric de Vries, Katherine Wainwright, Bernd Wanner, Andreas Welther, John Whitmore, Ella Zhang, Roberto Ziemer and Shirley Zinn.

The full list is much longer. I simply do not have the space to include everyone. I am sure I have forgotten some people who also deserve to be mentioned: To you I send my apologies.

Last, but not least, I wish to thank my partner, Christa Schreiber, for her practical, emotional and intellectual support. As a senior clinical psychologist, she has been instrumental in helping me to fine tune my ideas about the concepts of personal transformation included in this book.

Part I

Understanding values

Every excellent company we studied is clear on what it stands for, and takes the process of value shaping seriously. In fact, we wonder whether it is possible to be an excellent company without clarity on values and without having the right sorts of values.

Tom Peters and Robert H. Waterman, Jr., *In Search of Excellence*

The purpose of the Part I of this book is to provide the reader with a clear understanding of why values are so important, the role they play in our lives, and what it means to be a values-driven organization.

1 Values driven

What does it mean?

In order to understand why values-driven organizations are so successful, we must first understand what being "values-driven" means. To do that, we need to know what values are, where they come from and how values-based decision making is different from other forms of decision making.

What are values?

According to sociologists "values" are: "The ideals and customs of a society toward which the people have an effective regard." I prefer to define values in a more pragmatic way: "Values are a shorthand method of describing what is important to us individually or collectively (as an organization, community or nation) at any given moment in time." They are "shorthand" because the concepts that values represent can usually be captured in one word or a short phrase. For example, honesty, openness, compassion, long-term perspective and human rights can all be considered as values. Values are universal: They transcend contexts. Behaviours, on the other hand, are usually described in a "longhand" manner and are context dependent. For example, the behaviours associated with honesty, depending on the context, could be: (a) always tells the truth, (b) never tell a lie or (c) freedom from deceit or fraud.

What I am also suggesting is that because our values represent what is important to us *at any given moment in time*, our values are not fixed. The values that are important to you at this particular moment in your life are a reflection of the needs you are experiencing right now under your current life conditions. Examples of how value priorities change with age are shown in Figures 1.1 and 1.2.

Figure 1.1 shows the proportion of people in different age groups living in the UK who selected friendship as one of their top ten personal values.[1] You can see from this chart that friendship is an important priority for the young, but decreases in priority as we get older. One of the explanations for this could be because when we are single we have a greater need for companionship than when we get married and have families of our own.

Figure 1.2 shows the proportion of people in different age groups living in the UK who selected honesty as one of their top ten personal values. You can see from this chart that honesty takes on increasing importance as people get older,

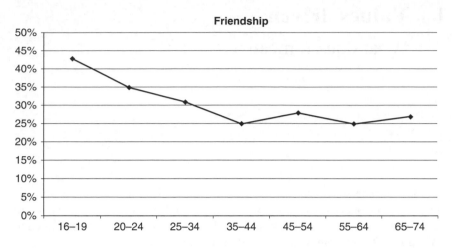

Figure 1.1 Proportion of people in different age groups in the UK who selected friendship as one of their top ten personal values.

but becomes slightly less of a priority for seniors. This does not mean necessarily that seniors are less honest than middle-aged people; it simply means that seniors have more pressing needs that may cause honesty to move to a lower priority ranking.

Not all our values change as we grow older. There are some values that we hold dear throughout our lives. For example, some people always have honesty as one of their core values. Others, as Figure 1.2 suggests, give more importance to

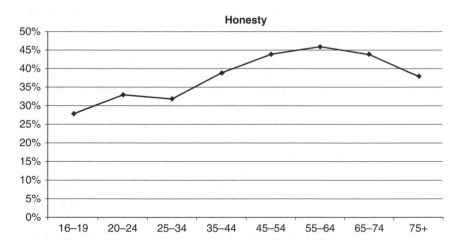

Figure 1.2 Proportion of people in different age groups in the UK selecting honesty as one of their top ten personal values.

honesty once they reach middle age. They begin to recognize that honesty is an important component of integrity, and integrity brings many benefits; not the least of which is that it is a significant enabler of trust. Trust facilitates personal and business interactions and enables us more easily to meet our needs. As soon as people recognize this, honesty begins to move up their value priority rankings.

You might find it useful to think about what unchanging (core) values you might have and write them down. Then think about how some of your values have changed; have become less important or more important over time as the circumstances of your life have changed, and also write them down. It is important to remember: *Your values are always a reflection of what you consider to be your needs.*

What are needs?

A need is something you want to get, have or experience that you believe will alleviate your suffering or distress, and make you happier or more aligned with who you are. Human beings experience three levels of needs.

I am well aware that the three levels of need shown in Table 1.1 are a gross simplification of the nuances that exist between needs, wants and desires. The distinction I have made however, between unfulfilled needs that cause us to be anxious and fearful and unfulfilled needs that are more like desires, is important. Let me explain why.

> The anxieties and fears that our leaders, managers and supervisors have about meeting their unmet needs, particularly their unmet emotional needs, are the principal source of the dysfunction we find in our organizations. They are also the principal source of the dysfunction we find in our own lives.

I will explore this topic in greater detail when I discuss the role and impact of the leader on an organization in Part III of this book. For now, let us simply focus on our human needs and how they relate to our values.

Table 1.1 Levels of need

Level of need	Description
Something you don't have you feel you absolutely need.	Something you consider important, that if you had you would feel less anxious or fearful.
Something you don't have enough of that you feel you absolutely need.	Something you consider important, that if you had more of you would feel less anxious or fearful.
Something you *would like to have* or desire that does not represent an immediate or pressing need.	Something that you don't have, that you believe would make you happier or improve your life in some way at some point in time in the future.

Basic needs and growth needs

One of the first researchers to make the link between needs, values and motivations was Abraham Maslow. Maslow (1908–70), who was a philosopher and one of the foremost spokespersons for humanistic and positive psychology, identified two basic types of human needs:

• Basic needs—also known as "deficiency" needs.
• Growth needs—also known as "being" needs.

A basic need is something that is important to get, have or have more of, in order to feel safe, happy and comfortable in your existing physical and social environment.

A growth need is something you would like to have in order to feel a sense of *internal* alignment—at ease or at peace with yourself—and a sense of fulfilment about the contribution you are making in the world.

You feel anxious and fearful when you are unable to satisfy your basic needs, but once they are met, you no longer pay much attention to them. The reason you feel anxious or fearful when these needs are not met is because you need to be able to satisfy these needs to ensure your physiological and emotional well-being.

When you are able to satisfy your growth needs, they do not go away, they engender deeper levels of attention and commitment. The reason you feel motivated to satisfy your growth needs is because they allow you to become more fully who you are. Satisfying these needs is an integral part of the process of self-actualization.[2]

Maslow describes the relationship between our basic needs and growth needs in the following way: "Man's higher nature rests on his lower nature, needing it as a foundation … The best way to develop this higher nature is to fulfil and gratify the lower nature first."[3]

Table 1.2 identifies three types of basic needs (survival, relationship and self-esteem) and four types of growth needs (transformation, internal cohesion, making a difference and service). The basic needs appear at the bottom of the table and the growth needs appear at the top of the table. A brief explanation of the needs associated with each stage of psychological development is provided in column three of Table 1.2.

The three basic needs and four growth needs represent distinct stages in our psychological development. If we are not able to satisfy our needs at a particular stage, we stay at that stage until we can meet those needs or overcome the fears that are preventing us from satisfying those needs.

For example, you may be in a high-paying job that you find unsatisfying. What you would like to do is follow your passion in a low-paying job that is more meaningful to you. Taking a significant cut in income may bring up survival fears. If you allow these fears to dictate your actions, you will not be able to move to the next stage of your development—satisfying your need to find work that is meaningful to you.

We begin our lives at the first stage of development. As babies, we are subconsciously programmed by our DNA to value survival. We do whatever we can to

Table 1.2 Basic needs and growth needs[4]

Types of needs	Development levels	Need requirements
GROWTH NEEDS (Being needs)	Service	Satisfying your need to leave a legacy—to have led a life of significance that will be remembered.
	Making a difference	Satisfying your need to actualize your purpose by influencing or impacting the world around you.
	Internal cohesion	Satisfying your need for authenticity and to find meaning and purpose for your life.
	Transformation	Satisfying your need for autonomy, freedom and independence.
BASIC NEEDS (Deficiency needs)	Self-esteem	Satisfying your emotional need to be recognized by others as valuable or important because of your skills, talents or qualities.
	Relationship	Satisfying your emotional need for belonging, protection and connection.
	Survival	Satisfying your physiological needs for security—staying alive and keeping your body healthy.

get our survival needs met. As young children, we value safety and love: We conform, cultivate friendships and build relationships in order to feel safe and loved. As teenagers, we value recognition: We try to excel or be the best at something so that people respect us. We want to feel a sense of our own self-worth. As young adults, we value adventure and opportunities to get on in the world: We want freedom, autonomy and equality. As mature adults, we want our lives to have meaning: We want to find work that aligns with what we are passionate about. Once we have found our vocation, we want to make a difference. We seek out others we can collaborate with to increase the impact we can have on the world. Once we have experienced the joy that making a difference brings, we want to lead a life of selfless service. We want to leave a legacy that people will remember us by.

Full spectrum development

I refer to someone who has learned how to master the satisfaction of their basic needs *and* their growth needs as a *full spectrum individual*. Table 1.3 shows some of the characteristics displayed by full spectrum individuals. Abraham Maslow described such a people as a "healthy human specimens."

For Marc Gafni, a spiritual philosopher and Director of the Centre for World Spirituality, one of the key attributes of full spectrum individuals is that they are willing to fully embrace their own sense of uniqueness. The desire to answer the call of your personal Unique Self, not as an expression of ego, but as a property of your essence, begins to show up when you focus on your internal cohesion and

Table 1.3 Characteristics of a full spectrum individual[5]

Clearer, more efficient perception of reality.
Increased objectivity, detachment, transcendence of self.
Recovery of creativity.
Democratic character structure.
Autonomy, uniqueness.
Ability to love.
Increased spontaneity and expressiveness; full functioning; aliveness.

making a difference needs. Your Unique Self is the place from which you discover your ultimate purpose in living. At the service level, a full spectrum individual feels called to work towards the creation of a world where every human being is able to grow and develop so they can live their own Unique Self story. By engaging with your unique self, you are called to live a values-driven and purpose-driven life.

As you actualize your unique self, you grow to understand that your personal existence and your being is utterly distinct, worthy and needed in the world. You begin to recognize that the world is desperately in need of your unique and extraordinary gifts. Your ability to give your gifts depends on your ability to free yourself of limiting beliefs and any false notions of who you are, and instead, to identify with your source and the larger service you offer to the world. When you are able to identify with your Unique Self and your unique gifts, your life becomes infused with meaning.[6]

According to Marc, the concept of Unique Self also applies to organizations. When an organization has a unique perspective on the world, it does not attempt to imitate its competitors; rather it turns inward to understand its own unique offerings of service or products and focuses on giving them to the world. When this uniqueness is understood and embraced by all employees, the organization shifts rapidly from surviving to thriving. The unique offerings encapsulate the energy that guides and directs the business.

The unique organization cultivates its particular set of eyes to gain unique insight into the needs of market place and the needs of its customers. This, in turn, yields new opportunities for the organization to give its unique gifts in ways that serve the highest interests of all parties involved.

Finally, it needs to be said that there is a direct connection between the Unique Self of the leader and the Unique Self of the organization. Leaders who live their Unique Selves manifest unique businesses. And, the values implicit and explicit in the Unique Self of the leader will often become the values of the company.

The needs we focus on

The amount of attention we give to satisfying a specific set of needs such as our survival, relationship or self-esteem needs, depends on three main factors: The stage we have reached in our psychological development; the life circumstances we were born into or which we are currently experiencing; and the situation in which we find ourselves at a specific moment in time.

Psychological development

The point I want to stress about our psychological development is that each stage is associated with specific needs and therefore results in the expression of different values. As we grow and develop, our values change in accordance with our changing needs. Annex 1 provides a detailed explanation of our psychological needs at the different stages of our lives.

As we progress through the different stages of our lives, particularly in our working environment, we find our values gradually changing. As children, we value safety (survival level) and protection (relationship level); as teenagers and young adults, we value looking good and recognition (self-esteem level); as a single person pursuing a career, we value autonomy and continuous learning (transformation level); as a team leader or supervisor we value trust (internal cohesion level); as an evolved mature professional, we value making a difference; and as a leader or elder we value leaving a legacy (service level).

This is important to understand, because people's values are a reflection of their needs and their needs are a reflection of the stage they have reached in their psychological development. As you enter each new stage of your life, you will find some of your values changing because you will have new, additional needs that you did not have before. You will also find your value priorities changing in line with your needs.

Values that depend on life circumstances

To understand how our life circumstances affect our values, let us compare two different individuals. Let us assume one of them was born into a wealthy educated family in a rich liberal democracy, and one of them was born into a poor, remote farming community in a country ruled by Generals—an authoritarian regime. The person in the rich liberal democracy would take the values of health and safety (survival level), and freedom and equality (transformation level), for granted. They would be more focused on higher order values such as fairness, openness, transparency and trust (internal cohesion level). Meanwhile the individual living in the poor authoritarian regime would have a daily focus on survival, safety, health. Only when this person felt that he was able to satisfy these needs, would he turn his attention to freedom and equality, and only when he had freedom and equality, would he focus on fairness, openness, transparency and trust.

This hierarchical order of values/needs was strongly demonstrated to me recently when I was watching a BBC news report from Cairo in Egypt. The Egyptians had just elected President Mohamed Morsi. They had established freedom and now, spontaneously, they were focusing on the next higher order democratic value—equality. The news report was about groups of men patrolling the streets of Cairo to punish anyone they found harassing women. Meanwhile the police, who had always turned to a blind eye to sexual harassment, stood by and watched. Having established freedom, the people of Cairo were feeling an automatic urge to establish equality. Just a few weeks later, a few days after the new constitution was unveiled, the issue of equality came up again. Women protested in the streets because the phrase guaranteeing them equality in the draft constitution had been removed. Having established freedom, the women of Egypt were now fighting for equality.

Situational values

To understand how the situation you find yourself in affects your values, let us assume that after several years of employment, with a salary that allowed you to live comfortably, you suddenly find yourself without a job, and with few job prospects. You will immediately start to give much more focus to the value of financial stability (survival need) than you had done in the past. Or if, as a single person, you move your home to a new location, a considerable distance from your existing home, you will find yourself giving much more focus to the value of friendship (relationship need).

Four years ago, when I left my home in the US to look after my ageing mother in the UK, I found myself lonely—I was living in a town where I knew practically no one. Consequently, I found myself giving much more focus to the values of family and friendship (relationship level). Things I had taken for granted in my life in the US now became important to me because they were lacking.

As I cared for my mother, who by this time was bedbound, I noticed another shift. I found myself experiencing a deep level of compassion. This awakening to compassion has stayed with me ever since. It is now more than two years since my mother died, and every time I see an old lady in the street, I find myself thinking, what can I do to help this woman? Compassion is alive in me now because of the year I spent caring for my mother in the last year of her life.

Motivation, happiness and needs

The reason we focus our attention on the satisfaction of our basic needs is because we want to feel safe, secure, respected and happy. It is intrinsic to our nature. There is one specific thing that stops us from feeling happy—our fears. You feel safe, secure, respected and happy when you are able to meet your deficiency needs, but you feel anxious or fearful when you are prevented from meeting these needs or when the satisfaction of these needs is under threat—when you lose a job, when you lose a friend, a partner or a close companion, or when you feel people do not respect you.

> Happiness is the feeling (an emotional reaction) you experience when you are able to let go of the anxiety or fear you are holding onto about not being able to meet one of your deficiency needs or when you remember an experience from the past when you felt supported and your needs were met in a loving way.

You feel happiness when a loved one returns home safe and sound from a long trip; you feel happiness when you pass an important exam; you feel happiness when you get positive feedback—praised or acknowledged by someone you respect; and you may feel happiness when you get a new or bigger car or house, or the latest mobile phone or computer. You also feel happiness when a situation you are currently experiencing triggers a memory of a time when you felt loved and cared for.

The problem with happiness is that it is usually short lived. Once you release the anxiety or fear you had about not being able to get, have or experience what you need, you quickly fall back into your normal way of being.

People who are normally optimistic do not usually get weighed down by trying to satisfy their needs. They are content and happy with what they have and are able to adapt to what life brings them. Their experience of life is that they have always been able to get their needs met. Hence they are conditioned into being optimistic. On the other hand, people who are normally pessimistic feel they have many unmet needs. Their experience of life is that they have never been able to get their needs met. Hence they are conditioned into being pessimistic.

Contentment, joy and needs

The ability to meet your growth needs engenders a deeper feeling than happiness, and consequently a deeper level of motivation and commitment to the satisfaction of these needs. You experience joy and contentment when you are able to satisfy your growth needs because you are discovering who you really are—you are discovering your authentic self and finding a meaning for your life.

Whereas the surge of happiness you feel when you are able to meet one of your deficiency needs quickly dissipates, leaving you operating with your normal background disposition—somewhere between pessimism and fear at one end of the scale and optimism and hope at the other end of the scale, what you feel when you are able to satisfy your growth needs is joy. When joy dissipates it leaves you with a feeling of contentment. The joy and contentment you feel arise from your inner sense of alignment or a feeling of personal fulfilment.

The key to finding joy and contentment is to find a sense of purpose for your life—a purpose that gives your life meaning. Having purpose and meaning in life increases overall well-being and life satisfaction, and improves mental and physical health. It also enhances resilience and self-esteem and decreases the chances of depression.[7]

In a recent study,[8] nearly 400 Americans aged 18 to 78 were asked whether they thought their lives were meaningful and/or happy. Examining their self-reported attitudes toward meaning, happiness and many other variables such as stress, spending patterns and having children, the researchers found that a meaningful life and happy life overlap in certain ways, but are ultimately very different.

Happiness is mainly about satisfying *your* needs: meaning comes from tapping into and expressing your true nature and helping *others* to satisfy their needs. Whereas happiness makes you feel good, meaningful involvements can sometimes make you feel bad: They can increase stress, worry and anxiety.[9] Having children for example, is associated with a meaningful life, but may make you less happy, because it involves worry and self-sacrifice. Similarly, putting in extra hours at the office to get a job done (going the extra mile) may involve self-sacrifice, but you do it because you feel you are making a contribution to a cause bigger than yourself, which brings meaning to your life.

Thus the key to employee engagement is to help the people in your organization meet their deficiency needs *and* find a sense of meaning and purpose to their lives. Once they have found their sense of purpose then you need to align their purpose with the organization's purpose by giving them work that aligns with what they are passionate about. When you do this, you will be giving your employees a sense of meaning and fulfilment.

In summary, the payoff you get from being able to satisfy your deficiency needs makes you happy by alleviating your fears. However, the happiness you feel is usually short lived. On the other hand, the payoff you get from being able to satisfy your growth needs goes much deeper, and is more long lasting. It brings a sense of meaning to your life.

Thus, your potential for happiness, joy and contentment depends on:

1. The stage you have reached in your psychological development: Your potential for joy and contentment increases significantly when you reach the stage in your development where you begin to focus on your growth needs and find meaning and purpose in your life.
2. The degree to which the environments in which you live and work are able to satisfy your deficiency needs and nurture/support you in meeting your growth needs.

Engendering loyalty and commitment

These findings have significant implications for organizations. If you want to have a loyal, committed and creative workforce in your organization then you need to make sure that your employees are able to satisfy their deficiency needs, *and* you also need to provide programmes and opportunities for them to pursue and satisfy their growth needs. You need to support the psychological development of your employees by implementing structures, policies, systems and procedures that enable them to take care of their families, form friendships with people with whom they work, excel at what they do best, nurture and cultivate autonomy, find authenticity, meaning and purpose, have opportunities to make a difference, and, if possible, leave a positive legacy. This is what it means to become a values-driven organization.

Values-driven organizations live the values that align with the needs that employees have at every level of their psychological development. When this happens organizations experience a high level of employee engagement. Employees feel engaged because the organization enables them to fully meet their needs.

Values versus beliefs

The shift in consciousness that I spoke of in the Foreword to this book, which is causing millions of the people all over the world to individuate and self-actualize, is normally accompanied by a shift from belief-based decision making to values-based decision making.[10] The main differences between using your beliefs and using your values to make decisions are as follows:

1. Beliefs are contextual and cultural, whereas values are universal: Values transcend contexts, because they arise from the experience of being human. Beliefs, on the other hand, arise from the experiences we have in specific situations, and relate only to those situations: They apply only to the context in which we learned the belief.

2. Beliefs are assumptions we hold to be true: They may be true, or they may not be true. We just don't know. They may lead to positive outcomes or they may not. They assume the causal relationships of the past which led to the belief will also apply in the future. In a rapidly changing world this may not be true. Positive values, on the other hand, we know, create beneficial experiences. They always have done, and they always will do in the future. Why? Because they enable us to meet our human needs: They support our individual and collective survival, and they help us to improve the social conditions in which we live. Positive values build connectedness and help us create the future we want to experience. Beliefs (especially cultural and religious beliefs), on the other hand, support separation. For example, you can gather a group of clerics from different religious denominations around a table and it will be very difficult for them to come to an agreement on their beliefs. Where they get stuck is in their ideologies. However, if you ask them what their values are, it is highly likely they will quickly come to a consensus. The same is true of politicians from different political parties. They will probably all share similar values, but their beliefs may be very different.

If you want to explore and understand the difference between values and beliefs, I recommend you go to www.valuescentre.com/pva and do the free personal values assessment. After accessing the website, write in your email address (to receive your results), and complete the five-minute survey. When you have received your report, carry out the values, beliefs and behaviours exercise which is at the end of the report. For those of you who do not have a access to the internet, or want to use this exercise in a group situation, a shortened version of this exercise can be found in Annex 3.

When you do the values, beliefs and behaviours exercise in a family or group situation, you will notice that while people are sharing and discussing their values the level of energy in the room will shift. People become more animated and excited. Once they have started sharing, it is difficult to get them to stop.

When they have finished (allow about ten to 15 minutes) ask the participants the following questions:

• What did it feel like sharing your values with other people?
• What did it feel like listening to the other people in your group share their values?

The answers you get are always the same. Some people find it scary to share their values; other people find it energizing. Almost everyone feels a strong sense of connection to the people they have been sharing with because they find that they share similar values. This is the reason why people become animated and excited when they do this exercise: They are connecting at a deep level with the people whom they are sharing with. It is not just the fact that they share similar values that creates the sense of connectedness; it is the openness and vulnerability of the sharing that makes the difference. That is why some people find this exercise scary. They have never been so intimate with people they do not know before. Mutually sharing (what is important to us) builds trust. When we share our values we find ourselves celebrating our human connectedness.

The reason that the mutual sharing of values builds trust is because our positive human values—known as virtues—are shared by all human beings. A virtue is a positive trait or quality deemed to be morally excellent. Virtues are universally recognized as promoting individual and collective well-being.

Potentially limiting values

Values can be positive or potentially limiting (negative). Examples of positive personal values include honesty, integrity and trust. Examples of positive organizational values include teamwork, creativity and financial stability. When we make decisions using our positive values, they either make us feel at ease with ourselves, at ease with others in our immediate environment or at ease in our larger social environment. They are connecting and life affirming.

Examples of potentially limiting personal values include control, blame and status. Examples of potentially limiting organizational values include hierarchy, bureaucracy and short-term focus. People exhibit controlling, blaming or manipulating behaviours because they consciously or subconsciously believe that by behaving in these ways they will be able to meet their deficiency needs.

Our potentially limiting values arise from the fears and anxieties we have about not being able to meet one, some or all of our deficiency needs. For example: If you have a limiting belief that you cannot trust other people, you will try to control everything in your life. If you have a limiting belief that you are not accepted or do not belong, you will blame others when things go wrong so you can avoid punishment and continue to be liked by the authority figures in your life. If you have a limiting belief that you are not good enough, you will try to outsmart or outmanoeuvre others—use status-seeking behaviours—so that you come out on top.

Unlike positive values that are connecting and arise from our hearts, potentially limiting values are separating and arise from our fears. What we forget when we let our potentially limiting values drive our behaviours is that they ultimately turn out to be counterproductive to what we want to achieve—we alienate people to our cause. This is because potentially limiting values always focus on our personal self-interest. When we let our potentially limiting values guide our decision making we send a message to other people that we care more about ourselves than we care about them.

The crux of the problem with potentially limiting values is that they are *potentially limiting*. They may satisfy our immediate need *to feel at ease with ourselves*—to meet our own needs—but in so doing, they create discord and conflict with the people in our immediate environment, and depending on the significance of the actions we take, they may create discord and conflict with people in our larger business environment or social milieu. The higher you move in the hierarchy of authority in an organization or in society, the greater your potential for creating discord and conflict if you let your potentially limiting values dictate your behaviours. This fact is self-evident when you recognize the negative impact that Hitler had on the lives of the people from Germany and Europe and the positive impact that Gandhi had on the lives of the people from India.[11]

Humans are basically social creatures: We depend on each other for our individual and collective survival, progress and success. When one person in a group is focused more on his or her needs or success than the group's needs or success, discord and conflict will ensue, and the group will become dysfunctional. The group will never be able to achieve its full potential.

When people, especially leaders, operate with pure self-interest, they not only compromise their own future well-being, they also compromise the well-being of the organization, group, community or nation they belong to. The collapse of companies such as Enron, Tyco International and WorldCom are a testament to this fact.

The term I have coined to describe these types of behaviours (behaviours driven by our potentially limiting values) is "personal entropy."

Personal entropy is the amount of fear-driven energy that a person expresses in his or her day-to-day interactions with other people.

Fear-driven energy arises from the conscious and subconscious fear-based beliefs (limiting beliefs) that people have about meeting their deficiency needs.

- Limiting beliefs at the survival level are about *not having enough of what you need to feel safe and secure*. These beliefs result in the display of potentially limiting values such as control, manipulation, greed and excessive caution.
- Limiting beliefs at the relationship level are about *not feeling loved enough to be accepted and protected*. These beliefs result in the display of potentially limiting values such as blame, being liked, competition and internal politics.
- Limiting beliefs at the self-esteem level are about *not being enough to engender the respect or acknowledgement of the authority figures in your life or your peers*. These beliefs result in the display of potentially limiting values

such as status seeking, power seeking, arrogance and an overly strong focus on self-image.

I will show in later chapters how personal entropy is measured, how it is related to cultural entropy (the amount of fear-driven energy that is found in a human group structure such as an organization, a community or nation), and the impact that personal and cultural entropy have on the performance of an organization.

Conclusions

Every individual and every organization is involved in making hundreds of decisions every day. The decisions we make are a reflection of our values and beliefs, and they are always directed towards a specific purpose. The purpose they are directed towards is the satisfaction of our individual or collective (organizational) needs. When we use our positive, life-affirming values to make decisions we create connection and trust. When we use our potentially limiting (negative) values to make decisions—those which reflect our subconscious fears—we create separation and mistrust.

People's priority needs, which are determined by where they are in their psychological development, what their current life circumstances are and the situation they currently find themselves in, are the drivers of their values. Their ability to get, have or experience what they value, together with their subconscious fear-based beliefs, drive their thoughts, feelings and emotions. Their thoughts, feelings and emotions then determine their actions and behaviours. Figure 1.3 shows these relationships.

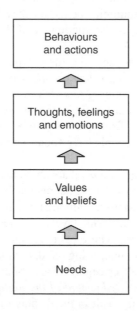

Figure 1.3 The relationship between needs, values, thoughts and behaviours.

In every interaction you have with other people, you must first understand what unmet needs they have—what they value—if you want to respond appropriately to their requests or demands. The values assessment instruments, which I will describe in Chapter 6, enable you to uncover and identify what people value, what their value priorities are and their most pressing unmet needs.

Summary

Here are the main points of Chapter 1:

1. Values are a shorthand method of describing what is important to us.
2. Your values are a reflection of your needs.
3. A need is something you want to get, have or experience that you believe will alleviate your suffering or distress, and make you happier or more aligned with who you are.
4. Abraham Maslow identified two basic types of human need—basic or deficiency needs, and growth or being needs.
5. We feel anxious or fearful if our basic/deficiency needs are not met.
6. When we are able to satisfy our basic/deficiency needs we no longer pay them attention.
7. When we are able to satisfy our growth/being needs they do not go away, they engender deeper levels of attention and commitment.
8. Someone who has learned how to master the satisfaction of their basic needs *and* their growth needs is called a *full spectrum individual*.
9. The amount of attention you give to satisfying a specific set of needs depends on three main factors: The stage you have reached in your psychological development, the life circumstances that you were born into or which you are currently experiencing and the situation in which you find yourself at a specific moment in time.
10. Happiness is the feeling you experience when you are able to let go of the anxiety or fear you have about not being able to meet your deficiency needs.
11. The ability to meet your growth needs engenders a deeper feeling than happiness, and consequently a deeper level of motivation and commitment.
12. If you want to have a loyal, committed and creative workforce in your organization then you need to make sure that your employees are able to satisfy their deficiency needs, *and* you also need to provide programmes and opportunities to enable them to pursue and satisfy their growth needs.
13. People all over the world are shifting from belief-based decision making to values-based decision making.
14. Sharing your values with other people builds trust.
15. Values can be positive or potentially limiting.
16. Potentially limiting values arise from the fears and anxieties we have about not being able to meet our deficiency needs.
17. When we let our potentially limiting values guide our decision making we send a message to other people that we care more about ourselves than we care about them.

18. When one person in a group is focused more on his or her success than the group's success, discord and conflict will ensue, and the group will become dysfunctional. It will never be able to achieve its full potential.

19. When people, especially leaders, operate with pure self-interest, they not only compromise their own future well-being, they also compromise the well-being of the organization, group, community or nation they belong to.

Notes

1 Data obtained from the UK National Values Survey carried out in October 2012.

2 Kurt Goldstein, a psychiatrist and pioneer in modern neuropsychology, first used the term "self-actualization" to describe the driving force in organisms that actualizes their individual capacities as much as possible. Abraham Maslow later used the term, not as a driving force, but as the desire in human individuals to become more and more of what one is and to become everything one is capable of becoming, thereby achieving the full realization of one's potential. Self-actualization is growth motivated, rather than deficiency motivated.

3 Abraham Maslow, *Toward a Psychology of Being*, second edition (New York: Van Nostrand Reinhold), 1968, p. 173.

4 This table forms the basis of the Seven Levels of Consciousness Model, which is discussed in detail in Chapter 5. The derivation of this model from Maslow's hierarchy of needs is presented in Annex 3.

5 Maslow, *Toward a Psychology of Being*, p. 157.

6 Marc Gafni, *Your Unique Self: The Radical Path to Personal Enlightenment* (Tucson: Integral Publishers), 2012.

7 Emily Esfahani Smith, There's More to Life Than Being Happy, *The Atlantic*, January, 2013.

8 Ray Baumeister, Kathleen Vohs, Jennifer Aaker and Emily Garbinsky, Some Key Differences between a Happy Life and a Meaningful Life, *Journal of Positive Psychology* (forthcoming, 2013).

9 Ibid.

10 There are six modes of decision making available to human beings—instincts, subconscious beliefs, conscious beliefs, values, intuition and inspiration. These are described in Annex 2.

11 For a more detailed discussion on the potentially limiting values of these two leaders and how they came about see pages 59–65 of *Love, Fear and the Destiny of Nations (Volume 1): The Impact of the Evolution of Human Consciousness on World Affairs*, by Richard Barrett.

2 The impact of values on performance

In the Foreword to this book, I made the bold claim that values-driven organizations are the most successful organizations on the planet. In this chapter, I am going to begin to substantiate this claim by pulling together information from various sources to show how a focus on values helps organizations to attract and retain talented and creative people, and positively impacts their financial performance.

The three main sources of data I am going to use are:

*   The financial returns of a selection of the *Best Companies to Work For in America* compared with the S&P 500 over a ten-year period from 2002 to 2012.[1]
*   The financial returns of a selection of the companies identified by Sisodia, Wolfe and Seth in *Firms of Endearment* compared with the S&P 500 over a ten-year period from 2002 to 2012.
*   The financial returns of the companies identified by Jim Collins in *Good to Great* compared with the S&P 500 over a ten-year period from 2002 to 2012.

I will also refer to various other studies and research results that link improvements in financial performance with improvements in culture, a focus on values or a focus on employee engagement. In later chapters, I will provide further evidence, from both small and large organizations, of the impact that a values focus has had on their growth, productivity and performance.

Cultural entropy and staff engagement

Before exploring the link between financial performance and values, I want to define two terms that I will be using frequently in this chapter and throughout the rest of this book—employee engagement and cultural entropy.

Employee engagement

Employee engagement is a measure of the level of emotional and intellectual involvement that employees have with an organization. This has a direct impact on the amount of enthusiasm and commitment they bring to their work. Engaged employees devote a high level of discretionary energy[2] to whatever they are doing.

They are willing to go the extra mile to get a job done on time and frequently put forward suggestions about how to improve performance. They want the company to be successful and they want to feel a sense of pride in being part of that success. Disengaged employees, on the other hand, don't really care about the company. They do what their job requires of them and no more. Actively disengaged employees actually erode an organization's bottom line through subversive activities and hostile attitudes to their work and their managers.

In the all-time bestseller, *In Search of Excellence: Lessons from America's Best-Run Companies*, Tom Peters and Robert Waterman put it like this:

> Let us suppose that we were asked for one all-purpose bit of advice for management, one truth that we were able to distil from the excellent companies' research. We might be tempted to reply, "Figure out your value system. Decide what your company stands for. What does your enterprise do that gives everyone most pride? Put yourself out ten or twenty years in the future: what would you look back on with greatest satisfaction?"[3]

According to Daniel Pink, author of *Drive: The Surprising Truth about What Motivates Us*,[4] there are three factors above all others that lie at the heart of engagement—autonomy, mastery and purpose.

Autonomy—the freedom to make choices about how, where, when and with whom we work. Researchers at Cornell University found that businesses that offer their employees autonomy grew four times faster than control-oriented firms and had one-third the turnover of staff.[5]

Mastery—the desire to get better and better at something that matters. A study of 11,000 industrial scientists and engineers found that the desire for intellectual challenge—that is, the urge to master something new and engaging—was the best predictor of productivity.[6]

Purpose—the most deeply motivated people hitch their desires to a cause larger than themselves. Researchers at the University of Rochester tracked the post-college success of students who had "extrinsic motivation"—to become wealthy or to achieve fame (profit goals), and "intrinsic motivations"—to help others improve their lives, to learn and to grow (purpose goals). They found that those who had purpose goals, and were attaining them, reported higher levels of satisfaction and subjective well-being than they did when they were at college. Those who had profit goals, and were attaining them, reported levels of satisfaction, self-esteem and positive affect lower or at the same level as when they were at college. Although they were reaching their goals, they did not feel any happier. On the contrary, they showed increases in anxiety, depression and other negative indicators.[7]

Based on his extensive review of research into what motivates people, Pink suggests the following formula for creating an engaged work force:

> The base line rewards must be sufficient. That is, the … basic compensation should be adequate and fair—particularly compared with people doing similar

work for similar organisations. Your [organisation] must be a congenial place to work. And the people … must have autonomy, they must have the opportunity to pursue mastery, and their daily duties must relate to a larger purpose. If these elements are in place, the best strategy is to provide a sense of urgency and significance—and then get out of the way.[8]

What Pink is describing here are the conditions required to create a highly engaged workforce. The conditions that lead to a highly disengaged work force are the opposite: Unfair compensation; benefits below the norm; a climate of stress and fear; hierarchical structures of control; bureaucratic procedures; and authoritarian managers who control, micro-manage and manipulate their staff. These are the conditions that create cultural entropy.

Cultural entropy

Cultural entropy[9] is a measure of the amount of energy that is consumed in doing unnecessary or unproductive work—the amount of conflict, friction and frustration that employees encounter in their day-to-day activities that prevent them and the organization from operating at peak performance. The main source of cultural entropy in an organization is the fear-based actions and behaviours of the leaders, managers and supervisors.

When leaders, managers and supervisors are anxious and fearful (when they have unmet deficiency needs and engage in dysfunctional behaviours such as control, manipulation, blame, internal competition, etc.) cultural entropy increases and employee engagement decreases. Conversely, when leaders, managers and supervisors engage in caring and trusting behaviours and the organization encourages its employees to be responsible and accountable for their work, allowing them free rein to take initiatives that boost performance, cultural entropy decreases and staff engagement increases.

The following graph (Figure 2.1) shows the relationship between cultural entropy and employee engagement as measured in 163 organizations in Australia and New Zealand in a joint research project carried out by Barrett Values Centre and Hewitt Associates in June 2008. The results of this analysis show that cultural entropy and employee engagement are highly inversely correlated—companies with low cultural entropy have high employee engagement and companies with high cultural entropy have low employee engagement.

In organizations with high cultural entropy (disengaged employees), the leaders, managers and supervisors are focused on addressing their own needs. In organizations with low cultural entropy (engaged employees), the leaders, managers and supervisors are focused on meeting *the needs of their direct reports and other colleagues, the needs of customers, the needs of investors and the needs of the people in the communities where they operate.* By focusing on the needs of all the organization's stakeholders they engender high levels of staff engagement, customer support, investor attention and societal goodwill.

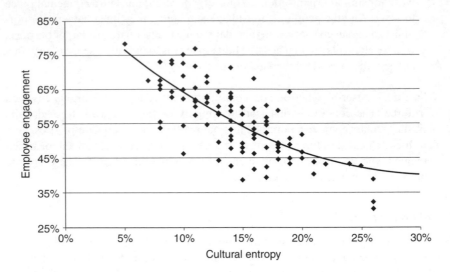

Figure 2.1 Employee engagement versus cultural entropy.

Employee engagement and performance

Gallup, a research-based performance-management consulting company, has found that organizations with highly engaged employees have 3.9 times the earnings per share growth rate compared with organizations with low engagement in the same industry.[10] Engaged workgroups are more productive, profitable and customer focused, and have higher retention rates, lower numbers of safety incidents and less absenteeism than disengaged workgroups.

According to Gallup, in 2008, 29 per cent of employees in the US were actively engaged in their jobs, 55 per cent were not engaged and 16 per cent were actively disengaged.[11] At this level of disengagement (71 per cent), the cost to US companies works out at about US$17,500 per employee.[12] This would mean for the US workforce as a whole, the cost of employee disengagement could be as much as US$2.6 trillion per year.[13]

Gallup concludes from its research that:

> In the best organizations, engagement is more than a human resources initiative—it is a strategic foundation for the way they do business. Increasing employee engagement correlates directly with a positive impact on key business metrics. The best-performing companies know that an employee engagement improvement strategy linked to the achievement of corporate goals will help them win in the marketplace.[14]

Gallup's employee engagement work is based on more than 30 years of in-depth behavioural economic research involving more than 17 million employees.

Another global human resource consulting firm, AON Hewitt, found that companies with high levels of engagement (65 per cent or greater) outperform the stock market, posting total shareholder returns 22 per cent more than the average. Companies with low engagement (45 per cent or less) had total shareholder returns that were 28 per cent lower than average.[15]

Based on their research with more than 7,000 organizations, AON Hewitt estimate that "a disengaged employee costs an organisation an average of $10,000 in profit annually; as a result organisations with high engagement are 78% more productive and 40% more profitable."[16]

They also found that in the most recent economic downturn (2008), organizations with high engagement scores were more resilient than companies with low engagement scores.

> They keep focused on the long-term; maintain a consistent employee proposition and a clear set of values. Rather than making large scale changes, the top performing organisations refine and adjust their programmes. They manage change in a way that is consistent with their values and aligned with their overall goals. Leaders remain visible and provide ongoing updates to reduce employee uncertainty and stress ... They use employee based information to drive their actions ... and involve multiple stakeholders in their decision-making.[17]

Research carried out by the UK retail giant Marks and Spencer shows that over a four-year period stores with improving engagement delivered £62 million more in sales to the business every year than stores with declining engagement. Research at Sainsbury's, another UK retail giant, found a clear link between sales performance and higher levels of engagement: High levels of engagement contributed up to 15 per cent of a store's year-on-year growth. RSA, a global insurance company, found that business units with higher levels of employee engagement had 35 per cent less downtime between calls.[18]

In their 2012 report, the UK Engage for Success Task Force identified four enablers of employee engagement:[19]

* Visible, empowering leadership providing a strong strategic narrative about the organization, where it's come from and where it's going.
* Engaging managers who provide focus for their people and give them responsibility, treat them as individuals, and coach, support and stretch them.
* Employees throughout the organization are given a voice to either reinforce or challenge existing views. Employees are seen as central to defining solutions.
* There is organizational integrity—the values pinned to the wall are reflected in day-to-day behaviours. There is no "say–do" gap.

Results supplied to the Task Force by Towers Watson showed that only 27 per cent of employees in the UK are "highly engaged."[20] This huge engagement deficit has a significant impact on UK productivity figures—output per hour in the UK was 15 points below the average for the rest of the G7 industrialized nations in 2011. On an output per worker basis, UK productivity was 20 points lower than the rest of the G7.[21]

The Task Force's report concludes:

> Releasing the potential of an engaged workforce holds the prospect of reducing costs associated with sickness, absence, employee turnover, production errors, accidents and inefficient processes. It also holds the prospect of improving productivity, customer satisfaction, customer retention and innovation. Any one of these mechanisms is capable of delivering substantial benefits to the bottom-line performance of organisations. The question of how to proceed remains unanswered, as this will depend on the specific circumstances of individual organisations, but the evidence in this report suggests that the best place to look for answers is with your employees.[22]

Employee centricity

Having established that there are strong links between employee engagement, cultural entropy and performance, let us now turn our attention to the financial returns that can be generated by a highly engaged workforce.

My first reference point is *Fortune Magazine's* "100 Best Companies to Work For." This survey, which selects the best companies to work for in America, is conducted by the Great Place to Work Institute.

Two-thirds of each company's final score in this survey is based on the responses to the Institute's Trust Index survey, which is sent to a random sample of employees. The survey asks questions related to their attitudes towards the management's credibility, job satisfaction and the general level of camaraderie that exists in the organization. The other third of the final score is based on the company's responses to the Institute's Culture Audit, which includes detailed questions about pay and benefit programmes, and a series of open-ended questions about hiring practices, internal communication, training, recognition programmes and diversity efforts.

In order to evaluate the financial performance of the best companies to work for (in America), I measured the growth in share price of the top 40[23] publicly traded best companies to work for over the period July 2002 to July 2012 and compared the result with the growth in share price of the S&P 500 over the same period. The results are shown in Figure 2.2.

An investment of $25,000 in each of the top 40 companies to work for (total investment of $1 million) over this ten-year period would have realized an average annualized return of 16.39 per cent, compared with 4.12 per cent for the S&P 500. Not only did the stocks of the top companies to work for significantly outperform the S&P 500 over this ten-year period, they also showed considerably more resilience in regaining their value after the global economic meltdown of 2008. They regained their pre-meltdown value in just over a year whereas it took

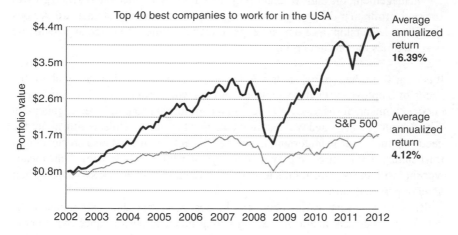

Figure 2.2 Growth in share price of the top 40 publicly traded best companies to work for in America July 2002–12 compared with the S&P 500.

three years for the S&P 500 companies to regain their value. I believe that the strong financial performance of these "people-focused" companies underlines the importance of the employee experience to the success of a company.

This leads directly to the question: What specific practices do "people focused" companies engage in that enable them to sustain high performance?

A report by the Boston Consulting Group (BCG) and the World Federation of People Management Federations (WFPMF) published in 2012 provides some answers to this question.[24] BCG and WFPMF compared the human resource practices of high-performing companies (the companies that made the list of 100 best companies to work for in America for three or more years) against lower performing companies in 22 key people-management areas. They concluded:

> High-performing companies consistently did more in all [areas] than their low-performing peers, but in certain activities their efforts truly stood out. For six topics in particular, the correlation between capability and economic performance was striking:
>
> • Recruiting
> • Bringing on new hires and employee retention
> • Talent management
> • Employer branding
> • Performance management and rewards
> • Leadership development
>
> For example, companies adept at recruiting enjoyed 3.5 times the revenue growth and 2.0 times the profit margin of their less capable peers. In talent

management, the highly capable enjoyed more than twice the revenue growth and profit margin of those less capable. And companies that are serious about leadership development experienced 2.1 times the revenue growth and 1.8 times the profit margin.[25]

It is clear from the reports, studies and research cited above that caring about the needs of employees (their basic needs and growth needs) is significantly correlated with financial success. However, let us not forget that employee engagement is also strongly correlated with cultural entropy; therefore, whilst caring about the needs of employees is important, it is not sufficient—you must also create a high-trust culture that inspires employees to bring their full selves to work. This means working with the organization's leaders, managers and supervisors to reduce their level of personal entropy.

If, as we have seen, caring about employees' needs and their experience in the company is a crucial factor in creating strong financial performance, what about caring for the needs of other stakeholders: How would such actions impact financial performance?

Stakeholder centricity

Raj Sisodia, David Wolfe and Jagdish Sheth provide an answer to this question in their book *Firms of Endearment: How World-class Companies Profit from Passion and Purpose*.[26]

This paradigm-shifting book compares the financial performance of the *Good to Great* companies identified by Jim Collins[27] with companies that embrace what have become known as the tenets of conscious capitalism—values driven, higher purpose, stakeholder orientation, conscious leadership and conscious culture. See Box 2.1.

Figure 2.3 shows a comparison in the growth in share price of eighteen of the thirty[28] *Firms of Endearment* identified by Sisodia, Wolfe and Seth—those that are publicly traded in North America—with the S&P 500. An investment of $25,000 in each of these eighteen companies over a ten-year period ending in August 2012 would have realized an average annualized return of 13.10 per cent. Like the best companies to work for, the *Firms of Endearment* outperformed the S&P 500 and also showed considerably more resilience in regaining their value after the global economic meltdown of 2008.

Finally, Figure 2.4 shows a comparison in the growth in share price of ten of the 11[29] *Good to Great* companies identified by Jim Collins in his book of the same name. Since this book was published, one of the companies failed (Circuit City), one was involved in a financial scandal (Fannie Mae) and one received a $25 billion bailout from the United States government (Wells Fargo). An investment of $25,000 in each of the ten *Good to Great* companies over a ten-year period ending in August 2012 would have realized an average annualized return of 5.32 per cent, only slightly better than the S&P 500.

Box 2.1 The tenets of conscious capitalism

Conscious capitalism is a philosophy based on a belief that a more complex form of capitalism is emerging that holds the potential for enhancing corporate performance while simultaneously continuing to advance the quality of life for billions of people. The conscious capitalism movement challenges business leaders to rethink why their organizations exist and to acknowledge their companies' roles in our modern, interdependent global society.

Values-driven: *Firms of Endearment* live and stand by their values.

Higher purpose: *Firms of Endearment* have a purpose that goes beyond profit maximization.

Stakeholder orientation: *Firms of Endearment* consider the impact their decisions have on all their stakeholders (employees, customers, partners, suppliers, investors, the local community and society in general).

Conscious leadership: *Firms of Endearment* employ conscious leaders who adopt a holistic worldview. They view their enterprises as part of a complex, interdependent social ecosystem with multiple constituencies. They see profit as one of the important purposes of the business, but not the sole purpose. They look for creative synergistic win-win approaches that offer value to all stakeholders.

Conscious culture: *Firms of Endearment* are democratically run, giving employees the freedom to organize themselves in a manner that best serves the company. They are committed to exemplary citizenship, and they embrace the concept of servant leadership. The authors of *Firms of Endearment* state: "If Firms of Endearment can be described by any one characteristic, it is that they possess a humanistic soul."

It is clear from a comparison of Figures 2.2, 2.3 and 2.4 that the samples of companies taken from *Best Companies to Work For* and *Firms of Endearment* have been significantly more successful over the long term than the *Good to Great* companies. In fact, the performance of the *Good to Great* companies has not been significantly better than the S&P 500.

It is interesting to note that there are only four publicly traded companies that share the distinction of being one of the top 40 of the *100 Best Companies to Work For* and also one of the *Firms of Endearment*. These are:

Amazon.com, Inc.
Google Inc.
Starbucks Corporation
Whole Foods Markets, Inc.

Figure 2.3 Growth in share price of the 18 *Firms of Endearment* July 2002–12 compared with the S&P 500.

The founders of these organizations were all named among the top 12 entrepreneurs of our time by *Fortune Magazine* in 2012. Jeff Bezos of Amazon was placed fourth. Larry Page and Sergey Brin of Google were placed fifth. Howard Schultz of Starbucks was placed sixth; and John Mackey of Whole Foods Markets was placed eighth.

Culture eats strategy for breakfast

I think it is important to state before concluding this chapter that it is clear to me from the evidence I have presented that Jim Collins' research did not get to

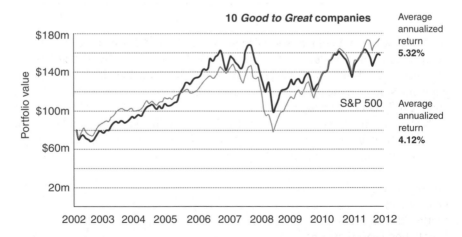

Figure 2.4 Growth in share price of ten *Good to Great* companies July 2002–12 compared with the S&P 500.

the heart of the matter—identifying the factors that create long-lasting organizational value for investors. I believe the mistake he made was to focus too much on exploring *strategies for success* rather than exploring *cultures for success*. I believe that this conclusion doesn't invalidate Collins' research in the least, it simply illustrates that the seven characteristics he identified in the so-called *Good to Great* companies (see Box 2.2), on their own, are not sufficient for long-term success. Focusing on the needs of your employees and the culture of the company are much more important.

I think Peter Drucker[30] had it right when he said "culture eats strategy for breakfast." I also agree with this web posting by Luther Johnson: "No matter how far reaching a leader's vision or how brilliant the strategy, neither will be realized if it is not supported by an organisation's culture."[31]

When you truly get to the heart of the matter—what creates long-lasting value for investors—you cannot fail to come to the conclusion that culture is everything! *Culture drives performance by unleashing human potential.*

The culture of an organization is defined by the values that are lived by the leaders, managers and supervisors; not necessarily by the espoused values—the values that the organization says it wants to embrace, but by the values that show

---

Box 2.2 The seven characteristics of *Good to Great* companies

Level-5 leadership: They had quiet, self-effacing leaders. People who had a "paradoxical blend" of humility and professional will.

First who, then what: The leaders placed the highest priority on surrounding themselves with great people. Rather than focus on vision or strategy, they spent most of their time trying to "put the right people on the bus and get the wrong people off the bus."

Confront the brutal facts: Confront the worst facts of your situation while maintaining an unwavering faith that you can overcome them.

Hedgehog concept: They found something they could do better than any other company in the world. Even if it meant abandoning their core concept and moving on to something else, they maintained that lofty standard.

Culture of discipline: They developed a corporate culture where employees were so committed to the company's core values that disciplinary rules were not necessary.

Technology accelerators: They used technology to support their core values, not as the driving force of the business.

The Flywheel: The process they used to make improvements was incremental, not revolutionary. It resembled "relentlessly pushing a giant heavy flywheel in one direction, turn upon turn, building momentum until a point of breakthrough and beyond."

up in the everyday interactions between leaders, managers and employees, and between employees and customers and suppliers. I believe that when you get the values right, and let them guide your decision making, you will stand a much better chance of getting your strategy right.

Don't get me wrong, I am not saying strategy is unimportant: It is vitally important. What *I am saying* is that no matter how good a strategy you have for your business, unless you have a cohesive culture that fosters employee commitment and engagement, you may find it difficult to implement your strategy no matter how wonderful it is.

Conclusions

The conclusion I have reached based on the results of the research presented in this chapter is that if you want to build a high-performing organization with superior financial returns, then you need to focus on satisfying the needs of all your stakeholders, especially the needs of your employees—their basic needs and their growth needs—the things they value in their lives.

The financial results from the publicly traded *Best Companies to Work for in North America* (companies that care about their employees) and the publicly traded *Firms of Endearment* (companies that care about all their stakeholders) presented in this chapter show that they not only have higher financial returns than the S&P 500, they showed more resilience in weathering the economic meltdown of 2008.

Summary

Here are the main points of Chapter 2:

1. There are two factors that significantly influence organizational performance—employee engagement and cultural entropy.
2. Employee engagement is a measure of the level of emotional and intellectual involvement that employees have with an organization.
3. Cultural entropy is a measure of the amount of energy in an organization that is consumed in doing unnecessary or unproductive work.
4. Employee engagement and cultural entropy are inversely correlated.
5. Low entropy leads to high engagement and high entropy leads to low engagement.
6. Organizations that focus on the needs of their employees and their stakeholders are significantly more successful and resilient than other organizations.

Notes

1 The S&P 500, or the Standard & Poor 500, is a stock market index based on the common stock prices of the 500 top publicly traded American companies. It is one of the most commonly followed indices and many consider it the best representation of the US economy.

2 Discretionary energy is the energy that employees choose to devote to their work over and above the normal amount of energy that is required for them to fulfil their duties or work contract.

3 Tom Peters and Robert H. Waterman, Jr., *In Search of Excellence: Lessons from America's Best-Run Companies* (London: Profile Books), 2004, p. 279. First published by Harper & Row, 1982.

4 Daniel H. Pink, *Drive: The Surprising Truth about What Motivates Us* (New York: River Head Books), 2009.

5 Ibid., p. 90.

6 Ibid., p. 91.

7 Ibid., p. 143.

8 Ibid., p. 66.

9 For a full description of cultural entropy and how to measure it see Chapter 6.

10 Employee Engagement: What's Your Engagement Ratio, Gallup Consulting (PDF).

11 http://hrcases.wordpress.com/tag/gallup-survey/ (last accessed 28 March 2013).

12 www.engagementisnotenough.com/pdfs/Cost_of_Engagement.pdf (last accessed 28 March 2013).

13 Assumes that there are 150 million people in the US workforce.

14 http://hrcases.wordpress.com/tag/gallup-survey/ (last accessed 28 March 2013).

15 *Trends in Global Employee Engagement*, AON Hewitt, 2011, www.aon.com/attachments/thought-leadership/Trends_Global_Employee_Engagement_Final.pdf (last accessed 4 April 2013).

16 Economic uncertainty creates a recession in employee engagement: How top organisations continue to prosper, AON Hewitt, Hewitt Engagement Recession Article HBR, www.aon.com.au/australia/attachments/human-capital-consulting/Hewitt_Engagement_Recession_Article_HBR.pdf (last accessed 4 April 2013).

17 Ibid.

18 Bruce Rayton, *Employee Engagement Task Force "Nailing the Evidence" Workgroup* (Bath: University of Bath School of Management), 2012, pp. iii–iv.

19 Ibid., p.1.

20 Ibid., p. 4.

21 Ibid., p. ii.

22 Ibid., p. 26.

23 See Annex 4 for a list of these companies.

24 Strack Rainer, Jean-Michel Cave, Carsten von der Linden, Horacio Quiros and Pieter Haen, *Realizing the Value of People Management: From Capability to Profitability*, 2 August 2012, www.bcgperspectives.com/content/articles/people_management_human_resources_leadership_from_capability_to_profitability/ (last accessed 4 April 2012).

25 Ibid.

26 Raj Sisodia, David Wolfe and Jagdish Sheth, *Firms of Endearment: How World-class Companies Profit from Passion and Purpose* (Upper Saddle River, NJ: Wharton School Publishing), 2007.

27 Jim Collins, *Good to Great* (New York: HarperCollins), 2001.

28 See Annex 5 for a full list of the *Firms of Endearment*.

29 See Annex 6 for a full list of the *Good to Great* companies and those that are no longer trading.

30 Peter Drucker was one of the best known and most influential thinkers and writers on the subject of management theory and practice in the twentieth century.

31 See www.relationaldynamicsinstitute.com/ (last accessed 28 March 2013), posted by lutherjohnson in Cuture Applications.

3   What employees want

In the last chapter, I presented data to show that organizations with strong financial returns focus specifically on satisfying the needs of their employees. When employees' needs are met, and employees feel aligned with the mission, vision and values of the organization, they respond with high levels of engagement and commitment: They come to work with enthusiasm and commitment and are willing to go the extra mile to support the organization in its endeavours.

The question I now want to address is: What do organizations need to do to create a highly motivated workforce where employees are willing to devote a significant amount of their discretionary energy, as well as their commitment and creativity, to making the organization a success?

I believe the research presented by Daniel Pink in *Drive: The Surprising Truth about What Motivates Us* points us in the right direction.

Baseline rewards that are sufficient and fair (fulfilling some of the employees' survival needs); a congenial working atmosphere (fulfilling some of the employees' relationship needs); freedom to make choices—autonomy (fulfilling some of the employees' transformation needs); opportunities to pursue mastery—learn and excel in their field of expertise (fulfilling some of the employees' self-esteem needs); and perform duties that align with a higher purpose—(fulfilling some of the employees' internal cohesion needs). In other words, Pink's research points us towards the seven human basic/growth needs presented in Table 1.2.

Thus, the answer to the question, what do organizations need to do to create a highly motivated workforce, is as follows: Organizations need to identify the needs that motivate their employees (what they value) and create a culture that addresses these needs.

Table 3.1, which is based on Table 1.2, provides a comprehensive list of the actions and opportunities that organizations need to focus on to serve employees' needs at all levels of psychological development. Also listed in this table are the feelings and experiences that are associated with the satisfaction of the needs associated with each level of development.

It is important to recognize that not all employees are the same: Different employees will have different needs (want and value different things) depending on the levels of consciousness they are operating from. The levels of consciousness they are operating from at any moment in time will depend on three

Table 3.1 Actions and opportunities that organizations need to provide to support the full spectrum of employees' needs

Level of development	Cause of happiness/joy	Actions and opportunities
7 Service	Leading a life of selfless service for the good of humanity.	Opportunities to serve others and/or care for the well-being of the Earth's life support systems.
6 Making a difference	Actualizing your sense of purpose by collaborating with others to make a difference in the world.	Opportunities to leverage your contribution by collaborating with others who share the same values and have a similar purpose.
5 Internal cohesion	Discovering your authentic self and finding a sense of meaning and purpose that is bigger and broader than meeting your own needs.	Opportunities for personal growth and development to support you in finding your life purpose and aligning your purpose with your daily work.
4 Transformation	Experiencing a sense of freedom, autonomy and responsibility by taking on challenges that stretch your capacities.	Opportunities to develop your skills by being made accountable for projects or processes of significance to yourself and/or the organization.
3 Self-esteem	Feeling acknowledged and recognized by those whom you respect.	Opportunities to learn and grow professionally with frequent support, feedback and coaching.
2 Relationship	Feeling accepted, cherished and nurtured by your family, friends or colleagues.	Opportunities to work in a congenial atmosphere where people respect and care about each other.
1 Survival	Feeling safe and secure, and being able to meet your physiological needs at home and in the workplace.	A safe working environment and pay and benefits that are sufficient to take care of employees' needs and the needs of their families.

factors: The employee's level of psychological development; the employee's general life circumstances; and the specific life challenges the employee is experiencing.

Three types of mind

In *Immunity to Change* Robert Kegan and Lisa Laskow Lahey identify three plateaus of adult psychological development—the socialized mind, the self-authoring mind and the self-transforming mind.[1] These are three different ways of seeing the world that reflect people's needs and motivations, their ability to handle complexity, and how they respond to change. As we grow and develop psychologically, and as long as we do not have any significant conscious or subconscious limiting beliefs about meeting our deficiency needs, we gradually evolve from operating with a socialized mind, to a self-authoring mind, to a self-transforming mind. Each shift represents a growth in consciousness in our personal developmental journey. The following descriptions of these three types of mind are based on my personal interpretation of Kegan and Lahey's concepts.

The *socialized mind* is a dependent mind. The way a socialized mind responds to a situation or a request is strongly influenced by what it believes others are expecting and how it can meet its survival, relationship, and self-esteem needs. The socialized mind prefers to be given instructions and told what to do. Those who operate with a socialized mind are unlikely to want to take on a leadership position. The level of responsibility and accountability they will have to endure will be too stressful or demand more than they are willing to give. People with this type of mind tend to think of their work as a job. They are motivated by incentives that allow them to satisfy their basic needs—money, friendship and respect. When these needs are met they feel happy, but they are not significantly engaged. They will quickly jump ship if they find an opening with another organization that gives them more of what they are looking for. They prefer simple, less complex tasks that can be easily mastered. The focus of the socialized mind tends to be on the needs associated with the first three stages of development—feeling safe and secure, accepted, cherished and nurtured, and acknowledged and recognized for their skills and talents.

The *self-authoring* mind is an independent mind. The self-authoring mind responds to a situation, opportunity or request by seeking to further its agenda. The self-authoring mind wants to be accountable and take initiatives, but it wants to do it its way. Those who operate with a self-authoring mind will be keen to take a leadership role. They will see this as a possibility to further their ambitions and goals. People with self-authoring minds may find themselves clashing with people who are also operating with self-authoring minds who hold different views on how things should be done. People with this type of mind tend to think of their work as a career. They are motivated by the ability to satisfy their first order growth needs—challenging situations that lead to advancement and work that has meaning to them. When these needs are met employees feel a strong sense of engagement. However, if the excitement and challenges they seek dry up or disappear for a period of time, they will be on the lookout for new opportunities to further their careers. They enjoy complex tasks that require them to tap into their innovation and creativity. The focus of the self-authoring mind tends to be on the needs associated with the fourth and fifth stages of development—finding freedom and autonomy, and meaning and purpose in life.

The *self-transforming* mind is an interdependent mind. The self-transforming mind responds to a situation or request by seeking out more information to find the best way forward. The self-transforming mind is not a prisoner to its beliefs, agenda or position. It is open to thoughts and ideas of others and can integrate them into a more inclusive worldview. People with self-authoring minds tend to think of their work as a mission or purpose. They are well suited to handling complex situations. They are motivated by the ability to satisfy their higher order growth needs—to make a difference in their world, and leave a legacy by serving humanity or the planet. When these needs are met, people experience the highest levels of engagement. They are prepared to put up with bureaucracy, and they will ignore internal politicking, just for the opportunity to experience the sense of fulfilment they get from being able to make a difference in the world. They bring clarity to complexity and are at easy with uncertainty. The focus of the self-transforming mind tends to be on the needs associated with the sixth and seventh stages of development—collaborating to make a difference, and selfless service.

The shift from one type of mind to the next is not something that can be taught: It has to be developed and nurtured. Some people take a lifetime to develop a self-transforming mind. Others get there more quickly. Many never get there at all.

We evolve from a socialized mind to a self-authoring mind to the extent we are able to overcome our anxieties and fears, individuate and feel confident about our ability to survive and thrive on our own. We evolve from a self-authoring mind to a self-transforming mind to the extent we can detach from the outcomes we think we need to satisfy our needs, self-actualize and be open to other perspectives. This way of being requires you to dissolve your attachment to a specific outcome and remain at ease with uncertainty.

Figure 3.1, which is based on the results of a survey of 4,000 citizens in the UK,[2] shows the proportion of people of different age groups whose top ten values align with the values associated with the three types of mind. The proportion of values associated with a socialized mind reaches a peak in the 20–24 age group and then, as one might expect, gradually falls as people age and mature. The proportion of values associated with self-authoring and a self-transforming minds is at its lowest in the 20–24 age group and then gradually increases as people age

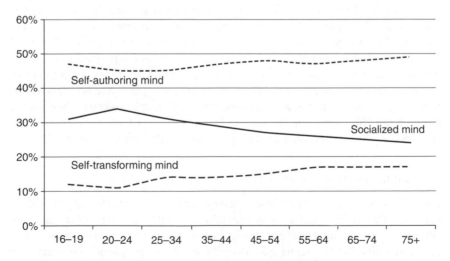

Figure 3.1 Proportion of UK population operating with the three types of mind in different age groups.

and mature. One would expect these trends to be magnified for college-educated people—those who have individuated and self-actualized.

Two large studies[3,4] of middle-class, college-educated professionals in the US showed that 58 per cent of them were operating with socialized minds, 36 per cent were operating with self-authoring minds and only 6 per cent were operating with self-transforming minds.[5]

This research by Robert Kegan led him to the following conclusion:

> Complexity is really a story about the relationship between the complex demands and arrangements of the world and our own complexity of mind. When we look at this relationship [at this point in time in history] we discover a gap: our own mental complexity lags behind the complexity of the world's demands.[6]

In my opinion, Kegan raises an important point. To meet the leadership needs of the complex world in which we live, we need to find ways to accelerate the human capacity for handling complexity by accelerating human development. *The New Leadership Paradigm* (the book, website and learning modules)[7] is my attempt to support this acceleration by making a world-class leadership development programme available to everyone on the planet at a modest cost.[8] People who cannot afford the downloadable learning modules for leading self, leading a team, leading an organization and leading in society, can, on application, receive these documents free of charge. My book, *What My Soul Told Me: A Practical Guide to Soul Activation* takes the topic of leading self to a deeper level, providing guidance on how to live a values-driven and purpose-driven life.[9]

Whilst classifying people into different types of mind may be useful in some situations, for example, selecting individuals for promotion to jobs that require more complex thinking, I think an alternative approach is needed when dealing with groups of people, such as teams, organizations, communities or nations. The approach I am suggesting is to map the values of the group to the Seven Levels of Consciousness Model, and from these results determine the proportion of values that are held by the group that correspond to the three types of mind. I believe this approach is useful where a government or an organization is attempting to determine what priorities to focus on in order to meet people's needs. Case studies highlighting this approach are shown in Chapter 7. Chapter 13 applies this approach to choosing espoused values that inspire different levels of workers.

Human development and change

Each of the three types of mind identified by Kegan responds to change in different ways. People who operate with a socialized mind tend to be vigilant and concerned about anything that is happening around them that involves change—they prefer stability and the status quo. Broadly speaking, people who operate with socialized minds tend to be focused on their basic needs (survival, relationship and self-esteem). They get anxious and fearful if they feel that the satisfaction of these needs might be threatened in any way. The socialized mind tends to filter whatever it is sensing in its external environment through its fear-based beliefs. People with socialized minds want to protect what they have and may see change as a potential threat to them being able to continue to meet their needs. Reorganization plans or cutbacks significantly affect the stress levels of these types of workers.

People who operate with a self-authoring mind are open to change and welcome the opportunities that change may bring. They interpret what is happening around them through the filter of "personal opportunity"—how they can use change to further their projects and careers. As long as their basic needs have been met, people who operate with self-authoring minds tend to be focused on their transformation needs, and, to some extent, their internal cohesion needs.

People who operate with a self-transforming mind tend to see change as part of the normal ebb and flow of life. They interpret what is happening around them through the filter of the "big picture"—how they can use the incoming information to further the mission or the purpose they are pursuing. As long as their basic needs and first-order growth needs have been met, people who operate with self-transforming minds tend to be focused on making a difference and their service needs.

Based on this understanding, it is clear that the answer to the question, what do organizations need to do to create a highly motivated workforce, depends to a large extent on the type of minds that are needed to perform the core work of the organization. This in turn depends on the level of complexity of the work that is required.

Organizations that employ a lot of labourers, retail or service personnel in low-complexity work—usually people who are operating with socialized minds—should give emphasis to satisfying their employees' basic needs. Organizations that employ a lot of knowledge workers, technicians and researchers in medium-level complexity work—usually people who are operating with self-authoring minds—should give emphasis to satisfying their employees' first-order growth needs (transformation and internal cohesion). Organizations that employ highly qualified professional advisors in work that impacts the way in which our society operates or in international relations should give emphasis to satisfying their employees' second order growth needs (making a difference and service).

Human development and complexity

In *Executive Leadership: A Practical Guide to Managing Complexity*,[10] Elliott Jaques, a Canadian-born organizational psychologist, suggests that we should match a person's level of cognitive complexity (psychological development) to the level of task complexity he or she has to perform. Jaques defines seven levels of role complexity that correlate more or less with the seven levels of psychological development.[11]

Table 3.2 shows Jaques' seven levels of job complexity (role complexity) for both the private and public sector and my interpretation of what people are

Table 3.2 Levels of job complexity and human motivation

Level of development	Private sector role	Public sector role	What people are looking for
7 Service	President/ CEO	President/ prime minister	Opportunities to serve humanity and/or care for the well-being of the Earth's life support systems.
6 Making a difference	Executive president	Minister	Opportunities to leverage your contribution by collaborating with other teams or groups that share the same values, have a similar purpose and want to make a difference in the world.
5 Internal cohesion	Vice president	Director general	Opportunities for personal growth and development to support you in finding your life purpose and aligning your purpose with your daily work.
4 Transformation	Department manager	Chief director	Opportunities to develop your personal mastery skills and explore your gifts and talents by being made accountable for projects or processes of significance to yourself and the organization.
3 Self-esteem	Unit manager	Director	Opportunities to learn and grow professionally with frequent support, feedback and coaching.
2 Relationship	Section manager	Assistant director	A congenial working atmosphere where people respect and care about each other.
1 Survival	Operator	Administrator	A safe working environment and pay and benefits that are sufficient to take care of employees' needs and the needs of their families.

looking for (the needs that are motivating them) at each level of development. The first three levels correspond to the needs of people operating with socialized minds. The next two levels correspond to the needs of people operating with self-authoring minds, and the top two levels correspond to the needs of people operating with self-transforming minds.

Based on the allocation of roles to levels of development shown in Table 3.2, an operator or administrator needs to be skilled in the core work of the organization.

A section manager or assistant director responsible for a work team needs to be skilled in relationship management to get the best out of his workers. A unit manager or director must have mastered relationship management *and* be confident and self-assured about the tasks he or she is asked to manage. A department manager or chief director must have mastered relationship management, be confident and self-assured about the tasks he or she is asked to manage, *and* be willing to take on challenging situations and be accountable for outcomes.

A vice president or director general must, in addition, ensure the people under his or her responsibility—his or her direct reports—share and operate with the same values, and are all heading in the same direction (have a sense of shared mission and a shared vision of the future they are trying to create).

An executive vice president or minister must, in addition, make sure that all the vice presidents that report to him or her act as one, and cooperate with each other to make a difference that impacts the well-being of the whole organization.

Finally, the president/CEO/prime minister must, in addition, make sure that everything that is done provides value-added benefits for all stakeholders and keeps a focus on the long-term future of the organization.

As people grow and develop, they naturally seek out roles that match the increasing level of complexity of their minds. As you move from operating with a socialized mind to a self-authoring mind you will want to take on more responsibility and accountability. As you move from operating with a self-authoring mind to a self-transforming mind you will want to be in a role where you can make a larger difference in the arena in which you work and make a contribution to society.

What this discussion about levels of development, complexity and roles suggests is that if you are running a large organization, the best way to ensure that you have a high performing team and highly committed and engaged workforce is to place people in roles that correspond to their level of psychological development—do not promote people to higher levels of role complexity until their mind can handle that level of complexity; and at the same time, care about and address the full spectrum of human needs, from pay and benefits at one end of the spectrum (to satisfy people's survival needs) to serving humanity at the other end of the spectrum (to satisfy people's service needs).

Alignment

You know when you have been successful at addressing employees' needs when you have a high level of staff engagement. There are two main dimensions to engagement: Emotional engagement and intellectual engagement.

Emotional engagement is principally a function of values alignment.

Everyone, no matter what stage they have reached in their personal development, is capable of feeling a sense of values alignment with the culture of their organization. When the lived values of the organization align with the values of employees at the level of personal development they have reached, values alignment will occur.

Intellectual engagement is principally a function of mission alignment.

There are two levels of mission alignment—the first occurs when you feel the organization is operationally on the right track; and the second occurs when you are able to spend your days working on what you are passionate about—on a topic or subject, or in a role that captivates your attention.

Everyone, no matter what stage they have reached in their personal development, is capable of experiencing the first stage of mission alignment—a sense that the organization is doing the right things—but to experience the second stage—working on what you are passionate about—you must have reached the internal cohesion level of personal development: You must have found your personal sense of purpose or your vocation, and in addition, you must have been given the opportunity to spend the majority of your time working on what you are passionate about.[12] When you are able to do this, and have the resources you need to make a difference, you will feel the highest levels of mission alignment. You will be living out your soul purpose.

You can feel a strong sense of mission alignment without necessarily feeling a strong sense of values alignment, especially if you work for a large bureaucratic, hierarchical organization, where there are high levels of cultural entropy. This was my case when I worked at the World Bank. I was able to overlook the lack of values alignment (mainly due to bureaucracy and internal politics) for many years because my work gave me the opportunity to experience a strong sense of mission alignment. I felt at that time that the organization was on the right track and I had the resources I needed to make a difference in the world.

You can also feel a strong sense of values alignment without necessarily feeling a strong sense of mission alignment—you love the pay, benefits and people, and get to use your skills in your day-to-day work, but what you are being asked to do is not challenging you to grow and develop or meeting your higher order growth needs: You are not able to make a difference and you do not have a direct line of sight between the work you do and the mission or vision of the organization. This is not an ideal situation for people with self-authoring or self-transforming minds. However, for someone operating with a socialized mind this may work very well.

Conclusions

We can conclude from the above that what employees want is to work in an organization that addresses their basic needs, and depending on the level of their psychological development, also addresses their higher order growth needs.

Therefore, to build a high-performing organization you will need to create a culture that:

- takes care of the basic needs of employees and their families;
- provides a high level of *emotional* engagement for employees (values alignment);
- provides a high level of *intellectual* engagement for employees (mission alignment);
- provides a low level of cultural entropy.

When you are able to do this, you will be able to increase employee engagement and tap into employees' discretionary energy. Discretionary energy shows up in the workplace either as a willingness to put in extra effort beyond the call of duty or as a willingness on the part of employees to bring their creative thinking to bear on their work or research.

In *A Business and Its Beliefs*, Thomas J. Watson, Jr., former President of IBM, has this to say about discretionary energy:

> I believe the real difference between success and failure in a corporation can very often be traced to the question of how well the organisation brings out the great energies and talents of its people. What does it do to help these people find common cause with each other? And how can it sustain this common cause and sense of direction from one generation to the next?[13]

Annex 7 provides a brief discussion and formula for understanding the relationship between the amount of value-added, discretionary energy that your organization can tap into and the level of cultural entropy your organization experiences.

Summary

Here are the main points of Chapter 3:

1. The source of all motivation and happiness is the satisfaction of our needs.
2. The levels of consciousness we operate from are a reflection of the needs/motivations that are uppermost in our minds.
3. There are three broad plateaus of human development that represent different ways of being in the world—the socialized mind, the self-authoring mind and the self-transforming mind.
4. The socialized mind is a dependent mind; the self-authoring mind is an independent mind; and the self-transforming mind is an interdependent mind.
5. People who operate with a socialized mind tend to be vigilant and concerned about anything that is happening around them that involves change—they much prefer stability and the status quo.
6. People who operate with a self-authoring mind are open to change and welcome the opportunities that change may bring.
7. People who operate with a self-transforming mind tend to see change as part of the normal ebb and flow of life.
8. The best way to ensure that you have a high-performing team and highly committed and engaged workforce is: (a) to place people in roles that correspond to their level of psychological development; and (b) to care about and address the full spectrum of employee needs.

Notes

1 Robert Kegan and Lisa Laskow Lahey, *Immunity to Change* (Boston, MA: Harvard Business School Publishing), 2009, pp. 16–21.

2 The UK National Values Survey carried out in October 2012, www.valuescentre.com/ uploads/2013-01-23/UK%20National%20Values%20Values%20Assessment%20 Report%20-%20Jan%2024th%202013.pdf (last accessed 4 April 2013).
3 Robert Kegan, *In Over Our Heads* (Cambridge, MA: Harvard University Press), 1994.
4 William Torbert, *Managing the Corporate Dream* (Homewood, IL: Dow-Jones), 1987.
5 Robert Kegan, *In Over Our Heads* (Cambridge, MA: Harvard University Press), 1994, pp. 27–28.
6 Ibid., p. 30.
7 Richard Barrett, *The New Leadership Paradigm* (Asheville, NC: Fulfilling Books), 2011.
8 A comprehensive leadership development programme with learning modules for leading self, leading others, leading an organization and leading in society can be accessed and downloaded by visiting www.newleadershipparadigm.com (last accessed 28 March 2013).
9 Richard Barrett, *What My Soul Told Me: A Practical Guide to Soul Activation* (Bath: Fulfilling Books), 2012.
10 Elliott Jaques and Stephen D. Clement. *Executive Leadership: A Practical Guide to Managing Complexity* (Malden, MA: Blackwell Business), 1991.
11 The correlation is mine, not Jaques'.
12 For a spiritual perspective on values alignment and mission alignment I recommend that you read *What My Soul Told Me: A Practical Guide to Soul Activation*.
13 Thomas J. Watson, Jr., *A Business and Its Beliefs* (New York: McGraw-Hill), 2003. First published in 1963.

4   Whole system change

In order to build and maintain a values-driven organization, you will need to know how to initiate and drive change: Not *change as a project* but *change as an ongoing process*. You will have to learn how to *manage the values* of your organization in the same way you manage the company's accounts: By taking regular frequent measurements of key performance indicators, and making adjustments based on the results. The main difference will be that the changes you make will be cultural changes rather than operational changes: Changes that increase employee engagement by reducing cultural entropy, and increasing values and mission alignment.

Measuring performance

In order to assess how well you are doing with your values management or change process, you will need to identify some key performance indicators. There are three types of indicators you should use:

*   *Output indicators*: These measure factors that relate to the delivery of products and services—productivity, efficiency, quality, etc.
*   *Outcome indicators*: These measure factors that relate to goals—income, sales, repeat business, new clients, market share, staff turnover, etc.
*   *Causal indicators*: As the name suggests, these measure factors that impact the output and outcome indicators. The three main causal indicators are cultural entropy, values alignment and mission alignment—the factors that influence employee engagement.

Output and outcome indicators are tangible indicators: They can be easily measured and determined. Causal indicators are known as intangible indicators: They are not so easily measured or determined. The Cultural Transformation Tools, which I will discuss in Parts II and III of this book, provide a way of measuring causal indicators. They have been designed to make the intangibles tangible and the invisible visible.

The ability to measure the intangibles is significantly important, because when you are able to measure causal indicators, you get to the root of the issues that are

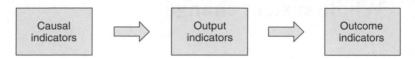

Figure 4.1 Relationship impact of indicators.

impacting your output and outcome indicators. In other words, causal indicators get you closer to the levers you need to adjust to improve your output and outcome indicators. Causal indicators primarily impact output indicators, which in turn impact outcome indicators as shown in Figure 4.1. For example, the level of cultural entropy (internal dysfunction) impacts productivity, which in turn impacts financial results.

As we shall see in Part III of this book, the three causal indicators—cultural entropy, values alignment and mission alignment—are themselves determined by three factors: The level of psychological development of the leader, the level of *personal entropy* of the current leaders, managers and supervisors, and the institutional legacy of the *personal entropy* of past leaders as experienced through the inherited systems, structures, processes, policies, procedures and incentives embedded in the organizational fabric. This deeper causal chain is shown in Figure 4.2. The shaded boxes represent the causal indicators that are measured by the Cultural Transformation Tools.

The principal tools for measuring the cultural entropy of the organization and the level of values alignment and mission alignment are the Cultural Values Assessment (CVA) and the Small Group Assessment (SGA) or Small Organization Assessment (SOA). The use of these tools is fully explained in Part II.

The principal tools for measuring the personal entropy of the current leaders, managers and supervisors are the Leadership Values Assessment (LVA) and the Leadership Development Report (LDR). The use of these tools is fully explained in Part III.

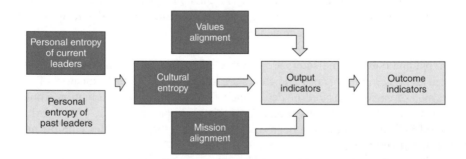

Figure 4.2 Causal chain of indicators.

Focusing on the whole system

Because all aspects of an organization are interconnected (performance is influenced by culture, culture is influenced by values and behaviours, and behaviours are influenced by motivations, and to a certain degree by incentives), it is important in any change management or cultural change process to affect the whole system, not just part of it. I can best explain what is meant by whole system change[1] by referring to Figure 4.3.

The four quadrants in this figure represent the four perspectives that can be taken of a human system such as an organization, a community or a nation.[2]

The four perspectives are:

- *Character*: The perspective as viewed from inside an individual (personal values and beliefs—top-left quadrant).
- *Personality*: The perspective as viewed from outside an individual (personal actions and behaviours—top-right quadrant).
- *Culture*: The perspective as viewed from inside a collective (cultural values and beliefs—bottom-left quadrant).
- *Society*: The perspective as viewed from outside a collective (social structures, systems, processes, actions and behaviours—bottom-right quadrant).

The two left-hand quadrants represent the intangibles—the things that are difficult to measure. The two right-hand quadrants represent the tangibles—the things that are relatively easy to measure. If you take the iceberg as a metaphor: What lies above the waterline are the things you can see—the tangibles; what lies beneath the waterline are the things you cannot see—the intangibles. If you take the tree as a metaphor: What lies underground sustains the life of what is above the ground: The roots are invisible, and the trunk and branches, which depend on

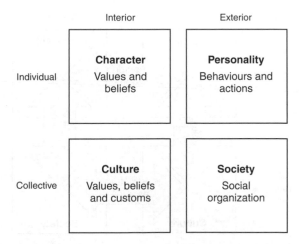

Figure 4.3 The four quadrants of human systems.

the health of the roots, are visible. What sustains and keeps humans healthy are their values and beliefs—the invisible. What are visible are their actions and behaviours.

In an organizational setting, the values, beliefs (top-left quadrant) and behaviours (top-right quadrant) of the leader and the leadership group (leaders, managers and supervisors) significantly influence the values and beliefs of the units, departments and teams that form part of the collective (the bottom-left quadrant) and the values and beliefs of the collective influence the behaviours of the collective (bottom-right quadrant). In other words, the culture of an organization is a reflection of the values and beliefs (consciousness) of the leader(s).

To be even more precise, the culture of an organization (the values and beliefs) is a reflection of the values and beliefs of the *present leaders* and the *institutionalized legacy* of the values and beliefs of past leaders as reflected in the structures, policies, procedures and incentives of the organization—the visible or tangible aspects of the culture.

Culture change

In order to successfully implement a change management or cultural change process four conditions must be met. These are shown in Figure 4.4.

The four conditions are described below:

*   *Personal alignment*: There must be an alignment between the values and beliefs of individuals and their words, actions and behaviours. This is particularly important for the leaders, managers and supervisors. The leaders, managers and supervisors must be authentic and walk their talk. If they say one thing and do another, there will be no trust in the organization.

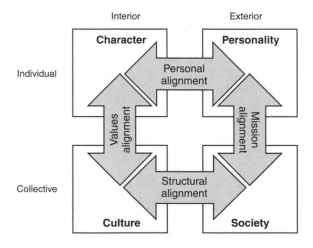

Figure 4.4 Four conditions for whole system change.

- *Structural alignment*: There must be an alignment between the stated values and beliefs of the organization as expressed in the espoused values, vision and mission, and the behaviours of the organization as reflected in the structures, policies, procedures and incentives of the organization. In other words, the organization, as a whole, must also walk the talk.
- *Values alignment*: There must be an alignment between the personal values of employees and the lived values of the organization. Employees need to feel at home in the organization so they can bring their whole selves to work. There must be no fear. There must be a sense of autonomy, equality, accountability, fairness, openness, transparency and trust.[3]
- *Mission alignment*: There must be an alignment between employees' sense of purpose or vocation and the role and duties they are asked to perform. The level of job complexity must also be in alignment with employees' level of personal development, and employees must feel that the organization is on the right track.

The process of culture change

Culture change in organizations requires a shift in the values and beliefs of the leaders, managers and supervisors (see Figure 4.5). When the values and beliefs of the leaders, managers and supervisors change (1), their actions and behaviours change (2). This, in turn, leads to a change in the values and beliefs of the culture of the organization (3), which in turn leads to a change in the actions and behaviours of the organization (4).

What I am effectively saying is that the culture of an organization is a reflection of the level of personal development (consciousness) of the leader(s). Similarly, the culture of a department is a reflection of the level of personal development (consciousness) of the director of the department, and the culture of

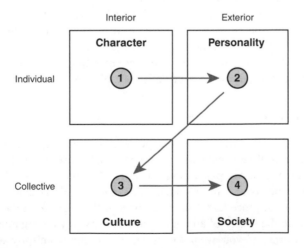

Figure 4.5 The process of culture change in an organization.

a team is a reflection of the level of personal development (consciousness) of the team leader.

When the leader of an organization with a strong, positive, high-performing culture retires or moves on, he or she is usually replaced by someone who is promoted from within the organization. This is done in order to preserve the culture. Organizations that have weak, negative, low-performing cultures usually replace their leaders with someone from outside the organization. The new leader comes with new values and beliefs and creates a new culture.

The extent to which the new leader is able to do this depends to a large extent on the strength of his or her character and personality, the commitment they have to the mission of the organization, and the power of the vision they hold for the future of the organization. If the new leader is weak in any of these areas, he or she may not have a discernible influence on the culture, especially if the institutional legacy of past leaders is deeply embedded in the organization's systems, processes and incentives. Some new leaders of institutions do not have the energy or the courage to take on a whole system change process, especially when they know their tenure as the head of the organization is limited to a specific timeframe.

Employee engagement

As discussed in the previous chapter, in addition to the level of cultural entropy, there are two other factors that significantly impact employee engagement—values alignment and mission alignment. These are the two vertical arrows in Figure 4.4. These two factors are profoundly influenced by the personal alignment of the leaders and the structural alignment of the organization. These are the two horizontal arrows in Figure 4.4.

Since the values of the organization and the way it is managed are a reflection of the values and beliefs of the present leaders *and* the legacy of past leaders, if you want to build a values-driven organization then the leaders must change how they operate (change their values, beliefs and behaviours by focusing on their personal mastery[4] and shift to a higher level of personal consciousness) or you must change the leaders. Furthermore, you must make sure that the structures, policies, procedures and incentives of the organization reflect the values of the organization and the values and needs of the employees—structural alignment.

Cultural entropy

The level of cultural entropy that is experienced in an organization is directly linked to the level of personal mastery and personal consciousness of the present leader(s) and the legacy of past leaders. The fear-based energies exhibited by the current leaders (personal entropy) and the fear-based energies that show up in the structures, policies, procedures and incentives of the organization (the legacy of past leaders) are the source of all the cultural entropy in your organization.

In other words, if you want to reduce the cultural entropy and improve employee engagement of your organization, you need to improve the level of personal alignment of the current leaders, managers and supervisors (reduce the level of their personal entropy) *and*, at the same time, change the structures, policies, procedures and incentives of the organization to align with the values of the organization and the values and needs of employees. How to reduce the personal entropy of the leaders and the cultural entropy of the organization is tackled in Part III of this book.

Ultimately, when everything is considered, there are three main factors you need to focus on if you want to build a high-performance, values-driven organization—*the personal alignment of the leaders, managers and supervisors, the structural alignment of the organization* and *the values and mission alignment of the employees.* The key objective in all these interventions is to increase the level of employee engagement.

The process of whole system change

Overview

Whole system change involves addressing the four conditions shown in Figure 4.4—personal alignment, structural alignment, values alignment and mission alignment—and addressing the system-wide causes of cultural entropy.

The starting point is to find out what is working and not working in the organization. This involves carrying out a cultural diagnostic (Cultural Values Assessment) for the whole organization, including data cuts for each business unit, department and team, as well as organization-wide demographic categories such as gender and age. The results of the assessment will allow you to identify the level of cultural entropy, values alignment and mission alignment for the whole organization, and for the individual business units, departments and teams. The results also provide you with a roadmap for change.

Change needs to happen at two levels: At the level of the organization as a whole, and at the level of the units, departments and teams that have the highest levels of cultural entropy and lowest levels of values alignment and mission alignment. When you compare the level of cultural entropy, values alignment and mission alignment in each business unit, department and team you will be able to develop a "league table" of the "best" and "worst." Those units, departments and teams with the highest levels of cultural entropy and the lowest levels of values and mission alignment are the ones that need the most attention.

This will involve working with the leaders of these units, departments and teams on their personal mastery to reduce their level of personal entropy, thereby reducing the level of cultural entropy they are creating in their units, departments and teams.

Part II of this book provides case studies showing how the results of Cultural Values Assessments (cultural diagnostic) are used to formulate recommendations for improving the performance of an organization. Part III provides case studies showing how the results of leadership values assessments (personal diagnostic) are used to formulate recommendations for improving the performance of individual leaders.

The process

The whole system culture change process can be divided into nine stages. These are shown in Figure 4.6 and described below in the following paragraphs. The first five stages apply to organizations that have not been involved in a cultural change programme in recent years. The last five stages represent the annual feedback loop that allows organizations to manage their culture and values on an ongoing basis.

The annual feedback loop involves carrying out Cultural Values Assessments and leadership values assessments, to identify the changes that need to be made, and then implementing these changes. The changes you make should eventually result in a drop in cultural entropy, and an increase in employee engagement (values and mission alignment): They should also result in an improvement in the output and outcome indicators. Every year the changes in causal indicators (cultural entropy, values alignment and mission alignment) should be correlated

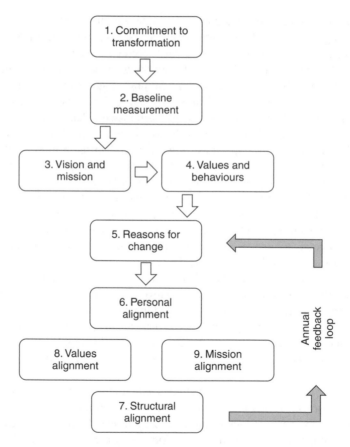

Figure 4.6 The whole system change process.

against the changes in output and outcome indicators as shown in the case studies included in Chapter 7.

It is usually not necessary to review the vision, mission and espoused values of the organization every year. However, you may notice over a period of three-to-four years that the results of the Cultural Values Assessments indicate employee value shifts that might cause you to consider reviewing your vision, mission and values. I know that in my own company, over a period of 15 years, we have twice found it helpful to change one of our values. We have never found it necessary to change our vision and mission.

Step 1: Commitment to transformation

Whole system change begins with the personal commitment of the leader and the leadership team to the change process. Without this commitment there is no point in proceeding. It is important for them to understand that, in making this commitment, the leader and the whole leadership team may have to focus on their own personal transformation, particularly those who head up units or departments that display high levels of cultural entropy.

The *sine qua non* of culture change is: To improve the culture of an organization, the leaders must change or you must change the leaders.

Organizational transformation begins with the personal transformation of the leaders. If there is no commitment by the leader and his or her leadership team to a shift in their values and behaviours, it will be pointless embarking on any form of whole system change process.

Additionally, the leader of an organization must own the process and be personally involved in the initiative. The leadership team must fully support the leader in this work. The process of cultural transformation is not something that can be delegated, nor can it be handed off to a team of consultants. Consultants can help guide the process, but they should not be in charge of the work. It is not a project: It is a process. Culture work is something that the organization has to do for itself, and it is always ongoing: It never ends. Culture has to be managed, and the way we manage culture is through values.

At the start of the cultural transformation process, it will be important, if the leader has not already done so, to handpick his or her leadership team. As Jim Collins says in *Good to Great*, getting the right people on the leadership team and sitting in the right seats is extremely important.[5]

It is quite usual for there to be one or two naysayers in the leadership team who are not willing to sign up to personal transformation. They are happy for others to do it, but they are not interested themselves. This is the point where they have to decide to get on or off the bus. There is no room on the bus for anyone who is not a willing participant and committed to the process. Usually at this point, the naysayers start looking for alternative employment. It is important that the leader be aware that this might happen and is willing to go ahead despite the fact that he or she might lose some of his or her best performers.

Step 2: Baseline measurement

After the leader and leadership team have made a personal commitment to the change process, then you can proceed by carrying out a Cultural Values Assessment (CVA) of the organization and, at the same time, build a scorecard of the organization's current performance, including output indicators such as productivity, efficiency and quality; outcome indicators such as profit, income and market share; and causal indicators—cultural entropy, values alignment and mission alignment—that you get from your CVA results. The object of the scorecard is to develop a set of baseline indicators from which you can measure the progress and impact of your whole system change process from year to year. This is also the best moment to do a values clarification exercise. This involves setting up focus groups across the whole organization to develop a deeper understanding of the impact and behaviours associated with the top positive and potentially limiting values that show up in the results of the Cultural Values Assessment. Instructions for carrying out a values clarification exercise are provided in Chapter 6.

Step 3: Vision and mission

After you have completed your baseline measurements, the next step is to review or redefine where the company is going. It is time to develop an internal and external vision and mission for the organization. A methodology for doing this, which is known as the Four Why's Process, is described in Annex 8.

In large and medium-sized organizations setting the vision and mission is the job of the leadership team. This task cannot be delegated. The direct reports of the leadership team (the leadership teams of the members of the leadership team) and a cross-section of the rest of the leadership group should be asked for their comments once the leadership team has sketched out some draft statements. The vision and mission statements should be short, easily memorable and inspirational. They should reflect a higher purpose. The purpose of the mission and vision statements is to give focus and direction to the organization so everyone is working towards the same goals. In small organizations, as long as it is manageable, it makes sense to involve as many people as possible in setting the vision and mission. Guidelines for developing mission and vision statements are provided in Annex 9.

Step 4: Values and behaviours

In addition to developing a vision and mission for the organization, it will also be important to define the values the organization wishes to embrace to guide its decision making. These are known as the *espoused* values. See Annex 9. The results of the CVA will be useful in this regard since it will highlight the values that are most important to employees in their personal lives and the desired cultural values. To the extent possible, all employees should be involved in this process.

The values should be single words or small phrases that are easily memorized and support the vision and mission. Normally, there should be no more than five values: Four is ideal. Preferably, the values should be spread over multiple levels of consciousness with at least one value at levels four and five. Some organizations who work with the Barrett model prefer to choose seven values—one at each of the seven levels of consciousness. Some organizations like to prioritize their values. What is important in this exercise is that the values can be easily recalled from memory. This can be difficult if you have a large number of values. The need to prioritize your values becomes important when you have more than four values. More information about the considerations involved in selecting espoused values is provided in Chapter 13.

The purpose of the espoused values is to provide a set of common principles that define how people in the organization should interact with each other and with the outside world.

Once the espoused values have been chosen, two or three behaviour statements should be developed for each value. To determine what behaviour statements are appropriate for each value you can use a technique such as appreciative inquiry.[6]

The purpose of developing behaviour statements is twofold:

- To give clarity to what each espoused value means in the context of the day-to-day operations of the organization so you can recognize the value in action.
- To provide a way of evaluating executive and employee performance—to measure the degree to which leaders, managers and supervisors as well as other employees are living the values of the organization.

Because behaviours are always contextual, it is not unusual for different behaviours to be used for the same espoused values in different parts of the organization. The behaviour statements should be short, memorable, one-sentence statements that describe the actions that support the value they represent, and they should be appropriate for the context of the work unit. For example, the value of "trust" on a factory floor may give more focus to competence-based behaviours, whereas "trust" in a sales or accounting department may give more focus to character-based behaviours.

Together, the values and behaviours, and the vision and mission, should define the unique character and personality of the organization, the levels of consciousness it operates from, and the key features of the brand. The ultimate purpose of defining the vision, mission, values and behaviours of an organization is to create a high-trust culture, a capacity for collective action and a sense of internal cohesion.

The process of building internal cohesion should begin with the leadership team. The leadership team can be regarded as a cultural fractal of the whole organization. If you don't have internal cohesion in the leadership team, you will not have internal cohesion in the rest of the organization. The only way to build internal cohesion in a leadership team is to create a climate of trust. This requires that the leaders spend quality time together, getting to know each other at more than a superficial level. You will find the Trust Matrix exercise, which is described in Annex 10, extremely useful in this regard.

Step 5: Reasons for change

For any significant change process or cultural adjustment there should be a clear understanding among the executive population about why the proposed changes are being undertaken. Whether you are involved in a one-off change project or carrying out an annual cultural adjustment (values management exercise), the results of the Cultural Values Assessment will direct you to what you need to do to improve your outputs and outcomes. The changes that are proposed should be clearly communicated to everyone along with the benefits the proposed changes are expected to bring.

When the changes that are being proposed are based on the results of a Cultural Values Assessment in which a large number of employees have participated, the changes are usually welcomed. The Cultural Values Assessment gives employees a voice. It provides a way for employees to communicate directly with the leaders of the organization about what they believe is working and not working, what is important to them and the needs they have that are not being met.

Organizations that use the Cultural Values Assessment on a regular basis have found that the number of employees taking the survey each year increases as employees realize that the leaders of the organization are not only taking note of what they say, they are also taking actions that address their needs. When this happens the year-on-year results of the Cultural Values Assessment will normally show a drop in cultural entropy and/or an increase in values alignment and mission alignment (see Chapter 7 for two case studies of values management spanning seven to eight years).

Step 6: Personal alignment

Personal alignment should begin with the leadership team. As shown in Figure 4.5, when the leaders transform—achieve a higher level of personal mastery or adopt a higher set of values—their behaviours change, and as their behaviours change, the culture changes.

To this end, it is important for all members of the leadership team and the extended leadership group to get feedback from their colleagues on the extent to which their values and behaviours support or detract from the desired organizational culture. One way of doing this is for all members of the leadership team and the extended leadership group to carry out a Leadership Values Assessment (LVA). The feedback from this assessment should include a coaching session to support the leader in lowering his or her level of personal entropy and shifting his or her focus to the higher levels of consciousness—helping them to find a sense of purpose, to collaborate with others to make a difference, and to leave a positive legacy. This will involve developing their empathy and compassion skills and tapping into their intuition and inspiration.

After the leadership team has embarked on the process of personal alignment, the direct reports of the leadership team should follow suit. Eventually, everyone in the organization who is a leader, manager or supervisor should participate in some form of LVA feedback process that enables them to grow and develop and improve their performance. Part III of this book is devoted to the topic of personal alignment.

Step 7: Structural alignment

The purpose of the structural alignment process is to reconfigure the structures, policies, procedures and incentives of the organization so they fully reflect the espoused values *and* the vision and mission of the organization. For change to happen, the espoused values must become pervasive at the institutional level. In large-scale organizations, the process of structural alignment can take up to two-to-three years to implement. In smaller organizations it can be done in less than a year. The responsibility for this usually falls to the human resource function. Part IV of this book is devoted to the topic of structural alignment.

Step 8: Values alignment

In order for the espoused values of the organization to be lived, everyone in the organization needs to know what the values are, and how the values relate to the role they are performing in the organization. This is usually communicated through a values alignment workshop.

As already stated, different behaviours may be associated with the same value depending on the functions that a particular unit, department or team performs. It is useful, as part of the values alignment process, for employees to define the behaviours of their unit during the values alignment workshop. Once employees in a particular unit have agreed on a set of behaviours, they should individually and collectively commit to them, and be accountable for supporting each other in living the agreed behaviours.

The purpose of values alignment is to inculcate the espoused values and behaviours of the organization into the executive and employee population. Apart from the informational content, the values alignment workshops should give participants the opportunity to explore their own values and understand and practise the concept of values-based decision making. The Personal Values Assessment (PVA), which can be found at www.valuescentre.com/pva, can be used as part of the personal values clarification process.

Step 9: Mission alignment

Just as everyone in the organization needs to be aware of and aligned with the espoused values and behaviours of the organization, they also need to be aware of and aligned with the vision and mission. This is usually communicated through a mission alignment workshop. The purpose of a mission alignment workshop is to make sure everyone has the same understanding of the mission and vision of the organization.

Apart from the informational content, the mission alignment workshop should give employees the opportunity to explore their own sense of purpose or mission to see if the role they are currently performing matches their skills and talents, and aligns with their passion. The workshop should also enable employees to get a clear line of sight between the work they do each day and the mission or vision of the organization. Every employee needs to know how the contribution they make on a daily basis makes a difference to the success of the organization. Part II of this book is devoted to the topic of values alignment and mission alignment.

Frequent mistakes

The four most frequent mistakes made in culture change programmes are as follows:

Forgetting to do structural alignment: This step—the realignment of the structural incentives—is the one that is most frequently ignored, poorly executed or forgotten in cultural transformation initiatives.

Many organizations put a great deal of energy and resources into personal alignment or personal development programmes for their executives without doing anything about structural alignment. This serves only to aggravate the level of discontent and disillusionment in the executive and employee population. When executives and employees return from personal development and personal mastery programmes, they usually come back with a higher personal awareness about how they should be interacting with their colleagues. They quickly become disillusioned when they realize that, although they have changed, the organization has not. The new behaviours they have learned are not practised by their superiors, and they are also not rewarded.

Unique focus on team building: Another frequent mistake that companies make is to invest in team building without first focusing on personal alignment. This significantly limits the potential for success: Without self-knowledge and personal mastery the impact of a team-building exercise may not last. For maximum impact, personal alignment (learning to lead yourself) should precede team building. This particularly applies to the top team where very often most of the dysfunction lies. Learning to lead yourself is a prerequisite to leading others.[7]

Failure to customize the transformation process: Change agents and consultants frequently make the mistake of using off-the-shelf personal alignment or team-building programmes that have not been tailored to the specific needs of the organization, unit, department or team they are working with. When you carry out a Cultural Values Assessment (CVA), a Small Group Assessment (SGA) or a Small Organization Assessment (SOA) you immediately know, when you get the results, what issues need to be tackled and what topics your personal alignment and team-building programmes should address. In addition I would also suggest that you use the Trust Matrix exercise described in Annex 10 to zero-in on the issues that the team needs to work on.

Failure to build internal capacity for values/culture management: Whole system change is an inside job and it is an ongoing process: It needs to be managed and facilitated by people who are trained. It cannot be handed off to consultants; but it can be guided by consultants—by experienced individuals who are able to transfer their knowledge and skills to the people in the organization who are charged with values/culture management. In large organizations, it is particularly important to train people throughout the organization in the use of the Seven Levels of Consciousness Model and the Cultural Transformation Tools. These people, once trained, become the organization's cultural ambassadors and culture navigators also known as change leaders or culture leads (see Chapter 15).

Conclusions

In order to build a high-performing, values-driven organization that engenders high levels of employee engagement (values alignment and mission alignment) and low levels of cultural entropy, you will need to develop a culture change process that targets both the personal alignment of the leaders and the structural alignment of the organization.

This work should not be approached as a project: It should be regarded as an ongoing process of values management that becomes deeply engrained into the measurement ethos of the organization. Using the Cultural Values Assessment and the Leadership Values Assessment, on an annual basis, you will be able to monitor the level of cultural entropy, the level of values alignment and mission alignment, and the level of personal entropy of the leaders, managers and supervisors. You should also monitor and review the level of structural alignment every year, after you have reviewed the results of the annual Cultural Values Assessment.

Carrying out an annual Cultural Values Assessment allows you to determine the personal needs of your employees, and monitor the extent to which they feel aligned with the culture of the organization (values alignment), and the extent they feel the organization is on the right track (mission alignment). Together with the level of cultural entropy, these indicators enable you to assess the level of employee engagement.

Summary

Here are the main points of Chapter 4:

1. To be effective, any change management or cultural transformation process should focus on the whole system, not just part of it.
2. In order to successfully implement a cultural transformation process, four conditions must be met—personal alignment, structural alignment, values alignment and mission alignment.
3. Personal alignment: There must be an alignment between the values and beliefs of individuals and their words, actions and behaviours. This is particularly important for the leaders, managers and supervisors.

4. Structural alignment: There must be an alignment between the stated values of the organization and the behaviours of the organization as they are reflected in the structures, policies, procedures and incentives of the organization.
5. Values alignment: There must be an alignment between the personal values of employees and the lived values of the organization. It is important that all employees feel at home in the organization and can bring their whole selves to work.
6. Mission alignment: Employees need to feel that the organization is on the right track. They must also feel a sense of alignment between their own sense of purpose or vocation and the role and duties they are asked to perform.
7. The culture of an organization is a reflection of the level of personal development (consciousness) of the leader(s).
8. The fear-based energies exhibited by the current and past leaders are the source of the organization's cultural entropy.
9. In order to build a high-performing, values-driven organization you will need to develop a process of ongoing values management.
10. The three main factors you need to focus on if you want to build a values-driven organization are the personal alignment of the leaders, managers and supervisors, the structural alignment of the organization and the values and mission alignment of employees.

Notes

1 The concept of whole system change described in this book is based on the work of Ken Wilber.
2 Ken Wilber, *A Brief History of Everything* (New York: Shambhala), 1996, p. 71.
3 These seven values represent distinct stages in the development of democracy. For a full discussion of these values read Part Two of Richard Barrett, *Love, Fear and the Destiny of Nations: The Impact of the Evolution of Human Consciousness on World Affairs* (Bath: Fulfilling Books), pp. 195–285.
4 Personal mastery: The process by which we bring our subconscious fears into our conscious awareness and thereby learn how to manage them and the emotions associated with them. See Richard Barrett, *The New Leadership Paradigm* (Asheville, NC: Fulfilling Books), pp. 151–190.
5 Jim Collins, *Good to Great* (New York: HarperCollins), 2001.
6 Appreciative Inquiry (AI) is a process or philosophy for involving individuals in a dialogue that focuses on renewal and change. See *The New Leadership Paradigm*, pp. 456–457.
7 These topics are dealt with a extensively in my book, *The New Leadership Paradigm*.

Part II

Mapping organizational values

The purpose of Part II of this book is to provide the reader with a clear understanding of how to map, measure and monitor the values of an organization, and how to use the results to reduce cultural entropy and increase the level of values and mission alignment.

You will recall from Chapter 4, Figure 4.4 (shown below), that there are four conditions necessary for whole system change. This part of the book focuses on two of these conditions—*values alignment* and *mission alignment*.

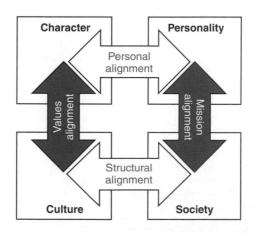

5   The model

The Cultural Transformation Tools, which I will describe in detail in the next two chapters of this book, are based on the Seven Levels of Consciousness Model, which was developed in 1996–7. The Seven Levels of Consciousness Model is based on Abraham Maslow's hierarchy of needs[1] and aligns with the seven stages of human psychological development. The Seven Levels of Consciousness Model applies to all individuals and all human group structures—organizations, institutions, communities, nations, etc. Annex 11 describes the origins and development of the model. Annex 12 defines what consciousness is and how it operates in our lives. The seven levels of personal consciousness and organizational consciousness are described below.

Seven levels of personal consciousness

As indicated earlier, each level of human need is associated with specific values. As people grow and evolve, their values change in accordance with their needs. Whatever we value is a reflection of the needs associated with the level of consciousness we are currently operating at, and the unmet needs we have not resolved from previous levels of development. The full range of human needs is shown in Table 5.1 along with the levels of consciousness at which they occur and the associated developmental tasks.

The developmental tasks represent the motivations associated with each stage of psychological growth (see Annex 1). Not everyone reaches the higher stages of development. Many people do not get much further than the differentiation stage (Level 3 consciousness). They stay entrenched in the cultural conditioning that they experienced during their childhood. Education, continuous learning and travel help us to move beyond this stage. When we learn more, and interact with people who were brought up in other cultures, we begin to see that ours is not the only way of looking at the world. We see that other cultures look at the world differently. This causes us to question our own way of viewing the world. This, in turn, leads us into the individuation stage of development where we begin to formulate our own unique view of the world based on our personal experiences; we begin to shift from dependence to independence. We begin to let go of our cultural beliefs and focus on our universal human values.

Table 5.1 Seven levels of personal consciousness

Levels of consciousness	Needs and actions	Developmental task
7 Service	Devoting your life to selfless service in pursuit of your purpose and the well-being of humanity.	*Serving*: Fulfilling your destiny by giving back to the world.
6 Making a difference	Actualizing your sense of purpose by collaborating with others to make a bigger difference in the world than you could on your own.	*Integrating*: Aligning with others who share the same purpose or vision to create a better world.
5 Internal cohesion	Uncovering your authentic self and finding meaning in your life by aligning with your passion and purpose and building a vision of the future you want to create.	*Self-actualizing*: Aligning fully with who you are so you can become all you can become and fulfil your potential.
4 Transformation	Exploring who you are and satisfying your need for autonomy, freedom and independence by developing your unique gifts and talents.	*Individuating*: Letting go of the aspects of your cultural and personal conditioning that no longer serve you or truly represent who you are.
3 Self-esteem	Satisfying your need to feel good about yourself by managing your life, having pride in your performance and feeling recognized by others.	*Differentiating*: Separating yourself from the crowd by honing your skills and talents and excelling at what you do best.
2 Relationship	Satisfying your need for belonging and feeling loved and respected by your family, friends and colleagues.	*Conforming*: Keeping safe and staying loyal to your family, kin and culture.
1 Survival	Satisfying your physiological survival needs.	*Surviving*: Staying alive and keeping healthy.

The focus of the first three levels of consciousness is on meeting the needs of the ego.[2] These include the need for physiological survival, the need for physical and emotional safety (love and belonging) and the emotional need for self-esteem.

The focus of the fourth level is transformation. This is where we learn to let go of the conscious and subconscious fears we have about meeting our physical, relationship and self-esteem needs, and begin to embrace our authentic selves by seeking freedom and becoming accountable for our lives. At this level we give primary attention to our mental needs.

The focus of the upper three levels of consciousness is on meeting the needs of the soul.[3,4] These include the need to find meaning in our lives, the need to make a difference and the need to be of service. These represent our spiritual needs.

Individuals who focus *exclusively* on the satisfaction of the lower needs tend to live narrow, unworldly lives, and may find themselves overly preoccupied with satisfying the conscious and subconscious fears of the ego. The fears of the ego lead us to believe that we do not have enough of our basic needs. Consequently, we are never fully happy either because: (a) we do not have enough money or security; (b) we do not have enough friendship and love; or (c) we are not acknowledged or recognized enough.

If you grew up without one, some or all of these basic needs being met, you may well find yourself trying to fill these needs in your adult life. This causes you to lead a dependency-based existence. You become dependent on others for your survival and safety, love and friendship, and your self-esteem or sense of self-worth. It is only when you release the subconscious and conscious fears of the ego that keep you in this dependency-based existence, that you become free to truly pursue your growth needs.

Individuals that focus *exclusively* on the satisfaction of the higher needs tend to lack the skills necessary to operate effectively in the physical world. They can be ineffectual and impractical when it comes to taking care of their basic needs. We describe such people as not being "grounded." To be successful in the world you need to learn how to master the satisfaction of all your needs so you can operate from full spectrum consciousness.

Mastering your personal needs

You master your Level 1 needs by developing the skills and capabilities that are necessary to ensure your physical survival including your ability to hold down a job and earn a living. You master your Level 2 needs by developing the interpersonal relationship skills that allow you to get along with people, and feel safe and loved. You master your Level 3 needs by nurturing and developing your skills and talents so you feel good about yourself. You master your Level 4 needs by learning to release the subconscious and conscious fears you hold about satisfying your basic needs (Levels 1 through 3) and developing your freedom, autonomy and independence. You master your Level 5 needs by discovering your personal meaning for existence—what you are passionate about and the work you love to do. You master your Level 6 needs when you are able to actualize your sense of purpose by making a difference in the world. You master your Level 7 needs when making a difference becomes a way of life and you embrace the concept of selfless service.

The most successful individuals are those that develop full spectrum consciousness—the ability to master the needs associated with every level of consciousness. They are able to respond and adapt appropriately to all the challenges that life throws at them.

The successful mastery of each stage of development involves two steps: First, becoming aware of the emergent need, and, second, developing the skills that are necessary to satisfy that need. You are always aware of the needs and values of the level of consciousness you are operating from, and the needs and values of the previous levels you have passed through, but you are unaware of the needs and values of the next and subsequent levels of consciousness. This makes it difficult for you to develop a deep sense of connection with people who are operating at a level of consciousness you have not yet reached, because you are operating at different psychological levels with different values. You do not feel the same sense of camaraderie as you do with people who are at the same level of consciousness and have similar values. It also makes it difficult for you to develop a deep sense of connection with people who are operating at a level of consciousness you have already transcended. You may feel a human connection to such people, but you will not have the same shared interests. You will be able to understand what motivates them, but they may not be able to understand what motivates you.

Before you become aware of an emergent need at a new level of consciousness, you are unconsciously incompetent at that new level. You do not know what you don't know. When you become aware of a need at an emergent level of consciousness, you are generally unskilled at satisfying it—you are consciously incompetent. You know what you don't know. As you learn the skills that are necessary to satisfy your needs at the new level of consciousness, you become consciously competent—you know what to do to satisfy the need, but you have to think about what to do every time the need comes up. Eventually, when you are adept at satisfying your needs at the new level of consciousness, you become unconsciously competent at that level—the skills you need have become second nature. You can automatically respond to and satisfy the need without conscious thought.

Seven levels of organizational consciousness

Organizations grow and develop in the same way as individuals—by successfully mastering their needs. The most successful organizations are those that develop full spectrum consciousness—the ability to master the needs associated with every level of organizational consciousness. They are able to respond and adapt appropriately to all the challenges that the market place (or in the case of a public sector organization, the institutional environment) throws at them.

The seven existential needs that constitute the seven stages in the development of *organizational* consciousness are shown in Table 5.2 along with the associated developmental tasks. The developmental tasks represent the stages that an organization goes through from start-up to full spectrum performance. These are similar to the development tasks associated with the seven stages of personal psychological development.

Mastering your organization's needs

The focus of the first three levels of organizational consciousness is on the basic needs of business—financial stability and profitability, employee and customer satisfaction, and high performance systems and processes.

Table 5.2 Seven levels of organizational consciousness

Levels of consciousness	Actions and needs	Developmental task
7 Service	Creating a long-term sustainable future for the organization by caring for humanity and preserving the Earth's life support systems.	*Serving*: Safeguarding the well-being of the planet and society for future generations.
6 Making a difference	Building the resilience of the organization by cooperating with other organizations and the local communities in which the organization operates.	*Collaborating*: Aligning with other like-minded organizations and communities for mutual benefit and support.
5 Internal cohesion	Enhancing the capacity of the organization for collective action by aligning employee motivations around a shared set of values and an inspiring vision.	*Bonding*: Creating an internally cohesive, high-trust culture that enables the organization to fulfil its purpose.
4 Transformation	Increasing innovation by giving employees a voice in decision making and making them accountable for their futures and the overall success of the organization.	*Empowering*: Empowering employees to participate in decision making by giving them freedom and autonomy.
3 Self-esteem	Establishing structures, policies, procedures and processes that create order, support the performance of the organization and enhance employee pride.	*Performing*: Building high-performance systems and processes that focus on the efficient running of the organization.
2 Relationship	Resolving conflicts and building harmonious relationships that create a sense of loyalty among employees and strong connection to customers.	*Harmonizing*: Creating a sense of belonging and mutual respect among employees and caring for customers.
1 Survival	Creating financial stability, profitability and caring for the health and safety of all employees.	*Surviving*: Becoming financially viable and independent.

The focus of the fourth level of consciousness is on adaptability—continuous renewal and transformation—a shift from fear-based, rigid, authoritarian hierarchies or silos to more open, inclusive, adaptive and democratic systems of governance that empower employees to operate with responsible freedom (accountability).

The focus of the upper three levels of consciousness is on organizational cohesion, building mutually beneficial alliances and partnerships, and safeguarding the well-being of human society.

Organizations that focus *exclusively* on the satisfaction of their basic needs are not usually market leaders. They can be successful in their specific niche, but in general they are too internally focused and self-absorbed, or too rigid and bureaucratic to become innovators in their fields. They are slow to adapt to changes in market conditions and do not empower their employees. There is little enthusiasm among the workforce and innovation and creativity get suppressed. Levels of staff engagement are relatively low. Such organizations are run by authoritarian leaders who operate by creating a culture of fear. They are not emotionally healthy places to work. Employees feel frustrated or disempowered and may complain about stress.

Organizations that focus *exclusively* on the satisfaction of the higher needs lack the basic business skills necessary to operate effectively and profitably. They are ineffectual and impractical when it comes to financial matters, they are not customer oriented and they lack the systems and processes necessary for high performance. They are simply not grounded in the reality of business.

Developmental tasks

The first task when you create an organization is to find ways of surviving financially. If you cannot survive—achieve an income stream that is larger than your expenses—then you will go bankrupt or fail.

Once a sustainable income stream has been achieved, the next task is to focus on relationships—managing internal conflicts, creating a sense of harmony and ensuring customers feel cared for and are happy with your products or services. If harmony cannot be achieved, frictions, frustrations and fragmentation will appear that undermine the organization's performance. If your customers are not happy they will quickly migrate to other providers.

The next developmental task is to create order and efficiency in the structure and operations of your organization by focusing on values such as excellence, quality and professionalism. You want to be productive, and you want your employees to feel a sense of pride in the organization. You need to develop a reputation for reliability and agility so you can be responsive to the needs of the market place.

To be responsive, you need to innovate. To innovate, you need to engage the minds of your employees. To engage the minds of your employees, you have to involve them in decision making—give them a sense of ownership.

An organization cannot move to the transformation stage of development if it does not give its employees a voice in decision making. This means empowering your employees by giving them responsible freedom—a felt sense of accountability for their contribution to the organization. This stage of development is critically dependent on the degree to which the leadership group chooses to embrace democratic principles. Box 5.1 provides an example of the principles of organizational democracy promoted by WorldBlu.[5]

I think it is important to recognize that you cannot transform an organization while you are operating from Level 3 consciousness. This was the problem with the re-engineering movement at the end of the last century. It failed to produce

Box 5.1 WorldBlu: Ten principles of organizational democracy

Purpose and vision: A democratic organization is clear about why it exists and what it hopes to achieve (its vision). These act as its true North, offering guidance and discipline to the organization's direction.

Transparency: Say goodbye to the "secret society" mentality. Democratic organizations are transparent and open with employees about the financial health, strategy and agenda of the organization.

Dialogue and listening: Instead of top-down monologue or dysfunctional silence that characterizes most work places, democratic organizations are committed to having conversations that bring out new levels of meaning and connection.

Fairness and dignity: Democratic organizations are committed to fairness and dignity, not treating some people like "somebodies" and other people like "nobodies."

Accountability: Democratic organizations point fingers, not in a blaming way but in a liberating way. They are crystal clear about who is accountable to whom and for what.

Individual and collective: In democratic organizations, the individual is just as important as the whole; meaning employees are valued for their individual contribution as well as for what they do to help achieve the collective goals of the organization.

Choice: Democratic organizations thrive on giving employees meaningful choices.

Integrity: Integrity is the name of the game, and democratic companies have a lot of it. They understand that freedom takes discipline and also doing what is morally and ethically right.

Decentralization: Democratic organizations make sure power is appropriately shared and distributed among people throughout the organization.

Reflection and evaluation: Democratic organizations are committed to continuous feedback and development, and are willing to learn from the past and apply lessons to improve the future.

lasting and profound change because it was top-down, hierarchically driven. It did not involve employees in the decision-making process and many employees lost their jobs in the drive for efficiency. You have to embrace the values of the transformation level to be successful in any form of change process.

Once you have empowered your employees by giving them responsible freedom, the next step is to get everyone heading in the same direction and living the same values. To do this, you need to create a shared vision to give clarity to your purpose, and a shared set of values to guide decision making. The vision should embrace a higher purpose—a purpose that supports the well-being of humanity or the planet. The values should be values that resonate with the hearts and minds of employees.

Only when the organization has achieved a strong sense of internal cohesion (a high-trust culture) will it be able to successfully move to the next stage of development—collaborating with other like-minded organizations, partners and communities for mutual well-being and support. The purpose of this stage of development is to ensure the long-term resilience of the organization.

Finally, the last stage of development is to support our human society. The organization must become a responsible global citizen by doing what it can to support and create a sustainable future for the local communities where it operates, and for humanity in general by helping the poor and disadvantaged and protecting the planet's life support systems.

Each of these developmental tasks corresponds to a different level of consciousness—the focus of each of the seven levels of organizational consciousness is explained below.

Survival consciousness

The first and most basic need of all organizations is to ensure their financial survival. Without profits or access to a continuing stream of funds, organizations quickly perish. Every organization needs to make financial stability a primary concern. A precondition for success at this level of consciousness is a healthy focus on cash flow and the bottom line. When companies become too entrenched in survival consciousness they develop an unhealthy short-term focus on shareholder value. In such situations, making the quarterly numbers—satisfying the needs of the financial markets—can preoccupy the minds of the leaders to the exclusion of all other factors including the needs of employees. This leads to excessive control, micro-management, caution and a tendency to be risk-averse.

Businesses that operate from survival consciousness are not interested in strategic alliances; takeovers are more their game. They will purchase a company and plunder its assets. They see people and the Earth as resources to be exploited for gain. When asked to conform to regulations, they do the minimum. They have an attitude of begrudging compliance.

The key to success at the first level of consciousness is strong financial performance and a focus on employee health and safety. Without profits, companies cannot invest in their employees, create new products or build strong relationships with their customers and the local communities where they work.

Relationship consciousness

The second basic need for all organizations is to create harmonious interpersonal relationships and good internal communications. Without good relationships with employees, customers and suppliers, a company's survival will be compromised. The critical issue at this level of consciousness is to create a sense of loyalty and belonging among employees, and a sense of caring and connection between the organization and its customers and suppliers. Preconditions for creating a sense of belonging are open communication, mutual respect and employee recognition. Preconditions for caring are friendliness, responsiveness and listening. When these are in place, loyalty and satisfaction among employees and customers will be high. Traditions and rituals help cement these bonds.

Fears about belonging and lack of respect lead to fragmentation, dissension and disloyalty. When leaders meet behind closed doors, or fail to communicate openly, employees suspect the worst: Cliques form and gossip becomes rife. When the leaders are more focused on their own success rather than the success of the organization, they begin to compete with each other. When leaders display territorial behaviours, blame, internal competition and internal politics ensue. Family businesses often operate from the second level of consciousness because they are patriarchal, built on family connections and are unable to trust outsiders in management positions.

Self-esteem consciousness

The focus of the third level of organizational consciousness is on performance, excellence, quality and professionalism. It is about keeping a balanced and watchful eye on all the key performance indicators. At this level of consciousness, the organization is focused on staying agile, becoming the best it can be through the adoption of best practices and focusing on productivity and efficiency. Systems and processes are strongly emphasized and strategies are developed to achieve desired results. Re-engineering, Six Sigma and Total Quality Management are typical responses to issues of performance at this level of consciousness. The purpose of all these initiatives is continuous performance improvement. A precondition for continuous performance improvement is the encouragement and reward of excellence.

Organizations that operate from the third level of consciousness tend to be structured hierarchically for the purposes of central control. Top-down is the primary mode of decision making. The hierarchical structure also provides opportunities for rewarding individuals who are focused on their own personal success. Steep hierarchies often serve no other purpose than to cater to managers' needs for recognition, status and self-esteem. To maintain central control, organizations that operate from the third level of consciousness tend to formulate rules to regulate and bring order to all aspects of their business. Companies that are predominantly focused at this level of consciousness can easily degenerate into power-based silos or rigid authoritarian bureaucracies. When this happens, failure or collapse will eventually occur unless the organization can shift to the next level of consciousness.

Transformation consciousness

The focus of the fourth level of organizational consciousness is on adaptability, employee empowerment, continuous renewal and continuous learning. The critical issue at this level of consciousness is how to stimulate innovation so that new products and services can be developed to respond to market opportunities. This requires the organization to be flexible and take risks. To fully respond to the challenges of this level of consciousness the organization must actively garner employees' ideas and opinions. Everyone must feel that his or her voice is being heard. This requires managers and leaders to admit they do not have all the answers and invite employee participation. For many leaders and managers this is a new role requiring new skills. That is why it is important to develop the emotional intelligence of managers. They must be able to facilitate high performance in large groups of people who are looking for equality and responsible freedom. Employees want to be accountable—not micro-managed and supervised every moment of every day.

One of the dangers at this level of consciousness is to become overly biased toward consensus. While some level of consensus is important, ultimately decisions must get made. Too much consensus can be the death knell of innovation.

A precondition for success at this level of consciousness is encouraging all employees to think and act like entrepreneurs. More accountability is given to everyone and structures become less hierarchical. Teamwork is encouraged and more attention is given to personal development and relationship skills. Diversity is seen as a positive asset in exploring new ideas. This shift, which brings responsible freedom and equality to workers, cannot fully achieve the desired results unless all employees and teams share similar values, have a common purpose and a shared vision of the future. This requires a shift to the fifth level of consciousness.

Internal cohesion consciousness

The focus at the fifth level of consciousness is on building an internally cohesive organization that has a capacity for collective action. For this to happen, leaders and managers must set aside their personal agendas and learn to work for the common good. The critical requirements at this level of consciousness are developing: a shared vision of the future that inspires employees; a shared set of values that provides guidance for decision making; and an organizational purpose that is more than making a profit. The shared vision, values and purpose should clarify the intentions of the organization with regard to all its stakeholders. The values should be translated into behaviours so they can be used for performance management. The values should be reflected in all the systems and processes of the organization with appropriate consequences for those who are unwilling to conform.

A precondition for success at this level of consciousness is to build a climate of trust that engenders responsible freedom. In order to build commitment and enthusiasm, every member of the organization should understand how their contribution relates to the overall success of the organization. In organizations that operate from the fifth level of consciousness, failures become lessons, and work becomes fun. The key to success at this level of consciousness is the establishment of a strong, positive, unique cultural identity that differentiates the organization from its competitors. The culture of the organization becomes a reflection of the brand. This is particularly important in service organizations where employees have close contact with customers and the general public. At this and subsequent levels of consciousness, organizations usually preserve their unique culture by promoting from within.

Making a difference consciousness

The focus of the sixth level of organizational consciousness is on deepening the level of internal connectedness in the organization and expanding the sense of external connectedness with stakeholders in order to make the organization more resilient.

Internally, the focus is on helping employees find personal fulfilment through their work. Externally, the focus is on building mutually beneficial partnerships and alliances with business partners, the local communities in which the organization operates and in certain circumstances with non-governmental organizations. The critical issue at this level of consciousness is that employees and customers see that the organization is making a difference in the world, either through its products and services, its involvement in the local community or its willingness to fight for causes that improve the well-being of humanity or the planet. Employees and customers must feel that the company cares about them, their futures and their needs.

Companies operating at this level of consciousness go the extra mile to make sure they are being responsible global citizens. They support and encourage employees' activities in the local community by providing time off to do volunteer work and/or making financial contributions to the charities in which employees are involved. At this level of consciousness, organizations create an environment where employees can find personal fulfilment. The organization supports employees in becoming all they can become, both in terms of their professional *and* their personal growth.

A precondition for success at this level is developing leaders with a strong sense of empathy. Leaders must recognize that they must not only provide direction for the organization, but they must also become the servants of those who work for them. They must create an environment that supports every employee in aligning their sense of purpose with the vision or mission of the company. At this level of consciousness leaders become mentors, thereby creating pools of talent that support succession planning. Leadership development is given significant emphasis at this level of consciousness.

Service consciousness

The focus at the seventh level of organizational consciousness is a continuation of the previous level—a further deepening of internal connectedness, and a further expansion of external connectedness. Internally the focus of the organization is on building a climate of humility and compassion. Externally, the focus is on local, national or global activism in building a sustainable future for humanity and the planet. The critical issue at this level of consciousness is developing a deep sense of social responsibility throughout the organization by caring about social justice, human rights and the ecology of the global environment.

A precondition for success at this level of consciousness is selfless service, displayed through a profound commitment to the common good and to the well-being of future generations. To be successful at this level of consciousness, organizations must embrace the highest ethical standards in all their interactions with employees, suppliers, customers, partners, investors and the local community. They should always give full consideration to the long-term impacts of their decisions and actions on all stakeholders.

Conclusions

Everyone views the world around them through the filters of their values, beliefs and fears. Your character (the values that govern your behaviours) and your personality (visible aspects of your character) are a reflection of these values, beliefs and fears.

Whatever values, beliefs and fears are most prominent in your mind determine the levels of consciousness that you operate from. The same is true in organizations. Whatever values, beliefs and fears are most prominent in the minds of the leaders determine the levels of consciousness the organization operates from.

With this understanding of the seven levels of personal and organizational consciousness, let us now explore how the seven levels of consciousness model enables us to develop a detailed diagnostic of an organizational culture and road map for improving leadership performance.

Summary

Here are the main points of Chapter 5:

1. Each level of human need is associated with specific values. As people grow and evolve, their values change in accordance with their needs.
2. The Seven Levels of Consciousness Model is based on Abraham Maslow's hierarchy of needs and aligns with the seven stages of psychological development.
3. The Seven Levels of Consciousness Model applies to all individuals and all human group structures—organizations, institutions, communities, nations, etc.
4. The most successful individuals are those that develop full spectrum consciousness—the ability to master the needs associated with every level of consciousness. They are able to respond and appropriately adapt to all the challenges that life throws at them.
5. The most successful organizations are those that develop full spectrum consciousness—the ability to master the needs associated with every level of consciousness. They are able to respond and appropriately adapt to all the challenges that the market place throws at them.

Notes

1 Maslow's hierarchy of needs is a theory in psychology, which he outlined in his 1943 paper "A Theory of Human Motivation." Maslow subsequently extended the idea to include his observations of humans' innate curiosity. His theories parallel many other theories of human developmental psychology.
2 Your *ego* is a field of conscious awareness that is associated with your body and your emotional needs.
3 Your soul is a field of conscious awareness that exists beyond space and time in the energetic realm of the quantum energy field.
4 For a detailed understanding of the ego and the soul, and the way they interact with each the reader is encouraged to read *What My Soul Told Me: A Practical Guide to Soul Activation*, by Richard Barrett.
5 www.worldblu.com/democratic-design/ (last accessed 28 March 2013).

6   The Cultural Transformation Tools

The Seven Levels of Consciousness Model described in the previous chapter has been used to create a set of survey instruments to map and manage the values of organizations and support the growth and development of individual leaders. Collectively, these survey instruments are known as the Cultural Transformation Tools (CTT). Annex 13 provides a full list of the survey instruments that are available for mapping and measuring the values of organizations.

At the time of writing (December 2012), the Cultural Transformation Tools have been used by more than 4,000 organizations (corporations, government agencies and non-governmental organizations) in over 50 countries to improve their performance by reducing cultural entropy, increasing employee engagement and improving revenue growth. The success of the CTT is due mainly to their ability to provide a detailed diagnostic and roadmap for organizational and personal change at the causal level.

More and more leaders are recognizing that the cultures of their organizations are the principle source of their competitive advantage. They are devoting a significant amount of time and resources to measuring and managing their values (monitoring their cultures) by listening to the feedback from their employees. There is an emerging consensus that cultural capital is the new frontier of competitive advantage—it is the key differentiator between a good company and a great company, and between long-term success and short-term failure.

The uniqueness of the CTT is that they make the invisible visible. They allow you to measure and map the intangibles—the underlying causal factors that promote or inhibit the performance of an organization. This is because the focus of the CCT is on values—the motivators that reflect our needs.

The CTT are used by some of the most prestigious companies in the world to monitor their cultures, and manage their values: They are also used by many small companies. They can be customized for any situation. The CTT are currently being used to map values of individuals, organizations, communities and nations.[1]

Since their inception, the basic understanding of how to use the CTT to map the values of individuals, organizations, communities and nations, and the basic techniques necessary to build a values-driven organization, have been taught to more than 4,000 consultants and change agents on six continents. Once a consultant or change agent has been accredited as a user of the Cultural Transformation Tools (by taking the CTT training), they are able to join a global network of practitioners that are connected through LinkedIn, Facebook and various other social networking sites. Because of the worldwide demand, the survey instruments have been translated into more than 30 languages.[2]

Before explaining how to use the CTT survey instruments and interpret the results, I would first like to give some explanations about the survey process and the different ways we categorize values. These value categorizations are at the heart of what makes the CTT unique, and a powerful diagnostic tool.

The survey process

The values data is typically collected anonymously. Collecting data by name is an option. Requesting names can be useful when working with small groups (SGA) or leadership teams, as it allows participants to review their individual data plots.

Once the survey is open, participants log on to a password-protected website where they are asked to identify themselves according to drop-down lists of demographic categories and sub-categories customized for their organization. They are then asked to select from a list of 80–100 words or phrases:

- Ten values/behaviours that represent who they are (personal values).
- Ten values/behaviours that represent how their organization operates (current culture).
- Ten values/behaviours that represent what they believe the organization needs to do to achieve its highest level of performance (desired culture).

The survey typically takes under 15 minutes to complete, and is usually left open for one or two weeks. The survey can be added to the frontend or backend of other employees' surveys. Paper versions of the survey can be made available to people who do not have access to a computer. Reports are normally transmitted within one week of the close of the survey. The whole process can be completed in three to five weeks depending on the size of the organization.

The templates of values/behaviours that are used in the survey can be customized for any organization. Reports are presented in English while the diagnostic diagrams (value plots) can be provided in any of the chosen survey languages. Additional questions may be added at the end of a survey in the following formats: Free text, yes/no, multiple choice and Likert scale. Responses to these additional questions are provided as raw data, categorized by demographic grouping.

Values by level

At the core of the CTT values technology is the concept that all values and behaviours are motivated by specific needs, and every need is aligned with one of the seven levels of consciousness. At any moment in time, whatever values we are focusing on in our personal lives reflect the needs of the levels of personal consciousness we are operating from; and whatever values our organizations are focusing on reflect the needs of the levels of organizational consciousness the leaders are operating from.

Positive or potentially limiting

As already stated values can be positive or potentially limiting. Positive values include words such as honesty, creativity and integrity. Potentially limiting values include words such as blame, internal competition and caution. We call these "negative" values *potentially limiting* because we do not know the extent to which these values are undermining the performance of the organization until we have been able to hold focus group sessions with employees after the survey is complete.

For example, every organization needs a certain amount of bureaucracy in order to function. When the level of bureaucracy is high, it can cause huge inefficiencies, frustration and employee disengagement. When the level of bureaucracy is low, it enables the smooth functioning of the organization. Finding the right level of bureaucracy depends on the organizational context and the type of people it employs. What works for one organization may not work for another. On the whole, the more trust you place in your people, the less bureaucracy you will need, and the more smoothly functioning your organization will be.

Some potentially limiting values that show up in the values assessment, such as blame for example, we know from the outset are going to be dysfunctional. The question is *how* dysfunctional: How pervasive is blame in the organization and to what extent does blame inhibit the performance of the organization? The answers to these questions are found by conducting focus group discussions with a broad range of staff in the organization. The focus group sessions are conducted after the results of the values assessment are known.

The focus groups are usually asked to concentrate on the top-scoring potentially limiting values. This exercise in values clarification can be facilitated by asking members of the focus groups four basic questions about the potentially limiting value being discussed:

1. What are the processes, procedures or behaviours associated with this value:
    a)   Inside the organization?
    b)   Outside the organization?
2. What is the impact of this value on employee engagement?
3. What is the impact of this value on performance?
4. What is the impact of this value on the bottom line?

It is also useful to carry out a similar exercise with the top-scoring positive values. The point of *this* exercise is to identify how important the value is to the performance of the organization (how does it contribute to the bottom line) and thereby identify to what extent more resources should be given to promoting this value.

Table 6.1 Allocation of values/behaviours to levels of consciousness

Levels of consciousness	Positive values/ behaviours (P)	Potentially limiting values/behaviours (L)
7 Service	Social responsibility, future generations, compassion, long-term perspective	n.a.
6 Making a difference	Environmental awareness, collaboration, employee fulfilment, partnering	n.a.
5 Internal cohesion	Trust, commitment, honesty, integrity, creativity, enthusiasm, passion	n.a.
4 Transformation	Adaptability, accountability, continuous learning, teamwork, personal growth	n.a.
3 Self-esteem	Productivity, efficiency, quality, professional growth, excellence, order	Bureaucracy, confusion, information hoarding, silo mentality, status, hierarchy
2 Relationship	Open communication, friendship, loyalty, customer satisfaction, caring, recognition	Blame, internal competition, manipulation, jealousy, back-stabbing
1 Survival	Financial stability, profit, employee health and safety, organizational growth	Control, caution, chaos, short-term focus, greed, risk-averse, ruthlessness

Positive values (P) can occur at all levels of consciousness. Potentially limiting values (L) only occur at the first three levels of consciousness. This is because potentially limiting values are associated with the conscious and subconscious fear-based beliefs of the ego about getting its basic needs met.

Table 6.1 provides some examples of the allocation of positive and potentially limiting values to different levels of consciousness. In this table, "n.a." means "not applicable": There are no potentially limiting values in the higher levels of consciousness.

Because an organizational template contains both positive values, such as trust, creativity and open communication, as well as potentially limiting values, such as bureaucracy, blame and control, it is possible to calculate the level of cultural entropy in an organization by dividing the number of votes cast for potentially limiting values by the total number of votes cast for all values.

Cultural entropy is defined as: The amount of energy in an organization that is unavailable for useful work. *It is a measure of the conflict, friction and frustration that exists within an organization due to relationship issues, system inefficiencies and values misalignment.* Cultural entropy arises from the fear-based behaviours of current leaders and the institutionalized fear-based beliefs that are embedded in the organization's operating policies and procedures—the legacy of past leaders.

Values by type

In addition to categorizing values by levels of consciousness, values can also be categorized into four types—individual values (I), relationship values (R), organizational values (O) and societal values (S).

Individual values are values that you hold that primarily relate to your relationship with yourself—the principles you live by, and what you consider important for your own self-interest. Relationship values are the values we hold that determine how we relate to other people in our lives, be they friends, family or colleagues in an organization. Organizational values are values that specifically relate to how organizations operate. Societal values are values that relate to how individuals and organizations relate to society.

Table 6.2 shows how the values listed in Table 6.1 are categorized according to the value types and sign (positive and potentially limiting).

Table 6.2 Allocation of values/behaviours to value types

	Individual (I) value/ behaviours	*Relationship (R) value/behaviours*	*Organizational (O) value/ behaviours*	*Societal (S) value/ behaviours*
Positive	Commitment Honesty Integrity Creativity Enthusiasm Passion Adaptability Personal growth Excellence	Compassion Trust Accountability Teamwork Recognition Open communication Friendship Loyalty Caring Collaboration	Long-term perspective Partnering Employee fulfilment Productivity Efficiency Quality Order Financial stability Profit Employee health/ safety Organizational growth Continuous learning Customer satisfaction Professional growth	Social responsibility Future generations Environmental awareness
Potentially limiting	Status Caution	Blame Control Internal competition Manipulation Jealousy Back-stabbing	Bureaucracy Confusion Ruthlessness Silo mentality Hierarchy Chaos Short-term focus Risk-averse Internal politics Information hoarding	

Values by business focus

A further values categorization we use is called the *business focus*. We have expanded the concept of the Balanced Scorecard, developed by Kaplan and Norton,[3] to create a six-part scorecard known as the Business Needs Scorecard (BNS). The six business categories, the principal stakeholders involved in each category and some of the values associated with each category are shown in Table 6.3.

The culture category is split into three subsections: Trust and Engagement—values that reflect intellectual and emotional engagement; Direction and Communication—values that reflect internal cohesion; and Supportive Environment—values that reflect care for employees.

Table 6.3 Categories of the Business Needs Scorecard

Category	Description	Stakeholder
Finance	Values and behaviours that have direct impact on growth, the bottom line and investor interests such as profit, cost-reduction and financial stability.	Investors
Fitness	Values and behaviours that have a direct impact on performance, quality and the effective delivery of products/services, such as productivity, efficiency, accountability and quality.	Employees
External stakeholder relations	Values and behaviours that have a direct impact on the relationship with customers, the market, suppliers and other strategic partners, such as customer satisfaction, customer collaboration and client focus.	Clients, suppliers and customers
Evolution	Values and behaviours that have a direct impact on the development of people, processes, products/services and ways of thinking, such as innovation, creativity, risk-taking and long-term perspective.	Employees
Culture	Culture is further broken down into three subcategories: Trust/Engagement: Values and behaviours that bring people together, build mutual confidence and encourage employees to participate. Direction/Communication: Values and behaviours that guide decision making and express how people communicate and exchange information. Supportive Environment: Values and behaviours that have a direct impact on how people are treated and looked after within the organization.	Employees
Societal contribution	Values and behaviours that have a direct impact on the relationship of the organization to the local community or society, such as environmental awareness, community involvement and human rights.	Society

The BNS scorecard is populated in two ways. The first diagram allocates the *top ten* current and desired culture values of the cultural values assessment to the scorecard and the second diagram allocates *all* the values chosen in a cultural values assessment to the scorecard. Two examples of the use of this diagnostic tool are shown in the following chapter (see Figures 7.5 and 7.13). High-performing cultures have an even distribution of the top ten current culture values across all six categories of the scorecard.

The BNS is used as a diagnostic tool to identify where an organization is currently focusing its business energies (values of the current culture), and where employees would like the company to focus its business energies (values of the desired culture)—the values that employees identify as important.

In addition to using the BNS as a diagnostic tool, it can also be used as a tool for developing indicators that lead to a balanced strategy for business growth. Annex 14 provides some ideas about how to use the BNS categories to establish a balanced set of strategy indicators.

Preparing for the CVA survey

The survey setup process consists of three main tasks:

1.   Customizing the values templates.
2.   Identifying the demographic groupings to be used in the survey.
3.   Choosing the survey languages.

Customization of the templates

Two templates are used in every survey:

•   A template of personal values.
•   A template of organizational values.

The personal values template consists of about 80 words or phrases that are categorized as individual, relationship or societal values. This template is used by participants to choose their personal values. There are no *organizational* values on the personal values template. The organizational values template is slightly larger than the personal values template—between 90 and 100 values. The organizational template contains individual, relationship, organizational and societal values. This template is used by participants to choose the values they see in the current culture of the organization, and the values they believe would help the organization to improve its performance (desired culture).

We refer to the words we use on the personal and organizational templates as "values/behaviours." We do this for two reasons. First, we want to make sure as part of the customization process that the templates represent an accurate portrayal of the collective culture of the employees and the vocabulary that is used in the organization; and second, we want to be able to include the espoused values of the organization in the template. In order to do this we need the flexibility of using both single word values, such as openness and teamwork, and short phrases, such as balance (work/life), making a difference, coaching/mentoring and ease with uncertainty.

Very often during the customization of the values templates, new words or phrases will be suggested. These "new" values/behaviours have to be translated into all the languages that are being used in the survey and categorized as positive or potentially limiting, individual, relationship, organizational or societal, and allocated to one of the seven levels of consciousness and one of the six categories of the Business Needs Scorecard.

In addition to choosing the words that go on the templates, the customization process can also involve changing the sign of a value—from positive to potentially limiting or vice versa. In some cultures, for example in South America, the word "image" when translated into Spanish is regarded as a positive value, whereas in the Western world "image" is regarded as a potentially limiting value: When you focus too much on your image, you are effectively attempting to project a false persona. Another example is the word "control." When it is used in a financial context, as in "financial controller," it can be regarded as positive. However, in most circumstances, the word "control" has negative connotations: It is usually associated with situations that reflect a lack of trust in other people's abilities.

Identifying demographic groupings

If a Cultural Values Assessment is carried out for a whole organization (or multiple types or categories of employees), the richness of the data collected can be increased significantly if participants are asked to indicate which demographic groupings they belong to. Typical demographic groupings used in large organizations include: Position (leaders, managers, staff), grade, business unit, location, gender, age ranges, ethnicity, length of service ranges, etc. Usually, for teams, small groups and small organizations, no demographic categories are necessary.

The fine tuning of the demographic categories and their sub-groupings at the setup stage is extremely important for the success of the survey. It allows the organization to develop a detailed diagnostic of what is working and not working for each of the demographic groupings. I always encourage clients to use multiple demographics. They don't have to ask for or use the results from all the demographics that are surveyed, but once the data is collected, they cannot go back and get the information. No charge is made for collecting the data from the different groupings: Only when a client requests the results from a particular grouping is a charge made for the analysis.

The results

In addition to a written report, the results of a Cultural Values Assessment are also presented in a series of diagrams (data plots) and tables. The following chapter provides a list of the plots and tables that can be produced.

Conclusions

The Cultural Transformation Tools are powerful diagnostic tools for supporting the growth and development of organizations and individuals. They make the invisible visible and the intangible tangible.

The diagnostic power of the tools stems from two factors: (a) they work at the causal level: They uncover what needs are being met and what needs are not being met; and (b) they categorize values in four ways:

- By level of consciousness.
- By sign—positive or potentially limiting.
- By type—individual, relationship, organizational and societal.
- By business focus—finance, fitness, external stakeholder relations, evolution, culture and societal contribution.

The transformational strength of the Cultural Transformation Tools lies in their ability to surface data that engenders new conversations: Conversations that have never happened before about values and beliefs that are prominent in the culture of the organization. They get people talking about what is fundamentally important to them—their values, their beliefs and their fears.

As we discussed earlier, in Chapter 1, such conversations are both clarifying and connecting. They touch our common humanity and make us realize that deep down in our hearts we are all very much the same. No matter what level of consciousness we are operating from, ultimately we all want the same thing. We all want to be happy. We feel happy when we feel safe and secure, when we feel loved and accepted, when we feel confident and respected, when we have freedom and autonomy, when we feel aligned with our work, when we are able to make a difference and when we are able to be of service to other people.

Summary

Here are the main points of Chapter 6:

1. The Cultural Transformation Tools (CTT) are based on the Seven Levels of Consciousness Model.
2. The CTT are used to map and manage the values of organizations and support the growth and development of individual leaders.
3. The success of the CTT is due mainly to their ability to provide a detailed diagnostic and roadmap for organizational and personal change at the causal level.
4. The uniqueness of the CTT is that they make the invisible visible. They allow you to measure and map the intangibles—the underlying causal factors that promote or inhibit the performance of an organization or of an individual.

Notes

1 Richard Barrett, *Love, Fear and the Destiny of Nations: The Impact of the Evolution of Human Consciousness on World Affairs* (Bath: Fulfilling Books), 2012.
2 At the time of writing, the CVA was available in Arabic, Brazilian, Chinese, Czech, Danish, Dutch, English, Finnish, Flemish, French, French Canadian, German, Greek, Hindi, Hungarian, Icelandic, Indonesian, Italian, Japanese, Korean, Lithuanian, Malay, Norwegian, Polish, Russian, Slovakian, Spanish, Swedish, Thai, Turkish and Vietnamese.
3 The Balanced Scorecard of Kaplan and Norton has four business categories: The financial perspective, the customer perspective, the internal business-process perspective and the learning and growth perspective.

7   Two longitudinal case studies

Before presenting examples of how the Cultural Transformation Tools have been used to support the growth and development of a small and large organization, I want to describe the typical outputs of a Cultural Values Assessment (CVA) and identify the key cultural indicators that can be found in the data plots and data tables.

There are six data plots and two data tables in a typical CVA report. An additional table that can be requested if desired is an espoused values analysis. Table 7.1 describes the cultural indicators that can be found in each data plot and data table, and provides comments on what level the indicators need to reach to be commensurate with high performance. A full description of each data plot and data table can be found in Annex 15.

Case Study 1: Small organization

The first example I want to highlight concerns a small organization operating out of three countries that has been using the Cultural Transformation Tools to monitor its culture for more than eight years. The data presented covers the period 2005 to 2012. Table 7.2 shows the key performance indicators during this period (income, number of staff, revenue per capita, values alignment, mission alignment and cultural entropy).

During 2005 and 2006 the organization had a high level of income per capita and an extremely low level of cultural entropy. Over the next two years the level of cultural entropy increased to 7 per cent and then 10 per cent. At the same time, the level of income per capita took a serious nose dive, dropping from $217,142 to $137,857. A new CEO was appointed from within the organization and a significant effort was made in each of the following years to reduce the level of cultural entropy and increase the level of values alignment and mission alignment. Between 2008 and 2012 the revenue per capita increased by 33 per cent.

Figures 7.1, 7.2 and 7.3 show plots of the revenue per capita, cultural entropy and mission alignment during this period. The data clearly indicates that the level of revenue per capita (a measure of productivity) was closely linked to the level of cultural entropy and mission alignment (causal indicators). As the level of

Table 7.1 CVA cultural indicators

Data plots	Cultural indicators	High performance/comments
Values plot	*Values alignment*: Number of matching top ten personal (PV) and current culture (CC) values. *Mission alignment*: Number of matching top ten current (CC) and desired culture (DC) values.	High-performing organizations have three or more matching personal (PV) and current culture values (CC).[1] High-performing organizations have six or more matching current (CC) and desired culture values (DC) and no potentially limiting values in the top ten current culture values (CC).
Values distribution	*Cultural entropy*: The proportion of overall votes for potentially limiting values.	High-performing cultures have entropy at or below 10%.
Positive values distribution	Indicates the levels of consciousness where there are significant gaps between the distribution of positive personal (PV), current (CC) and desired culture (DC) values.	High-performing cultures have approximately the same proportion of personal (PV), current culture (CC) and desired culture (DC) values at each level of consciousness.
CTS	Indicates the distribution of personal (PV), current culture (CC) and desired culture values (DC) between the common good (C)—levels 5, 6 and 7, transformation (T)—level 4, and self-interest (S)—levels 1, 2 and 3.	High-performing cultures display a strong alignment between the common good (C), transformation (T) and self-interest (S) for the personal (PV), current culture (CC) and desired culture values (DC).
Business Needs Scorecard	Maps the top ten current (CC) and desired culture values (DC) in the Values Plot to a six-part scorecard including: Finance, Fitness, External Stakeholder Relations, Culture (Trust/Engagement, Direction/Communication and Supportive Environment), Evolution and Societal Contribution.	High-performing cultures show an even distribution of values across all six categories of the scorecard for the current culture, and a similar distribution for the desired culture.
Business Needs Scorecard values distribution	Indicates the areas of the Business Needs Scorecard where there are significant gaps between what people currently experience (CC) and their desired culture (DC).	High-performing cultures have a relatively similar distribution of focus in each area between current culture (CC) and desired culture (DC).

(Continued)

Table 7.1 Continued

Data tables	Cultural indicators	High performance/comments
Cultural Entropy Report	This table breaks down the cultural entropy by level of consciousness and shows how many votes each potentially limiting value received.	It is easier to reduce the impact of potentially limiting values at Level 3 than at Level 2, and easier to reduce the impact of potentially limiting values at Level 2 than at Level 1.
Value jumps	Lists the values that have the largest jump in votes between the current culture (CC) and desired culture (DC). These are the values that participants are asking to see more of in the organization.	High-performing cultures tend to have low value jumps.
Espoused values analysis	Lists the number of votes for each of the espoused values in the current (CC) and desired culture (DC).	This table tells you to what extent the espoused values are being lived (CC) and to what extent employees feel the espoused values are important (DC).

cultural entropy went down and the level of mission alignment went up, the productivity of the employees increased.

You will also notice that during the global economic meltdown in 2009–10 the company maintained the same level of income (many companies suffered a significant reduction in income) and managed to increase both the number and productivity of its staff. During the following two years—2011 and 2012—the company demonstrated its resilience by increasing its revenues by 22 per cent and 13 per cent respectively.

One of the key factors in the improvement of the values and mission alignment from 2011 to 2012 (from four to five and six to seven, respectively) was the decision to take the company virtual: The head office was closed and every member of the company was given the opportunity of working from home.

Table 7.2 Key performance indicators

Year	Income ($ millions)	Number of staff	Revenue/ capita ($)	Values alignment	Mission alignment	Cultural entropy
2005	1.52	7	217,142	5	7	1%
2006	1.55	8	193,750	4	9	1%
2007	1.73	12	144,166	3	5	7%
2008	1.93	14	137,857	5	6	10%
2009	2.37	15	158,000	6	4	8%
2010	2.37	14	169,285	5	6	8%
2011	2.91	18	161,666	4	6	3%
2012	3.30	18	183,333	5	7	2%

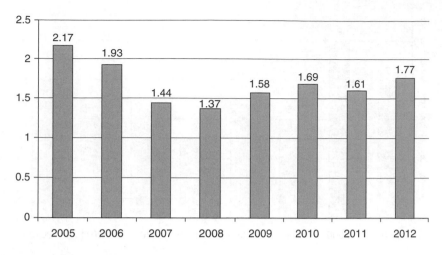

Figure 7.1 Revenue per capita ($100,000).

Values plot

The values data plot for 2012, which includes input from 16 of the 18 employees, is shown in Figure 7.4.[2] Each dot on the diagrams represents one of the values listed in the table below the diagrams.

The first point you will notice from a rapid visual scan is the alignment of levels of consciousness: The top personal values, the top current culture values and the top desired culture values are all concentrated at the fourth, fifth and sixth level of consciousness. These are the levels of transformation, internal cohesion

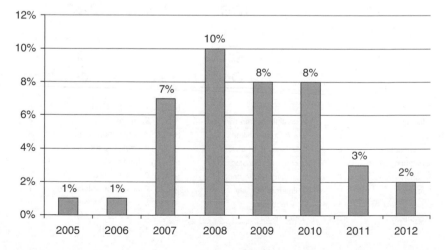

Figure 7.2 Cultural entropy.

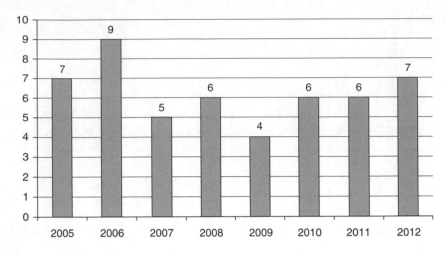

Figure 7.3 Mission alignment.

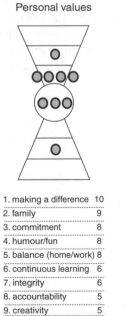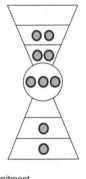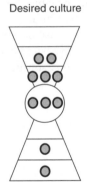

Personal values		Current culture		Desired culture	
1. making a difference	10	1. commitment	12	1. accountability	9
2. family	9	2. continuous improvement	10	2. commitment	8
3. commitment	8	3. employee fulfilment	10	3. continuous improvement	8
4. humour/fun	8	4. balance (home/work)	9	4. employee fulfilment	8
5. balance (home/work)	8	5. customer satisfaction	9	5. humour/fun	8
6. continuous learning	6	6. making a difference	9	6. shared vision	8
7. integrity	6	7. financial stability	8	7. customer collaboration	7
8. accountability	5	8. humour/fun	8	8. customer satisfaction	6
9. creativity	5	9. teamwork	8	9. financial stability	6
				10. teamwork	6

Figure 7.4 Data plot for 2012.[3]

and making a difference. The values distribution plot (not shown) indicates that the percentage of values at these three levels combined was 67 (personal values), 73 (current culture) and 78 per cent (desired culture). The percentage of values at the first three levels of consciousness was 25 (personal values), 24 (current culture) and 20 per cent (desired culture). We can conclude from these results that this company has mastered its deficiency needs and is focused on its growth needs.

Another strong indicator of alignment is the number of top ten values that are the same in the personal, current culture and desired culture. There are four such values—making a difference, commitment, humour/fun and balance (home/work).

Business Needs Scorecard (BNS)

The distribution of top current and desired culture values on the Business Needs Scorecard is shown in Figure 7.5.

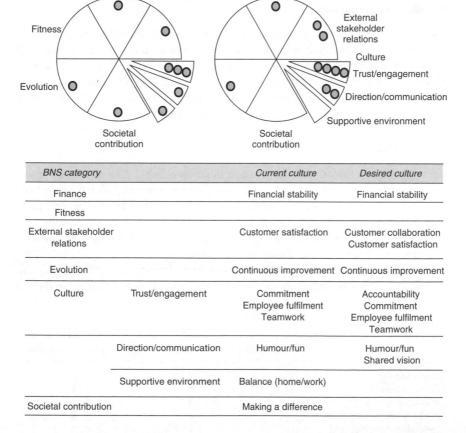

BNS category		Current culture	Desired culture
Finance		Financial stability	Financial stability
Fitness			
External stakeholder relations		Customer satisfaction	Customer collaboration Customer satisfaction
Evolution		Continuous improvement	Continuous improvement
Culture	Trust/engagement	Commitment Employee fulfilment Teamwork	Accountability Commitment Employee fulfilment Teamwork
	Direction/communication	Humour/fun	Humour/fun Shared vision
	Supportive environment	Balance (home/work)	
Societal contribution		Making a difference	

Figure 7.5 Business Needs Scorecard.

The first point of note is that the top values in the current culture are reasonably well distributed: The desired culture has values in every category and subcategory except fitness. The company is taking care of employees, investors, clients and society. The only gaps in the desired culture are in the categories of fitness and societal contribution.

In the current culture the category of societal contribution was filled with the value of making a difference. This does not mean that employees no longer think making a difference is important, it simply means that they believe that at this point in time the company needs to give more focus to the values of accountability, customer collaboration and shared vision, which are not present in the top values of the current culture. The gap in fitness in the current and desired culture represents a potential blind spot.

With such a relatively well-aligned culture, and such excellent results, you may be wondering what's next for this company in terms of cultural adjustment. We can get clues as to what's next by looking at the espoused values analysis and the value jumps table.

Espoused values analysis

The company has four espoused values—commitment, shared vision, customer satisfaction and employee fulfilment. Three of these values are alive and well in the current culture: Commitment is the number one current culture value with 12 votes; employee fulfilment is number three and customer satisfaction is number five. The only espoused value not appearing in the top nine values is shared vision. This is one of the areas that should receive more attention.

Value jumps

Let's now take a look at the value jumps table (see Table 7.3). It is notable that every one of the top value jumps except innovation is concerned with the employee experience. Accountability and shared vision reflect the need of people operating with self-authoring minds. Coaching/mentoring and leadership development reflect the needs of people operating with self-transforming minds. Innovation is concerned with the future evolution of the company.

The biggest value jump and the number one desired culture value is accountability. Shared vision, which is the only espoused value not appearing in the top

Table 7.3 Value jumps

Values	Current culture votes	Desired culture votes	Value jump
Accountability	4	9	5
Shared vision	4	8	4
Innovation	1	5	4
Coaching/mentoring	0	4	4
Leadership development	0	4	4

nine current culture values, is also one of the important value jumps. It is clear from this analysis that accountability and shared vision are two of the most important values that the organization needs to focus on during 2013. Other values that employees want to see given more emphasis in 2013 are innovation, coaching/ mentoring and leadership development.

Summary

The data shows that this is an extremely high-performing organization and the employees are highly engaged: There are five matching personal and current culture values (values alignment); there are seven matching current and desired culture values (mission alignment); cultural entropy is well below 10 per cent; and commitment is the number one current culture value. We do not often find such a high level of alignment in an organization.

Case Study 2: Large organization

The second example I want to highlight concerns a large South African company that has been using the Cultural Transformation Tools since 2005. The data presented covers the period 2005 to 2011. Table 7.4 shows the key performance indicators during this period (income, number of staff, revenue per capita, values alignment, mission alignment and cultural entropy).

Since this company started mapping their values in 2005, the level of cultural entropy decreased from 25 per cent to 12 per cent. At the same time, revenue per capita increased from 713,000 ZAR to 987,000 ZAR—a 38 per cent increase— and the mission alignment increased from three to seven (matching CC and DC values).

You will also notice that during the global economic meltdown in 2009–10 the level of income only showed a slight dip (other companies in the same sector in South Africa suffered a more significant reduction in income). The productivity of staff also dipped, but quickly rebounded by 2010, and has since grown significantly.

Table 7.4 Key performance indicators

Year	Income (ZAR millions)	Number of staff	Revenue/ capita (ZAR thousands)	Values alignment	Mission alignment	Cultural entropy
2005	15,809	22,188	713	1	3	25%
2006	18,948	24,034	788	1	4	19%
2007	22,428	26,522	846	1	4	17%
2008	22,077	27,570	801	1	5	14%
2009	21,570	27,037	798	2	6	13%
2010	23,635	27,525	859	2	6	13%
2011	28,115	28,494	987	2	7	12%

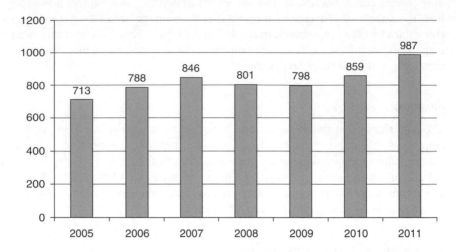

Figure 7.6 Revenue per capita.

Figures 7.6, 7.7 and 7.8 show the revenue per capita, cultural entropy and mission alignment from 2005 to 2011. These graphs clearly indicate how the level of income per capita (a measure of productivity) was closely linked to the reduction in cultural entropy and the increase in mission alignment (causal indicators). As the level of cultural entropy decreased and the level of mission alignment increased, the productivity (revenue per capita) of employees increased.

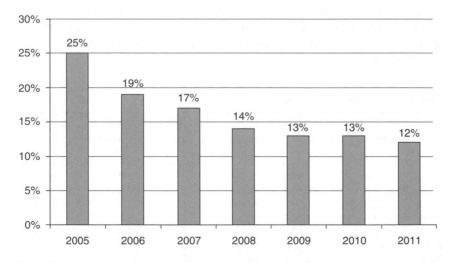

Figure 7.7 Cultural entropy.

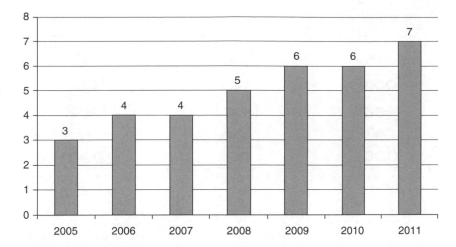

Figure 7.8 Mission alignment.

Values plot

The values data plot for 2011, which includes input from 22,102 employees out of the total of 28,115, is shown in Figure 7.9.

The first point you will notice from a rapid visual scan is the strong alignment between the levels of consciousness of the personal values and the levels of consciousness of the desired culture values. This was also true for the small company. However, in the small company, the levels of consciousness of the current culture were also in alignment with the levels of consciousness of the personal values and the desired culture. This is not true for the large company. The large company has not yet quite reached the same level of cultural alignment as the small company. It is quite likely in this large company that as long as the leaders stay focused on managing the organization's values, the level of cultural entropy will stabilize around 10 per cent, and the level of values alignment and mission alignment will fluctuate slightly from their current levels. It is difficult for a large company to get below 10 per cent cultural entropy because of the large diversity of the stages of development of employees in large companies. In small, knowledge-based companies there is much less diversity in the stages of development.

Differences due to level of cultural entropy

The alignment in consciousness between the personal values and desired culture values in these two case studies is typical of organizations with low levels of cultural entropy (approaching 10 per cent or less). In organizations with medium to high levels of cultural entropy, the values chosen for the desired culture tend to concentrate at the transformation level of consciousness (see Figure 8.3 in the following chapter). This is because many of the values found at the transformation

Personal values	Current culture	Desired culture
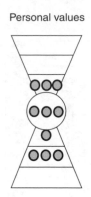	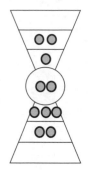	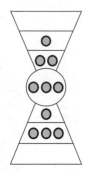

accountability	15133	accountability	9526	accountability	12215
honesty	11007	client-driven	7991	balance (home/work)	7061
commitment	9729	client satisfaction	6343	client satisfaction	6829
respect	8042	brand reputation	4699	client-driven	6736
integrity	7198	teamwork	4626	employee recognition	5803
family	6840	achievement	4534	commitment	5542
caring	6649	commitment	4238	honesty	5430
balance (home/work)	6193	employee recognition	4020	achievement	5066
responsibility	5896	environmental awareness	4017	teamwork	5005
efficiency	5365	being the best	3944	employee satisfaction	4948

Figure 7.9 Values plot.

level of consciousness are remedies for the potentially limiting values that show up in the first three levels of consciousness. For example, when bureaucracy (Level 3) and/or blame (Level 2) show up in the top current culture values, accountability (Level 4) will frequently show up in the top desired culture values: Accountability is a remedy for bureaucracy and blame. The topic of remedial or correcting values is discussed in more detail in the following chapter, where more case studies are presented.

As a general rule we can say that employees choose correcting or remedial values (for the desired culture) in medium-to-high-entropy organizations, and once the level of cultural entropy gets to around 10–15 per cent—a level of cultural entropy that employees can tolerate—they choose desired culture values that are more in alignment with their personal values.

This means that the ideal culture in a low-entropy organization, from the employee perspective, is one that aligns with the levels of consciousness they personally operate from; and the ideal culture in a medium-to-high-entropy organization is one that brings the current culture into alignment with the desired culture.

This suggests that employees give priority to mission alignment (current and desired culture alignment) rather than personal values alignment. When mission alignment has been achieved, they transfer their focus to values alignment (personal and current culture alignment). What this means is that above 15 per cent cultural entropy, we tend to see improvements in mission alignment as cultural entropy falls, and as cultural entropy gets to around 15 per cent or below, both values alignment and mission alignment tend to increase. This is when we see more of employees' personal values showing up in the desired culture. As cultural entropy gets to around 10 per cent, it often stabilizes, especially in large companies, and instead of cultural entropy continuing to decrease, we tend to see increases in values alignment (increase in the number of personal and current culture value matches) and/or mission alignment (increase in the number of current and desired culture matches).

Impact of stages of development on alignment

One further point worth noting about the alignment between personal consciousness and desired culture consciousness in the small and large organizations is how different they are. In both cases, there is an alignment in consciousness between the personal values and the desired culture values, but the levels of consciousness that the employees are operating from are different. Figures 7.10 and 7.11 compare the personal values from Case Study 1 (small company) and Case Study 2 (large company). Figure 7.10 shows the personal values plots, and Figure 7.11 shows the personal values distribution.

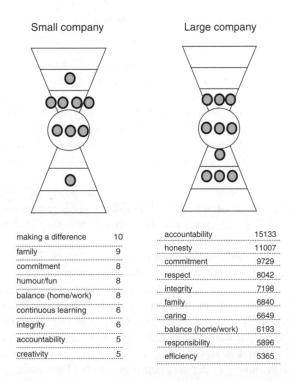

Small company		Large company	
making a difference	10	accountability	15133
family	9	honesty	11007
commitment	8	commitment	9729
humour/fun	8	respect	8042
balance (home/work)	8	integrity	7198
continuous learning	6	family	6840
integrity	6	caring	6649
accountability	5	balance (home/work)	6193
creativity	5	responsibility	5896
		efficiency	5365

Figure 7.10 Comparison of personal values plots for Case Studies 1 and 2.

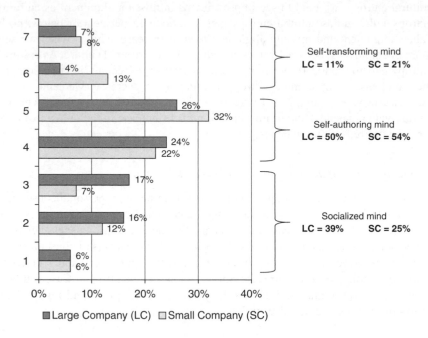

Figure 7.11 Comparison of personal values distribution.

We can see from the comparison of values plots that the employees from the two companies only share four values—accountability, family, commitment and balance home/work. The priorities for each of these values, except for commitment, are different. The number one personal value in the small company is making a difference (a Level 6 value), which is typical of people operating with self-transforming minds, whereas the number one personal value in the large company is accountability (a Level 4 value), which is typical of people operating with self-authoring minds.

A more detailed exploration of the differences is shown in Figure 7.11, which compares the distribution of personal values (all the votes cast for personal values) for the small and large company and how this distribution relates to the three types of mind discussed in Chapter 3.

We see from this analysis that the proportion of votes for values that correspond to the needs of a socialized type of mind is significantly higher for the large company than the small company—39 per cent, compared with 25 per cent. The proportion of votes for values that correspond to the needs of a self-authoring mind is slightly higher in the small company—54 per cent, compared with 50 per cent. The proportion of votes for values that correspond to the needs of a self-transforming mind is significantly higher in the small company compared with the large company—21 per cent compared with 11 per cent.

These differences are mainly due to the fact that practically all the people working in the small company are involved in relatively demanding, complex, knowledge-orientated tasks, whereas a substantial number of the people working in the large company are working in less complex, customer-facing tasks and administrative support. This means that the smaller company has a requirement for people at a higher average stage of development than the large company: And because they are at a higher stage of development, they have higher order needs and values, and more complex minds.

Consequently, it is extremely important for the employees of the small company to see and feel that their work efforts are making a difference in the world—they are less concerned about meeting their deficiency needs—whereas in the large company employees give more emphasis to meeting their survival, relationship and self-esteem needs, particularly their need to feel accepted and nurtured (Level 2—16 per cent of values chosen), and acknowledged and recognized (Level 3—17 per cent of values chosen). Not surprisingly therefore, employee satisfaction (Level 2) and employee recognition (Level 2) score highly in the desired culture of the large company.

Of course, there will be many senior people in the large organization who are working on demanding, complex, knowledge-orientated tasks, who are at a higher stage of development than the average employee, but in terms of numbers, they represent a relatively small proportion of the population and consequently have less impact on the overall results. Figure 7.12, which shows the level of development of the top team, senior managers, middle managers and junior managers in the large company illustrates this point.

The levels of development follow the pattern one might expect: The top team has more values in the self-transforming mind range (18 per cent) than the senior managers (14 per cent), and the senior managers have more values in this range than the middle managers (12 per cent), which have more values in this range than the junior managers (10 per cent). The average of all employees in this range is 11 per cent (see Figure 7.11). Conversely the junior managers have more values in the socialized mind range (40 per cet) than the middle managers (37 per cent),

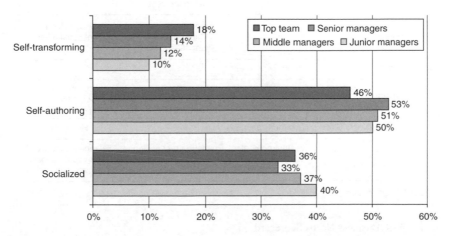

Figure 7.12 Types of mind by management level.

and middle managers have more values in this range than the senior managers (33 per cent). Interestingly, the top team has more values (36 per cent) in the socialized mind range than the senior managers (33 per cent) but less than the middle managers and junior managers.

Business Needs Scorecard (BNS)

Three other points in the Cultural Values Assessment of the large company that are worthy of note can be seen from the analysis of the Business Needs Scorecard data (see Figure 7.13).

The first point is that the top values in the current culture are relatively well distributed: They are in all areas of the BNS except the evolution and finance categories. The company is taking care of employees, clients and society.

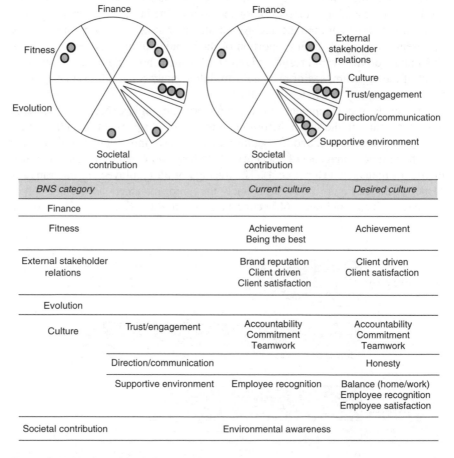

BNS category		Current culture	Desired culture
Finance			
Fitness		Achievement Being the best	Achievement
External stakeholder relations		Brand reputation Client driven Client satisfaction	Client driven Client satisfaction
Evolution			
Culture	Trust/engagement	Accountability Commitment Teamwork	Accountability Commitment Teamwork
	Direction/communication		Honesty
	Supportive environment	Employee recognition	Balance (home/work) Employee recognition Employee satisfaction
Societal contribution		Environmental awareness	

Figure 7.13 Business Needs Scorecard.

The second point is that the lack of values in the evolution category seems to represent a blind spot. There are no values in this category in the current *or* desired culture. This means the organization is not giving enough emphasis to values such as long-term perspective, creativity and innovation. This is potentially worrisome, especially since this blind spot has shown up in several consecutive assessments. One could make a similar comment about the finance category. However, in this case previous assessments have shown values in this category and the financial position of the company is quite sound. This is not so much a blind spot as an area where the company has become quite proficient: Making a profit is not an issue.

The third point to note is even though the company has a low level of cultural entropy and a relatively high level of mission alignment, employees want to see even more emphasis given to cultural improvements—there are seven values in the culture category of the desired culture as opposed to four in the current culture. Employees want the organization to create a more supportive environment through more balance (home/work) and employee satisfaction and improve communication through more honesty.

Value jumps

The value jumps table gives us more indications of what this large organization needs to focus on in the coming year.

It is interesting to note that every one of the top seven value jumps shown in Table 7.5 is associated with the employee experience. This is unusual. Normally we would expect to see at least one or two values focusing on the needs of customers or the organization. The two highest jumps—balance (home/work) and employee satisfaction, and the sixth—employee recognition, reflect the needs of people operating with socialized minds. Accountability, fairness, honesty and trust reflect the needs of people operating with self-authoring minds. Fairness, honesty and trust are Level 5 values that contribute to internal cohesion. Accountability is a Level 4 value that speaks to autonomy and freedom.

When we dig deeper into this data we find differences at each management level. Table 7.6 shows the top five value jumps, expressed in number of votes for

Table 7.5 Value jumps

Values	Current culture votes	Desired culture votes	Value jump	Percentage increase
Balance (home/work)	2,889	7,061	4,172	144%
Employee satisfaction	1,846	4,948	3,102	168%
Accountability	9,526	12,215	2,689	28%
Fairness	1,908	4,131	2,223	117%
Honesty	3,258	5,430	2,172	67%
Employee recognition	4,020	5,803	1,783	44%
Trust	1,686	3,390	1,704	101%

Table 7.6 Value jumps by level of management

Senior managers (637)	Middle managers (5,457)	Junior managers (9,723)
Balance (home/work) (148)	Balance (home/work) (1,477)	Balance (home/work) (1,915)
Accountability (146)	**Accountability** (1,192)	*Employee satisfaction* (1,553)
Innovation (87)	*Employee satisfaction* (1,025)	Fairness (1,433)
Employee satisfaction (79)	Transparency (708)	**Accountability** (1,082)
Adaptability (73)	Fairness (691)	Honesty (1,072)

the same set of senior managers, middle managers and junior managers included in Figure 7.12.

It is interesting to notice that whereas balance (home/work) is the top priority for every management level, employee satisfaction (in italics) is much more important at the junior level than the middle or senior level. Accountability (in bold) is less important at the junior level than at the higher levels. This is exactly what one would expect: The greater the influence of the socialized mind, the more people are focused on satisfaction (meeting their deficiency needs) and the less focused they are on being accountable. Conversely, people with self-authoring minds are more interested in accountability than satisfaction.

The data from this large company also shows another interesting characteristic that is often found in large organizations—the level of cultural entropy of senior management decreases below the senior management level, and the cultural entropy observed by the top team is lower than the senior managers (see Table 7.7).

The reason for the low level of cultural entropy in the top team, in this case, is: (a) that they work very well together; and (b) they delegate to their senior managers. The reason why the senior managers have the highest level of cultural entropy of the different management levels is that they have a lot of accountability (accountability is the number one current culture value in the organization): They are under pressure from above to perform, and under pressure from below to manage their staff and resources. Clearly, there is a high level of commitment in the organization (number seven in the top ten current culture values), which is contributing to the felt need across all levels of management to get a better grip on their home/work balance.

Very often, when the overall level of cultural entropy in an organization is high, shall we say 30 per cent or above, the level of cultural entropy of the top team is also high. This is an indication that there is a lack of trust within the

Table 7.7 Cultural entropy by level

Top team	Senior management	Middle management	Junior management
1%	14%	13%	9%

Table 7.8 Espoused values analysis

Espoused value	Current culture votes	Desired culture votes	Positive difference
Accountability	9,526	12,215	+28%
Integrity	3,766	4,606	+22%
People-centred	3,371	3,548	+5%
Pushing boundaries	2,966	2,383	−20%
Respect	3,343	4,606	+38%

leadership team and a lot of infighting. This is not the case here. The top team appears to be working quite well together, but appears to be a little out of touch with what is happening with their direct reports and other senior managers.

Espoused values analysis

Only one of the five espoused values of this large organization (shown in Table 7.8) appears in the current culture top ten and the desired culture top ten—accountability. Except for *pushing boundaries*, which shows a 20 per cent drop in votes, the rest of the espoused values show an increase in the number of desired culture votes over the number of current culture votes of between 5 and 38 per cent.

If one considers that honesty, which was the fifth highest value jump (see Table 7.4), is closely linked to integrity, then one might consider that the demand for integrity in the current culture should be increased by 3,258 votes and the demand for integrity in the desired culture should be increased by 5,430.

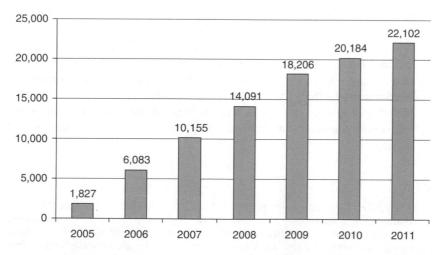

Figure 7.14 Participation rates.

This would give integrity a score of 44 per cent—by far the most positive difference and the largest value jump.

Participation rates

The Cultural Values Assessment gives employees a voice about things that matter to them. This is evidenced by the increase in the number of people participating in the survey in the large organization—from 8 per cent in 2005 to 77 per cent in 2011 (see Figure 7.14).

This increase in participation is attributed to the fact that the leaders of the organization act on the results of the survey. Each year they chose to focus on three actions to bring down the level of cultural entropy and/or increase the level of values and mission alignment. Knowing this, and seeing these actions being undertaken, more and more employees wanted to participate in the Cultural Values Assessment each year so they could get their needs met.

Conclusions

This brief overview of longitudinal data from a small and large company that have acted on the results of their Cultural Values Assessments over a period of several years shows that their efforts to manage their values have paid off. They have both increased their revenues and revenue per capita (productivity), and because of their focus on values, they were able to ride through the global economic meltdown in 2009 relatively unscathed and quickly bounced back to growth.

Summary

Here are the main points of Chapter 7:

1. There are six data plots and two data tables in a typical CVA report. An additional table that can be requested is an espoused values analysis.
2. When leaders follow up on the results of a cultural values assessment by making changes, the participation rate of employees in the survey increases.
3. In both case studies, the focus on values has led to an increase in revenues, employee productivity and organizational resilience.
4. In both case studies, the values in the current culture were spread across the four most important stakeholders—employees, customers, investors and society.

Notes

1 The template of values used to map employees' personal values is slightly different from the template used to map the current and desired culture values of the organization: It does not contain any organizational values. Consequently, the number of matching personal and current culture organizational values would not normally exceed five,

whereas it is possible to have ten matching current and desired culture organizational values.

2 The reason why there are only nine values in the personal and current culture values is that there were more than five personal values that scored five votes, and more than five current culture values that scored seven votes. Plotting these extra values would have made the diagram less clear. With larger groups, usually more than 20, there is almost always a clear cut-off point for the top ten values.

3 Each of the values listed is represented by a dot at the appropriate level on the seven levels of consciousness diagram.

8   More case studies

Whereas my intention in Chapter 7 was to show the long-term impact of focusing on values management using case studies from two organizations that have been carrying out cultural values assessments over a significant period of time, my intention in Chapter 8 is to highlight the diagnostic powers of the Cultural Values Assessment (CVA) in specific situations. To this end, I will be using various indicators taken from the Cultural Values Assessments of the companies concerned. Chief among them will be: Cultural entropy; the number of matching personal and current culture values (values alignment); the number of matching current and desired cultural values (mission alignment); and the Business Needs Scorecard results. I will also indicate how the types of values (IROS) can be used to gain insights into what is working and not working in an organizational culture.

Cultural entropy

Since cultural entropy is one of the key indicators of performance, you will find the following table useful. Table 8.1 describes the broad-brush corrective measures that are associated with different levels of cultural entropy.

In 2012, Barrett Values Centre conducted a research project to examine the impact of cultural entropy on the values of organizations in 40 industries and 36 countries using 1,011 Cultural Values Assessments carried out during the period 2007 to 2011.

The assessments were separated into the five cultural entropy bands shown in Table 8.1. Figure 8.1 show that only 15 per cent (147) of the organizations surveyed had a culture entropy score in the healthy range (0–10 per cent). Five per cent (50) had a cultural entropy score in the critical range (≥41 per cent).

The top ten values by level of consciousness of the 147 healthy organizations, and the 50 critical organizations are shown in Figure 8.2. Alongside each value are: (a) the percentages of organizations in these ranges that had that particular value in the top ten of their current culture—for example, 58 per cent of low-entropy organizations had teamwork in their top ten current culture values, and 90 per cent of high-entropy organizations had bureaucracy in their top ten current culture values; and (b) the level and type of value—for example, teamwork occurs at the transformation level (4) and is a relationship (R) value, and bureaucracy is

Table 8.1 Implications associated with different levels of cultural entropy

Cultural entropy	Implications
0–10%	Healthy: This is a low and healthy level of cultural entropy.
11–20%	Minor issues: This level of cultural entropy reflects the need to make some cultural or structural adjustments.
21–30%	Significant issues: This level of cultural entropy reflects the need for cultural and/or structural transformation and leadership coaching.
31–40%	Serious issues: This level of cultural entropy reflects the need for cultural and/or structural transformation, leadership development and coaching.
41% +	Critical issues: This level of cultural entropy reflects the need for cultural and/or structural transformation, selective changes in leadership, and leadership development and coaching.

a potentially limiting (L) self-esteem value (Level 3), and an organizational (O) value. The white dots represent potentially limiting values. These values are followed by an (L). Positive values are shown as grey dots. This figure also shows the Business Needs Scorecard charts for the current culture of low and high cultural entropy organizations.

The top scoring values amongst the low-entropy organizations were teamwork, customer satisfaction, continuous improvement and commitment—all positive values. The top scoring values among the high-entropy organizations were bureaucracy, short-term focus, hierarchy and blame—all potentially limiting values.

The low-entropy organizations are mainly focused at Level 3 (self-esteem) and Level 4 (transformation). The high-entropy organizations are mainly focused at Level 3 (self-esteem) and Level 1 (survival). In the high-entropy organizations,

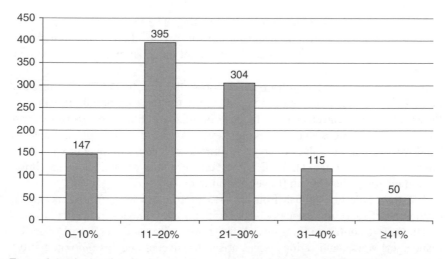

Figure 8.1 Distribution of cultural entropy scores by entropy band (2007–11).

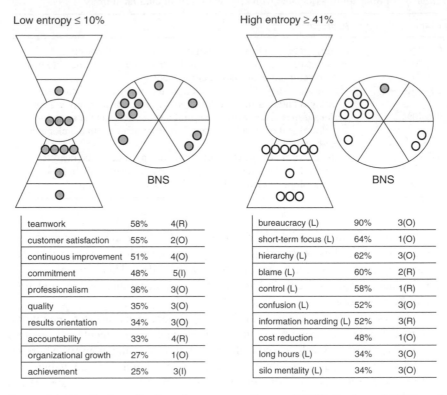

Low entropy ≤ 10%   High entropy ≥ 41%

teamwork	58%	4(R)
customer satisfaction	55%	2(O)
continuous improvement	51%	4(O)
commitment	48%	5(I)
professionalism	36%	3(O)
quality	35%	3(O)
results orientation	34%	3(O)
accountability	33%	4(R)
organizational growth	27%	1(O)
achievement	25%	3(I)

bureaucracy (L)	90%	3(O)
short-term focus (L)	64%	1(O)
hierarchy (L)	62%	3(O)
blame (L)	60%	2(R)
control (L)	58%	1(R)
confusion (L)	52%	3(O)
information hoarding (L)	52%	3(R)
cost reduction	48%	1(O)
long hours (L)	34%	3(O)
silo mentality (L)	34%	3(O)

Figure 8.2 Distribution of values in current culture and BNS for low- (≤10%) and high- (≥41%) entropy organizations.

the self-esteem values are all potentially limiting. The high level of control and the strong focus on short-term results at the survival level are also inhibiting the performance of these organizations. There is not much autonomy and accountability in these organizations.

When we explored the shift in values across the entropy bands we found that potentially limiting values start to appear in the top ten current culture values in the 21–30 per cent entropy band. The first potentially limiting values to appear are bureaucracy, hierarchy and confusion (Level 3). In the 31–40 per cent entropy band we also find the values of control, short-term focus, silo mentality and long hours (Level 3 and Level 1). In the highest entropy band we find blame and information hoarding showing up (Level 2 and Level 3).

We were able to establish from this research that low performance and the disintegration of a culture usually begins with poor accountability and teamwork,[1] which leads to confusion, causing a shift to bureaucracy and hierarchy. As performance gets worse, and serious issues arise, divisiveness begins (silo mentality), and panic sets in—people start to work long hours to get things back on track.

Table 8.2 Distribution of potentially limiting values by level for the highest entropy band

Level of consciousness	Values occurring in highest entropy band
Self-esteem (3)	Bureaucracy, hierarchy, confusion, long hours, silo mentality
Relationship (2)	Blame
Survival (1)	Short-term focus, control, (cost reduction)

At the same time, more focus is given to control, cost reduction[2] and short-term results. Then, as conditions get critical, people start to think about how to protect their jobs by blaming others and hoarding information.

The distribution across levels of consciousness of the potentially limiting values appearing in the high cultural entropy band is shown in Table 8.2. Although cost reduction is essentially a positive value—it can improve financial performance— in high-entropy organizations cost reduction is usually recognized by employees as a potentially limiting value. For this reason, it is shown in parentheses in Table 8.2.

Table 8.3 shows the allocation of the top ten values of the low and high cultural entropy organizations to the Business Needs Scorecard.

High-entropy organizations are slow in making decisions—they get bogged down by bureaucracy and hierarchy. They lose the commitment of their employees—there is very little accountability and teamwork (resulting in confusion). They forget about their customers. They get overly focused on short-term results, cutting spending on continuous improvement and investments for their future, and everyone starts to focus on their own self-interest.

The distribution of the value types in the low- and high-entropy organizations is shown in Table 8.4. The individual values of commitment and achievement in the low-entropy organizations are instrumental in creating a high performance ethic. The relationship values of teamwork and accountability ensure that people

Table 8.3 Allocation of values to BNS categories for low- and high-entropy bands

Category	Low entropy (0–10%)	High entropy (41%+)
Finance	Organizational growth	Cost reduction
Fitness	Achievement, professionalism, quality, results orientation	Bureaucracy, hierarchy, long hours
External stakeholder relations	Customer satisfaction	
Evolution	Continuous improvement	Short-term focus
Culture	*Trust/Engagement*: Accountability, commitment, teamwork	*Trust/Engagement*: Silo mentality, control, blame *Direction/Communication*: Confusion, information hoarding
Societal contribution		

Table 8.4 Value types for low- and high-entropy organizations

Low-entropy organizations (0–10%)

I	R	O	S
Commitment Achievement	Teamwork Accountability	Customer satisfaction Continuous improvement Professionalism Quality Results orientation Organizational growth	

High-entropy organizations (41%+)

I	R	O	S
	Blame (L) Control (L) Information hoarding (L)	Bureaucracy (L) Cost reduction (L) Hierarchy (L) Confusion (L) Results (L) Short-term focus (L) Long hours (L)	

work well together and take responsibility for outcomes. The organizational values of continuous improvement, quality and professionalism are instrumental in guaranteeing customer satisfaction. The attention given to results and organizational growth keeps the organization focused on success. All these values are missing from the top values of the high-entropy organizations we examined.

A high-entropy organization

Figure 8.3 shows the values data plot of a high-entropy organization. This plot represents the opinions of 80 senior managers. You will notice immediately from the distribution of the top values (the dots) that there is a significant misalignment in consciousness between the managers' personal values (a focus at Level 5), the current culture (a focus at Levels 1 and 2) and the desired culture (a focus at Level 4 and Level 2). There are no matching personal and current culture values (low values alignment) and only one matching current and desired culture value, accountability (low mission alignment).

What is typical about this data plot, which we frequently find in high-entropy organizations, is the desired culture values are concentrated at the level of transformation (Level 4). The values at this level are the remedies to many of the issues (potentially limiting values) at Levels 1, 2 and 3. Due to the difficulties they are having, this company has become internally focused: You will notice that customer satisfaction does not occur in the top ten values of the current culture but is the number two value in the desired culture.

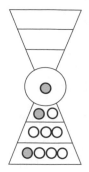

Personal values · Current culture · Desired culture

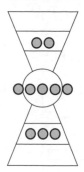

1. commitment	39	1. cost reduction (L)	64	1. continuous improvement	40
2. honesty	33	2. profit	40	2. customer satisfaction	36
3. making a difference	31	3. results orientation	36	3. accountability	29
4. positive attitude	29	4. blame (L)	34	4. coaching/mentoring	28
5. achievement	27	5. demanding (L)	32	5. leadership development	26
6. humour/fun	27	6. long hours (L)	29	6. teamwork	23
7. integrity	27	7. accountability	27	7. open communication	22
8. fairness	26	8. job/insecurity (L)	26	8. adaptability	21
9. performance	26	9. lack of appreciation (L)	25	9. employee recognition	21
10. initiative	23	10. control (L)	25	10. information sharing	21

Figure 8.3 A high-entropy organization.

Additionally, there are three positive relationship values in the desired culture (accountability, open communication and employee recognition), which act as a counterbalance to the four potentially limiting relationship values in the current culture (blame, demanding, lack of appreciation and control).

Figure 8.4 shows the values distribution diagram for the personal, current and desired culture of the same group of senior managers. The level of cultural entropy is 48 per cent (in the critical range). The entropy is relatively evenly spread across Levels 1 (18 per cent), 2 (16 per cent) and 3 (14 per cent).

What is disturbing about this result is the high level of cultural entropy at Levels 1 and 2 (it is more difficult to reduce entropy at Levels 1 and 2 than at Level 3). This suggests that the leaders are operating with high levels of personal entropy, which will be difficult to rectify. This conclusion is borne out by the fact that 2 per cent of their personal values are potentially limiting, and 3 per cent of their desired culture values are potentially limiting. Normally, we do not see any potentially limiting values in the desired culture of low-entropy organizations. New blood in the leadership group may be necessary to rectify this situation.

Figure 8.5 shows the distribution of positive values across the seven levels of consciousness. This is the same diagram as shown in Figure 8.4 except it is turned on its side and the potentially limiting values have been removed.

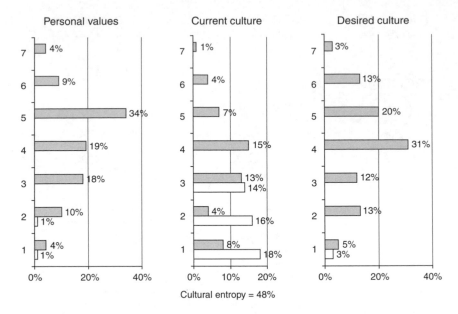

Figure 8.4 Values distribution diagram.

The senior managers in this organization want to see more focus on Level 2 values such as customer satisfaction, open communication and employee recognition; more focus on Level 4 values such as continuous improvement, accountability, teamwork, adaptability, empowerment and information sharing; more focus on Level 5 values generally (no specific values at this level came through in the

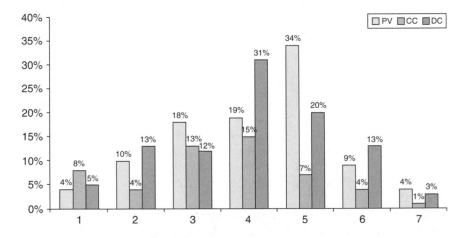

Figure 8.5 Distribution of positive values.

Table 8.5 Value jumps table

Values	Current culture votes	Desired culture votes	Value jump
Coaching/mentoring	1	28	27
Customer satisfaction	15	36	21
Employee recognition	0	21	21
Continuous improvement	21	40	19
Open communication	21	40	19
Information sharing	4	22	17
Leadership development	10	21	16
Empowerment	3	26	16

top ten desired culture or the value jumps); more focus on Level 6 values such as coaching/mentoring and leadership development; and more focus on Level 7 values. The only levels where there is adequate coverage of values in the current culture compared with the desired culture are Levels 1 and 3. There is a significant gap between the senior managers' personal values and the current culture at Levels 2, 3, 5 and 6, and small gaps at Levels 4 and 7. The personal values do not add up to 100 per cent because 2 per cent of these values were potentially limiting and not therefore included.

Table 8.5 shows the top value jumps of this group of 80 managers. You can see from this table that the key issue for this company is the quality of leadership. The top value jumps include coaching and mentoring, employee recognition, open communication, information sharing, leadership development and empowerment. Accountability is not a significant issue: There are 27 votes for accountability in the current culture and almost the same (29) in the desired culture.

Figure 8.6 is a graphical representation of Table 8.4 showing the results for the top five value jumps.

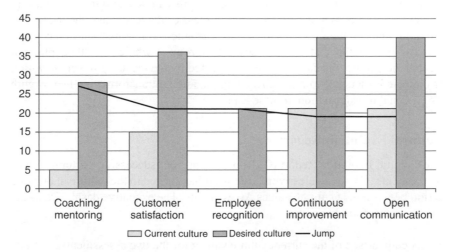

Figure 8.6 Top five value jumps.

The high level of cultural entropy and the seven potentially limiting values showing up in the top ten current culture values are a clear sign that the leaders are not performing: They are letting their fears dictate their behaviours.

Blame, demanding, long hours, cost reduction and control are all signs that the leadership group has lost its way. The organization is focused on profit, but not on customers. Neither is the company taking care of its people—lack of appreciation and job insecurity are potentially limiting values showing up in the current culture.

The desired culture values point the way to improving the quality of leadership: Coaching/mentoring, leadership development, open communication, employee recognition and information sharing are all desired culture values that do not appear in the top ten current culture values and are high-scoring value jumps. These are the values that the leadership team needs to focus on if they want to turn this company around.

Cognitive dissonance

When I feedback a result like this to a leadership team, I pose the question:

> How is it that with this set of personal values—pointing to the top ten personal values—did you create this culture—pointing to the current culture and all the potentially limiting values—when you all agree that what you want is this—pointing to the desired culture?

This question creates cognitive dissonance. Cognitive dissonance is the term used to describe the feeling of discomfort that people experience when holding two or more conflicting ideas simultaneously. This is an uncomfortable mental state that can only be relieved by doing something to reduce the dissonance. What cognitive dissonance does, in a situation like this, is point to a lack of authenticity or integrity among the decision makers of the group. This can be enough, sometimes, to trigger a shift in consciousness and a willingness of the leader and the leadership group to focus on their own personal transformation. It is important to recognize in situations like this that it is not usually the group as whole (the 80 people) that created the culture; the culture is always created by the leader of the organization or the core leadership team members. Organizational transformation begins with the personal transformation of these leaders.

Cultural Evolution Report

The Cultural Evolution Report (CER) uses data from successive Cultural Values Assessments (CVAs) to clearly indicate what has shifted in the culture in the time period between the Cultural Values Assessments. The executive dashboard of the CER contains four diagrams:

• A comparison of the current culture values for the two assessments.
• A comparison of the cultural entropy for the two assessments.

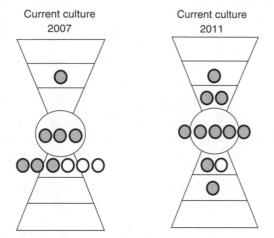

Figure 8.7 Comparison of current culture values 2007 and 2011.

- A comparison of the distribution of positive current culture values across all levels of consciousness for the two assessments.
- A comparison of the values matches for the two assessments.

Figure 8.7 shows a comparison of the current culture values in an organization between 2007 and 2011. There is a significant shift from Level 3 to Level 4. There are 11 top values in the 2011 results because the last two values scored the same number of votes.

Figure 8.8 shows a comparison of the cultural entropy between 2007 and 2011. The cultural entropy fell from 19 per cent to 13 per cent.

Figure 8.9 shows a comparison of the distribution of positive current culture values across all levels of consciousness. There has been a significant jump in

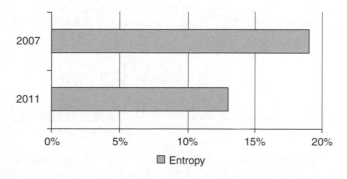

Figure 8.8 Comparison of cultural entropy 2007 and 2011.

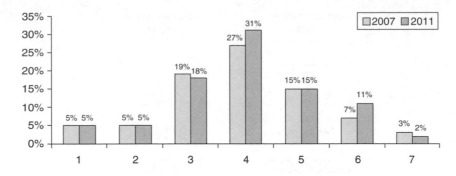

Figure 8.9 Comparison of distribution of positive values 2007 and 2011.

Level 4 values from 27 per cent to 31 per cent, and in Level 6 values from 7 per cent to 11 per cent.

Figure 8.10 shows a comparison of the values matches PV/CC (values alignment) and CC/DC (mission alignment). The number of PV/CC matches increased from zero to three and the number of CC/DC matches increased from two to five resulting in an increase in employee engagement.

In addition to the executive dashboard, the CER also provides the following diagrams and tables:

* A table outlining what values have remained in the top ten, what values have dropped out of the top ten, and what values have come into the top ten personal, current culture and desired culture values in the intervening time period between the two cultural values assessments.
* The shifts in the types of values (IROS) in the top ten personal, current culture and desired culture values in the two Cultural Values Assessments.
* A comparison of the distribution of values by level in the current culture of the two Cultural Values Assessments similar to Figure 8.9 including potentially limiting values.
* A comparison of the percentage of employees voting for each of the potentially limiting values by level in the two Cultural Values Assessments.

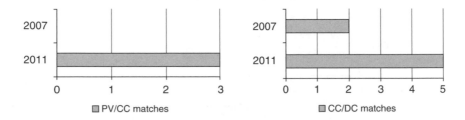

Figure 8.10 Comparison of PV/CC and CC/DC matches.

- A comparison of the Business Needs Scorecards for the two values assessments.
- A comparison of the percentage increase of the top value jumps in the two Cultural Values Assessments.
- A comparison of the distribution of values by level for the desired culture of the first assessment compared with the current culture of the second assessment and the desired culture of the second assessment.
- A comparison of the Business Needs Scorecards for the desired culture of the first assessment compared with the current culture of the second assessment and the desired culture of the second assessment.
- A comparison of the results of the espoused value analysis for the two cultural values assessments. This is an optional extra.

Merger/Compatibility Assessment

The Merger/Compatibility Assessment enables leaders to anticipate and plan for the cultural issues that could arise in a merger, an acquisition or the joining together of two departments or units to create a single entity.

The example I have chosen is of two medium-sized organizations that are not highly evolved, but are relatively compatible. Each company is comprised of about 1,000 employees and they have a significant number of matching personal, current culture and desired culture values.

Figure 8.11 shows the top ten personal values plotted to the Seven Levels of Consciousness Model. The people from the two companies share seven matching personal values—teamwork, humour/fun, honesty, commitment, positive attitude, balance (home/work) and integrity. They operate from the same levels of consciousness and consequently have very similar needs.

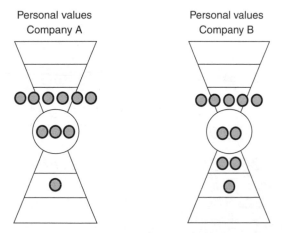

Figure 8.11 Personal values of people in Company A and Company B.

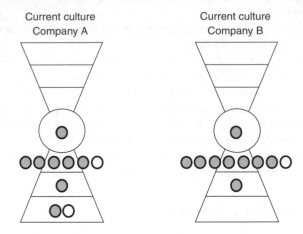

Figure 8.12 Current culture of Company A and Company B.

Figure 8.12 shows the distribution of the top ten current culture values for the two companies. Both companies are heavily focused at Level 3 consciousness. They share seven matching values—client focus, professionalism, teamwork, long hours (L), excellence, quality and being the best. Company A, which is struggling financially, also has cost reduction, profit and hierarchy in its top ten current culture values. Company B, on the other hand, has market orientation, achievement and best practice.

Figure 8.13 shows the distribution of the top ten desired culture values. Employees in both companies want to see a strong focus at Levels 3 and 4. They share eight matching desired culture values—client focus, teamwork, excellence,

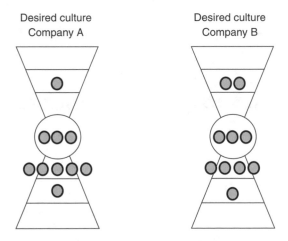

Figure 8.13 Desired culture of Company A and Company B.

professionalism, balance (home/work), leadership, best practice and market orientation. Employees in Company A also want to see an increased focus on being the best and information sharing. Employees in Company B, on the other hand, want to see an increased focus on accountability and coaching/mentoring.

The results of this compatibility analysis suggest that these two companies should not have too many cultural problems when they merge together. The people have very similar personal values; the current cultures are similar, except that Company A has 22 per cent cultural entropy compared with 12 per cent for Company B; and the desired cultures are also very similar. One of the key benefits of the merger is that Company B will be able to help Company A improve their market orientation and best practices. These are desired culture values for Company A that Company B has in its current culture. This would be a timely merger for Company A since it is not doing well financially (focus on cost reduction and profit in the current culture).

A typical Merger/Compatibility Assessment provides the following diagrams and tables:

- A comparison of the personal, current culture and desired culture values of the two groups—what values are shared and what values are different.
- A comparison of the levels of cultural entropy of the two groups.
- A comparison of the types of values in the current culture of the two groups.
- A comparison of the distribution of values across the seven levels of consciousness for the two groups.
- A comparison of the Balanced Needs Scorecards for the two groups.
- A comparison of the current culture strengths of one group with the desired culture values of the other group. This tells you how the two groups can help each other.

Conclusions

This brief overview of the evolution of cultural entropy in an organization and the data produced by a Cultural Values Assessment (CVA) highlights the diagnostic powers of the Cultural Transformation Tools. This chapter specifically focused on: (a) diagnosing the problems in a high-entropy organization; (b) comparing the cultural evolution of a company between two specific time periods; and (c) assessing the cultural compatibility of two companies that are about to merge.

Summary

Here are the main points of Chapter 8:

1. Only 15 per cent of over 1,000 organizations surveyed between 2007 and 2011 had a cultural entropy score of 10 per cent or below. Forty-six per cent had a cultural entropy score of 21 per cent or more.

2. The top-scoring values among low-entropy organizations are teamwork, customer satisfaction, continuous improvement and commitment.
3. The top-scoring values among high-entropy organizations are bureaucracy, short-term focus, hierarchy and blame.
4. In low-entropy organizations the levels of desired culture consciousness reflect the levels of employees' personal consciousness.
5. In high-entropy organizations the desired culture consciousness tends to be focused at the level of transformation.
6. The disintegration of a culture usually begins with poor accountability and teamwork, which leads to confusion, causing a shift to bureaucracy and hierarchy. As performance gets worse, and serious issues arise, divisiveness begins (silo mentality), and people start to work long hours to get things back on track. At the same time, more focus is given to control, cost reduction and short-term results. As conditions go critical, people start to think about how to protect their jobs by blaming others and information hoarding.
7. Organizations that display high cultural entropy in their current culture usually find the answers to their problems at the transformation level of the desired culture.
8. The Cultural Evolution Report (CER) enables you to measure in detail the cultural changes that have occurred over a specific time period.
9. The Merger/Compatibility Assessment enables you to evaluate potential issues that might arise from two organizations or units merging together.

Notes

1 Accountability and teamwork are the two top desired cultural values in high-entropy organizations. They are also two of the top ten values in low-entropy organizations.
2 Normally speaking, the value of "cost reduction" can be considered as a positive value. However, we have found that at moderate-to-high levels of cultural entropy cost reduction becomes a potentially limiting value, causing increased levels of frustration.

Part III

Mapping leadership values

The purpose of Part III of this book is to provide the reader with a clear understanding of how to measure, map and monitor the values of leaders, managers and supervisors, and how to use the results to improve their level of personal alignment, reduce their level of personal entropy, and thereby reduce the level of cultural entropy in their unit, department or organization.

You will recall from Chapter 4, Figure 4.4 (shown below), there are four conditions necessary for whole system change. This part of the book focuses on *personal alignment*. Personal alignment is about leaders, managers and supervisors walking the talk—being authentic and operating with integrity.

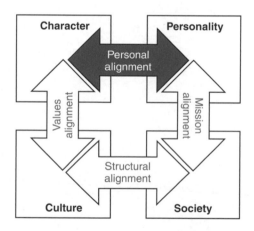

9   Leadership performance

The overall purpose of carrying out regular assessments of the operational values of the leaders, managers and supervisors is the same as the reason for carrying out regular assessments of the culture of an organization—to systematically reduce the level of cultural entropy of the organization and thereby increase the level of employee engagement.

By focusing on the personal entropy of the current leaders, managers and supervisors you are able to get to the main source of the organization's cultural entropy. The other source of cultural entropy is the legacy of the personal entropy of past leaders that has been institutionalized in the structures, policies, procedures and incentives of the organization. I will deal with how to reduce the institutionalized entropy from past leaders in Part IV of this book.

The purpose therefore of carrying out regular leadership values assessments of leaders, managers and supervisors is:

1. to monitor their level of personal entropy;
2. to help them take actions to reduce their level of personal entropy; and
3. to help and support them in their personal growth and development.

Reducing a leader's, manager's or supervisor's personal entropy directly impacts the level of cultural entropy of their organization, department or team; and promoting the leader's, manager's or supervisor's personal development directly impacts their ability to improve the levels of values alignment and mission alignment of their staff.

The leader of an organization must make it his or her personal duty to not only reduce his or her level of personal entropy and increase his or her level of values alignment and mission alignment, but also encourage and support every other leader, manager and supervisor in the organization to do the same. The leader must also spearhead the charge in revamping the structures, processes, policies, procedures and incentives of the organization to more clearly meet the physical, emotional, mental and "spiritual"[1] needs of employees and other stakeholders. In this regard, the following quote from Peters and Waterman in *In Search of Excellence*, published in 1982, is as timely as ever: "The institutional leader should primarily be an expert in the promotion and protection of values."[2]

What is personal entropy?

Personal entropy is the amount of fear-driven energy that a person expresses in his or her day-to-day interactions with other people.

Almost everyone, except perhaps for some of the most highly evolved souls, operates with some level of personal entropy. The problem with personal entropy is that, if you don't learn to master it, it becomes counterproductive to meeting your individual short-, medium- and long-term goals. If you are leader, manager or supervisor, you will find your personal entropy showing up in your organization, department or team as cultural entropy. It will undermine the performance of your team, reduce their level of commitment and decrease their level of engagement.

Where does personal entropy come from?

Personal entropy arises from your early life experiences about not being able to meet your deficiency needs—not being able to get enough of what you need to feel safe and secure (the survival level of development); not being able to get enough of what you need to feel loved and accepted (the relationship level of development); and not being able to get enough of what you need to feel acknowledged and respected (the self-esteem level of development). It is closely associated with the parental and cultural programming you received while you were growing up.

When, as young children, we are unable, for whatever reason, to satisfy our deficiency needs, our ego-minds develop subconscious fear-based beliefs about not having enough, not being loved enough and not being enough. The reason children develop these beliefs is because up to the age of about seven or eight the neo-cortex—the reasoning part of the brain—is not fully developed. Only the reptilian brain and limbic brain are operational. These are the parts of the brain that process our emotions. Therefore, when we are young we evaluate every situation we experience according to whether it brings us emotional pleasure or emotional pain. We do not have the capacity to evaluate our experiences cognitively through the filters of logic and reason because those faculties are not yet fully available to us. In order to make meaning from our experiences as children, we establish beliefs based on our emotional reactions to situations.

The emotional feelings of hurt, anger and sadness we experienced in our childhood, in situations where we were unable to get our needs met, are stored in our memory banks along with the beliefs we learned. These beliefs become the mental models we use to understand how the world works. When, as an adult, a situation we are currently experiencing subconsciously reminds us of a childhood experience involving one or several of these emotionally charged memories, we emote—the negative emotions stored in our memory flood our mind and we get angry or upset.

In the psychological literature the subconscious fear-based beliefs learned during childhood are called "Early Maladaptive Schemas (EMS)."[3] Jeffrey Young,

Founder and Director of the Cognitive Therapy Centres of New York and Fairfield County (Connecticut), describes EMS in the following way:

> Early Maladaptive Schemas [beliefs] seem to be the result of dysfunctional experiences with parents, siblings, and peers during the first few years of an individual's life. Most schemas [beliefs] are caused by on-going everyday noxious experiences with family members and peers which cumulatively strengthen the schema [belief]. For example a child who is constantly criticized when performance does not meet parental standards is prone to develop the incompetence/failure schema.[4]

A brief list and description of the principal types of maladaptive schema, including the incompetence/failure schema, is presented in Annex 16.

These early negative experiences gradually become hardwired into your mind as limiting beliefs. They become the default mental models you use to give meaning to your experiences and the filters that condition your reality.

Our subconscious fear-based beliefs are aligned with the first three stages of personal development—survival (not having enough), relationship (not being loved enough) and self-esteem (not being enough). Thus, we can state: *Our fear-driven energy—our personal entropy—arises from our early childhood experiences about not being able to meet our deficiency needs.*

Limiting survival beliefs

Limiting beliefs at the survival level are about *not having enough* to feel safe and secure. These beliefs result in the display of potentially limiting values such as control, manipulation, greed, excessive caution, impatience and generally result in a lack of trust.

During the first stage of your psychological development, the surviving stage, your primary task is to establish a separate sense of identity from your mother, and learn how to exercise control over your environment so you can get your survival needs met. If, for whatever reason, you had difficulties accomplishing this task, either because your parents were not vigilant enough to your needs, or you were left alone or abandoned for long periods of time and/or your parents were fearful for their own survival, your nascent ego will very likely have formed subconscious fear-based beliefs (early maladaptive schema) that the world is an unsafe place and that other people cannot be trusted. This either leads you to want to control and manipulate your environment, so you can get what you want, or operate with excessive caution and become risk-averse to make sure what you already have does not get taken away.

If on the other hand, your parents were attentive to your needs, and were watchful for signs of distress, then you will grow up with a sense of security and the feeling that others can be trusted. You will feel confident about being able to meet your survival needs, and consequently will not spend much time or energy worrying about having enough. Feeling safe and secure is the first and most important need of the ego-mind.

Limiting relationship beliefs

Limiting beliefs at the relationship level are about *not being loved enough* to feel accepted or protected—not belonging. These beliefs result in the display of potentially limiting values such as jealously, blame and being liked. Being liked is potentially limiting because your overriding need to be accepted may cause you to lie or possibly embroider the truth so people do not think badly about you. The desire to be liked can also lead to dishonesty and blame. You lie about your actions and deflect responsibility for your "wrongdoings" onto other people to avoid punishment and stay in good favour. If as a child, you are constantly blamed for things that others did, you will grow up wanting to be treated fairly and strongly concerned about justice.

During the second stage of psychological development, the conforming or self-protective stage, your primary task is to learn how to feel loved and safe in your family or social group. Adherence to rules and rituals (conforming) becomes important, because they consolidate your sense of belonging, and enhance your sense of safety. If for any reason you grow up feeling unloved or unaccepted, not getting your share of love or not belonging, your ego may have developed a subconscious fear-based limiting belief that you are not lovable, not accepted, not preferred or that you are an outsider. Later on in life, you may find yourself constantly seeking affection or searching for a group or community that accepts and welcomes you as you are.

If on the other hand, you always felt loved no matter what you did, and that love was given unconditionally, then you will grow up with a sense of being accepted. You will feel confident about being able to meet your relationship needs, and consequently not spend much time or energy worrying about being loved enough. Feeling loved, accepted and a sense of belonging is the second most important need of the ego-mind.

Limiting self-esteem beliefs

Limiting beliefs at the self-esteem level are about *not being enough* to feel confident in your capabilities or respected. These beliefs result in the display of potentially limiting values such as status seeking, power-seeking, political manoeuvring, being highly competitive and wanting to be top dog.

During the third stage of psychological development, the differentiation stage, your primary need is to be recognized by your parents or peers for excelling or doing well. The task at this stage is to develop a healthy sense of pride in your accomplishments and a feeling of self-worth. You want to feel good about who you are and you want to feel respected by your peers. If, for whatever reason, you are denied this recognition, you will grow up with the subconscious fear-based belief that you are not good enough. You will always feel driven to prove your self-worth. You may become a workaholic. You will want to be acknowledged by your peers or those in authority as someone who is important or someone to be feared. If your ego-mind does not get the reinforcement that it needs, you could grow up with a feeling that no matter how hard you try, recognition escapes you: The successes you achieve may never be enough to satisfy your needs.

If on the other hand, your parents encouraged you to try out new things, and praised your efforts no matter how well you did, you will feel a sense of self-worth or pride in your accomplishments. You will feel confident about who you are and your abilities, and consequently not spend much time worrying about being enough. Feeling a sense of self-worth is the third most important need of the ego-mind.

Object referral and subject referral

When you constantly need others to protect you, to demonstrate their love for you and tell you how great you are, you live in a state of dependence: You have become dependent on others to meet your deficiency needs. You will operate with a social-ized mind and you will define who you are by your job, your income, your friends and your possessions. This way of being is called object referral. Leaders who surround themselves with "yes men" are leaders who are operating from object referral: Their egos need to be stroked in order to feel good about themselves.

If, on the other hand, your experience of life is determined by what you think about yourself, who *you* believe you are, and not what others believe, you live in a state of subject referral with a self-authoring or self-transforming mind. Only when you become self-sufficient and have mastered your deficiency needs can you operate from a place of independence. Such leaders appreciate constructive feedback and hearing other people's points of view. They are not wedded to their own perspectives.

If you were able to successfully transition through the first three stages of your psychological development without significant trauma about meeting your defi-ciency needs and without developing too many subconscious fear-based beliefs, your level of personal entropy will be relatively low and you will find it easy to get along with people and make your way in life.

It is important to recognize that everyone has subconscious fear-based limiting beliefs. If you have ever been upset, stressed, angry or impatient, or ever judged yourself for not having the skills you need to survive, not being handsome or pretty enough to be loved or not being successful enough to be respected or acknowledged, you have a conscious or subconscious fear-based belief (limiting belief) operating in your mind. Only you can rectify this situation. The process of releasing, managing or overcoming your subconscious fear-based beliefs is called personal mastery.

What is personal mastery?

I define personal mastery as: *The ability to manage one's emotional stability at the ego level of existence.* You achieve personal mastery when you are able to successfully manage your emotions so that you become responsible for how you feel and are no longer dependent on others to meet your survival, relationship and self-esteem needs.

To become proficient in managing your emotions, you have to develop mindfulness. Mindfulness is the ability to stand back and observe the thought processes going on inside you. When you become proficient in practising mindfulness, you come to the realization that most of your reactions and upsets are sourced from your memories of unresolved past hurts about not getting your deficiency needs met.

Whatever emotions you are experiencing at a given moment in time are either driven by the instincts of your reptilian brain, or the fear-based beliefs of your ego-mind. Every bout of impatience, frustration, anger, rage or self-judgment is self-generated, usually subconsciously. The actions or words of other people trigger your early maladaptive schemas. It is these schema (your subconscious fears) that cause you to react negatively, projecting the unresolved hurt of past emotional scars into the world. If you want to manage your anger, frustration and upsets, you need to make yourself accountable for every emotion, feeling and thought you have. You must learn that your reactions to situations are the product of your unmet needs and your limiting beliefs. They don't have to control you: You *can* control them.

The first step you need to take in overcoming your limiting fear-based beliefs is to identify them and name them. Because most fear-based beliefs are subconscious, you may not be aware you have them. Your upsets are the only clue you have that they exist. An upset is any form of emotional reaction that disturbs your energetic balance—causes you to lose your composure. Apart from self-coaching, which I will explain in the following section, the best way to uncover your fear-based beliefs is to get feedback from the people you work with or the people with whom you share your personal life.

Two of the tools you can use to get this type of feedback, which I will describe later in this chapter, are the Leadership Values Assessment and the Leadership Development Report. The results from these assessments are delivered in a two-to-three hour session by someone with coaching skills.

Getting such feedback is usually just the starting point. You then have to do something about it. Ultimately, if you are serious about developing your personal mastery skills, and overcoming your limiting fear-based beliefs, you will have to learn how to become your own self-coach.

In *The New Leadership Paradigm* and again in *What My Soul Told Me: A Practical Guide to Soul Activation*, I have outlined an eight-step process for managing and mastering your limiting conscious or subconscious fears. This self-coaching process is described in Annex 17.

Emotional intelligence and personal mastery

How is personal mastery related to emotional intelligence? Since Daniel Goleman published his book, *Emotional Intelligence: Why it Can Matter More than IQ*[5] in 1996, there has been a considerable amount of interest in business circles in helping leaders to understand the role that emotions play in their lives and the impact on their performance. We can define emotional intelligence as: *The ability to understand, manage and use your emotions to guide you in making wise decisions.*

Emotional intelligence requires:

- *Self-awareness*: The ability to read your emotions and feelings, recognize their impact on you and others, and use them to guide your decision making.
- *Self-management*: The ability to manage or master your emotions and feelings so you can adapt more readily to changing circumstances and meet your own needs.

The feedback process from a 360° assessment such as the Leadership Values Assessment or the Leadership Development Report enables you to recognize the impact *you* have on others compared with the impact you think you have. In other words, the feedback you get from a values assessment helps you to identify your dysfunctional, life-depleting behaviours (limiting values), your blind spots, as well as your life-enhancing behaviours (positive values).

Basically, we can say that: *Personal mastery is the process by which you build your emotional intelligence*, and the feedback process from a values assessment is one of the ways *to bring to light the values and behaviours that are undermining your emotional intelligence.*

Once you have raised your emotional intelligence, you can then start to work on your social intelligence. We can define social intelligence as: *The ability to understand and use the emotions of others to guide you in making wise decisions.*

Social intelligence requires:

- *Social awareness*: the ability to sense, understand and respond to others' emotions in a group situation.
- *Relationship management*: the ability to inspire, influence and develop others while managing conflict.

Because social intelligence is focused on understanding the emotions of others, it not only demands strong listening skills, it also requires a high level of empathy. You need to be able to focus on and understand what is going on with others and take yourself out of the equation. Consequently, developing your social intelligence usually comes after developing your emotional intelligence.

Your ability to lead others is severely compromised if you cannot lead yourself. What happens, if you attempt to lead others before first developing your self-leadership skills, is the fears of your ego—your self-interest in meeting your own needs—get in the way of supporting the people you are leading—making sure their needs are met. This is particularly true if you are holding onto any subconscious fear-based beliefs (potentially limiting values) about not being safe enough, loved enough or not enough.

This is the problem with potentially limiting values: They handicap you in working with others. They may satisfy *your* need to satisfy your *own* needs, but in so doing, they alienate other people and create discord and conflict with the people around you in your immediate environment; and perhaps, depending on what actions you take to satisfy your unmet deficiency needs, with people in your larger social environment too. Those who go on shooting rampages represent an extreme case of such behaviours. Their actions are in some way designed to meet their unmet needs. The higher you move in the leadership ranks, the more your potentially limiting values will contribute to the cultural entropy of the group you are responsible for.

Why is it important to reduce personal entropy?

This is the reason why: If you do not find a way to release, reduce or master your personal entropy, you will find it blocking your happiness, progress or advancement in both your personal and professional life. Your subconscious fears will keep you locked into the first three levels of consciousness, thereby preventing you from becoming all you can become. Your subconscious fears inhibit you from individuating and self-actualizing—reaching the fourth and fifth stages of psychological development. As you release or overcome your fears, you increase your ability to trust, and you open a space in your mind to experience and manifest love. Love is the great connector, whereas fear is the great separator.

I am not saying that all fears should be judged as negative. We all have natural fears about keeping the body safe and secure. This is the purpose of the ego, to keep you safe and sound. These are "good" fears because they enable you to stay alive and keep your body healthy. The "bad" fears, those that do not support you in your growth and development, are the conscious and subconscious fears the ego has about not having enough, not being loved enough and not being enough. When these fears are present, they cause you to be highly vigilant: Your reptilian and limbic mind/brains constantly evaluate your environment for threats or for opportunities to meet your unmet needs. They cause you to react to situations, sometimes saying things you will later regret or they cause you to focus on your own self-interest without regard for how your actions or behaviours affect other people. When this happens you lose the trust and the loyalty of the people around you: You isolate yourself. People become fearful of being overly exposed to you, and as soon as that happens, they are no longer willing to contribute their discretionary energy to their work and they avoid any form of commitment, contact and cooperation. This is when, as a leader, your fear-based behaviours become counterproductive to your personal and organizational goals.

Conclusions

Personal entropy is the source of cultural entropy. Who you are as a leader—what you stand for and the needs/values that drive your decision making—significantly influence the culture of your organization, department or team. If you are committed to the success of the organization then you also need to be committed to your own personal mastery and development. You will need to recognize that the cultural entropy you see around you may in some way be due to the personal entropy you display every day.

Summary

Here are the main points of Chapter 9:

1. Personal entropy is the amount of fear-driven energy that a person expresses in his or her day-to-day interactions.
2. Reducing a leader's personal entropy directly impacts the level of cultural entropy of the organization, and promoting the leader's personal development directly impacts his or her ability to improve the levels of values alignment and mission alignment of the people in the organization.
3. Personal entropy arises from your early life experiences about not being able to get your deficiency needs met.
4. Only when you have mastered your deficiency needs can you become fully independent (individuate).
5. Personal mastery is the ability to manage one's emotional stability at the ego level of existence. You achieve personal mastery when you are able to successfully manage your emotions so you are no longer dependent on others to meet your survival, relationship and self-esteem needs.
6. Emotional intelligence is the ability to understand, manage and use your emotions to guide you in making wise decisions.
7. Social intelligence is the ability to understand and use the emotions of others to guide you in making wise decisions.
8. Your ability to lead others (social intelligence) is severely compromised if you cannot lead yourself (emotional intelligence).
9. If you do not find a way to release, reduce or master your personal entropy, you will find it blocking your happiness, progress or advancement in both your personal and professional life.

Notes

1 Spiritual in this context refers to the need for employees to find a sense of meaning in their work, to actualize that meaning by making a difference, and to lead a life of selfless service.
2 Tom Peters and Robert H. Waterman, Jr., *In Search of Excellence*: *Lessons from America's Best-Run Companies* (London: Profile Books), 2004, p. 281. First published by Harper & Row, 1982.
3 Jeffrey E. Young, *Cognitive Therapy for Personality Disorders: A Schema-focused Approach*, revised edition (Sarasota, FL: Professional Resource Press), 1994.
4 Ibid., p. 11.
5 Daniel Goleman, *Emotional Intelligence: Why It Can Matter More than IQ* (London: Bloomsbury Publishing), 1996.

10 Measuring leadership performance

The Seven Levels of Consciousness Model described in Chapter 5 has not only been used to create a set of survey instruments to help organizations manage their values, it has also been used to create a set of survey instruments to help leaders, managers and supervisors monitor and manage their values and behaviours, as well as measuring their level of personal entropy. These survey instruments form part of the Cultural Transformation Tools (CTT) described in Chapter 6. Annex 18 provides a list of the CTT survey instruments that can be used by leaders, managers and supervisors to reduce their personal entropy, support their development and evaluate their level of values and mission alignment. Annex 19 describes the data plots associated with each of these instruments.

Before explaining how to interpret the results of the three main instruments available for these purposes—the Individual Values Assessment (IVA), the Leadership Values Assessment (LVA) and the Leadership Development Report (LDR), I would first like to give some explanations about the survey processes. The major difference between the IVA and the LVA and LDR is that the IVA is a self-assessment instrument. The LVA and LDR are feedback assessments with a self-assessment component that is used to compare the feedback from assessors with the leader's evaluation of his or her values.

The survey process

Individual Values Assessment (IVA)

The main purpose of the IVA is to help leaders, managers and supervisors evaluate the level of values alignment and mission alignment they have with their organization. The Individual Values Assessment is the same instrument that is used for collecting information for a Cultural Values Assessment.

Once the IVA survey website is open, participants login using a password and are then asked to select from a list of 80–90 words or phrases:

- Ten values/behaviours that represent who they are (personal values).
- Ten values/behaviours that represent how their organization operates (current culture).

- Ten values/behaviours that represent what they believe the organization needs to do to achieve its highest level of performance (desired culture).

The survey typically takes less than 15 minutes. Standard templates for personal and organizational values are used which can be customized if requested. Reports are presented in English while the diagnostic diagrams (value plots) can be provided in the chosen survey language. The chosen values are analyzed in the same way as a CVA—by sign (positive or potentially limiting), by level of consciousness (1–7), by type (IROS) and by business focus (BNS). The number of potentially limiting values/behaviours the individual ascribes to the current culture is indicative of the level of cultural entropy in the organization.

Leadership Values Assessment (LVA)

The purpose of the LVA is to get feedback from your peers, subordinates and superiors about their perspective on how they see you operating as a leader and compare their perspective with yours.

The LVA process begins with the customization of the leadership values template for the organization. Leaders are then asked to go to a password-protected website to select ten values that most represent their operating style. They also list what they believe are their strengths, and the areas of improvement they are currently working on. Fifteen to 20 assessors, chosen by the leader, also go to the password-protected website to select ten values that represent the leader's operating style; the behaviours they believe the leader needs to stop, start or improve; and any other comments they may wish to give as feedback to the leader. Assessors can choose whether to provide their name with their feedback or take the survey anonymously. The LVA feedback is given by a coach in a two-to-three hour one-on-one session. Based on the feedback, the leader and the coach together develop a detailed action plan to improve the leader's performance.

When a group of leaders in the same leadership team are having LVAs produced at the same time, a collective Group Leadership Plot can be produced. This plot shows the amalgamated responses of the leaders and the feedback they all received. This plot highlights the common strengths of the group and common issues.

Leadership Development Report (LDR)

The purpose of the LDR is the same as the LVA. The main difference between the LDR and LVA is that the LDR is automated. It uses a standard leadership values template based on the most common values that have been recorded for hundreds of leaders over a period of several years. Clients can choose to customize this template at an additional cost. Once the survey website is open, and leaders have logged on using a personal password, they are asked to select ten values that most represent their operating style. They are then asked to rate themselves against 26 leadership behaviours indicating to what extent each of the statements represents an existing strength or area for development. Fifteen to 20 assessors, chosen by the leader, also go to the password-protected website to select ten values that represent the leader's operating style, and ten values they believe are important for the leader to integrate into his or her operating style. They then rate the leader against the 26 leadership behaviours and provide any other comments they wish to give as feedback to the leader. The results of the LDR, like the LVA, are delivered by a coach in a two-to-three hour one-on-one feedback session. Based on the feedback, the leader and the coach together develop a detailed action plan to improve the leader's performance.

Levels of personal entropy

One of the key outputs from this process is the level of personal entropy. The following table (Table 10.1) provides an overview of the implications associated with different ranges of personal entropy.

Values associated with high and low personal entropy

In order to more fully understand the leadership values/behaviours that are consistent with low personal entropy and high personal entropy, we analyzed the results of 100 Leadership Values Assessments conducted during 2008–9 across 15 business sectors in 19 countries. The countries represented in this study include: Australia, Belgium, Brazil, Canada, Czech Republic, France, Germany, India, the Netherlands, Norway, Peru, Poland, South Africa, Sweden, Trinidad and Tobago, Turkey, the UK, the US and Venezuela.

Table 10.1 Implications associated with different levels of personal entropy

Personal entropy	Implications
0–6%	*Healthy*: This is a low and healthy level of personal entropy suggesting decision making is not driven by subconscious fears.
7–10%	*Minor issues*: This level of personal entropy reflects the need for leaders to examine how their fear-based behaviours are affecting people around them and/or their own degree of work/life balance.
11–15%	*Significant issues*: This level of personal entropy reflects the need for leaders to examine how their fear-based behaviours are compromising their relationships with peers and subordinates, and negatively impacting their professional goals.
16–20%	*Serious issues*: This level of personal entropy reflects the need for leaders to examine how their fear-based behaviours are undermining their personal integrity and trustworthiness, and negatively impacting their professional and personal goals.
21%+	*Critical issues*: This level of personal entropy reflects the need for leaders to examine how their fear-based behaviours are compromising their ability to inspire and support their subordinates and collaborate effectively with their peers.

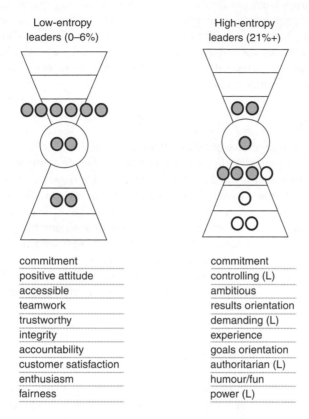

Low-entropy
leaders (0–6%)

High-entropy
leaders (21%+)

commitment	commitment
positive attitude	controlling (L)
accessible	ambitious
teamwork	results orientation
trustworthy	demanding (L)
integrity	experience
accountability	goals orientation
customer satisfaction	authoritarian (L)
enthusiasm	humour/fun
fairness	power (L)

Figure 10.1 Values associated with high and low personal entropy.

The results of this research are presented in Figure 10.1, which shows the top ten values most frequently found in leaders who are operating in the lowest entropy range (0–6 per cent) and the top ten values most frequently found in leaders who are operating in the highest entropy range (21 per cent+).

There is only one matching value between the low- and high-entropy leaders—they are all committed; the main difference is the high-entropy leaders employ at least four fear-driven behaviours to get their needs met.

High-entropy leaders feel they have to control, demand and use their power in an authoritarian way to get what they want. Low-entropy leaders, on the other hand, get their needs met by working with their people (teamwork), being accessible, focusing on accountability and customer satisfaction, listening to their employees and treating their employees with fairness. Low-entropy leaders are trustworthy, enthusiastic and bring a positive attitude to their work. High-entropy leaders are focused on results and goals rather than people. On average they display four potentially limiting relationship values, whereas low-entropy leaders display five positive relationship values.

In summary, we can say that low-entropy leaders display values that engender high levels of employee engagement—a focus on Level 5 consciousness (internal cohesion) and Level 4 (transformation). They let their people know they are appreciated, and they support them in being successful. By contrast, high-entropy leaders are more concerned about their own success (achievement and ambition) than the success of their people.

Conclusions

Leaders grow and develop when they get regular feedback. The LVA and LDR are designed for this purpose. They are coaching tools for promoting self-awareness, reducing personal entropy and improving emotional and social intelligence. The LVA and LDR compare a leader's perception of his or her operating style with the perception of his or her superior, peers and subordinates. The LVA and LDR reveal the extent to which a leader's behaviours help or hinder the performance of an organization, and to what extent their decision making is influenced by the fears they have about not getting their deficiency needs met. Reducing the level of personal entropy (conscious and subconscious fear-based behaviours) of the leaders of an organization is one of the most important ways of reducing cultural entropy.

Summary

Here are the main points of Chapter 10:

1. There are three main instruments for measuring the values of individuals—the Individual Values Assessment (IVA), the Leadership Values Assessment (LVA) and the Leadership Development Report (LDR).
2. The purpose of the IVA is to help leaders, managers and supervisors evaluate their level of values alignment and mission alignment with their organization.
3. The purpose of the LVA and LDR is to get feedback from peers, subordinates and superiors about what values their leaders display compared with how the leaders see themselves. The LVA and LDR also measure the level of personal entropy.
4. The LVA and LDR results are fed back to the leader, manager or supervisor in a two-to-three hour one-on-one coaching session. Based on the feedback, the leader and the coach together develop a detailed action plan to improve the leader's performance.
5. High-entropy leaders feel they have to control, demand and use their power in an authoritarian way to get what they want.
6. Low-entropy leaders get their needs met by working with their people, being accessible, focusing on accountability and customer satisfaction, listening to their employees and treating them with fairness.
7. Low-entropy leaders display values that result in high levels of employee engagement. High-entropy leaders display values that result in low levels of employee engagement.

11 Leadership case studies

The cultural entropy of an organization is a reflection of the personal entropy of the current leaders and the institutional legacy of the personal entropy of past leaders. In the next two figures, I show how the level of personal entropy of two leaders, both founders of their organizations (therefore no legacy of cultural entropy from past leaders) affected the cultural entropy of their organizations. In both cases the organizations concerned have between 20 and 30 employees.

Figure 11.1 shows the results from a low-entropy organization, and Figure 11.2 shows the results from a high-entropy organization. The CVA result is on the left-hand side of the figure, and the LVA result is on the right-hand side. Each dot represents one of the top values—the values that received the most votes by employees. Potentially limiting values are shown as white dots and designated with an (L). Positive values are shown as shaded dots. The levels of personal and cultural entropy are indicated on the figures. The level of cultural entropy was measured using a Cultural Values Assessment (CVA). The level of personal entropy was measured using a Leadership Values Assessment (LVA).

Briefly, in order to understand the following two figures, what you need to know is that personal entropy is measured in a similar way to cultural entropy. Each person giving feedback on the leader is asked to pick ten values that reflect how the leader operates. The level of personal entropy is the proportion of potentially limiting values that are picked by the assessors. The top values picked by the assessors and the number of votes are shown below each diagram.

The key point to notice from Figure 11.1 is that the level of personal entropy and cultural entropy are both relatively low: The personal entropy of the leader is 9 per cent and the cultural entropy of his organization is 7 per cent.

The key point to notice from Figure 11.2 is the level of personal entropy and cultural entropy are both high: The personal entropy of the leader is 64 per cent and the cultural entropy of the organization is 38 per cent.

What these figures clearly show is that cultural entropy is significantly affected by the personal entropy of the leader of the group. This is why it is important, if you want to reduce the overall level of cultural entropy of an organization, to focus not only on reducing entropy at the organizational level, but also focus on

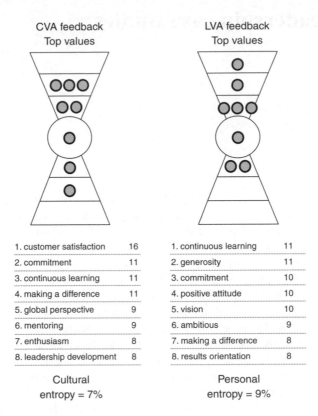

CVA feedback
Top values

LVA feedback
Top values

1. customer satisfaction	16
2. commitment	11
3. continuous learning	11
4. making a difference	11
5. global perspective	9
6. mentoring	9
7. enthusiasm	8
8. leadership development	8

Cultural
entropy = 7%

1. continuous learning	11
2. generosity	11
3. commitment	10
4. positive attitude	10
5. vision	10
6. ambitious	9
7. making a difference	8
8. results orientation	8

Personal
entropy = 9%

Figure 11.1 Low-entropy organization.

reducing the personal entropy of the leaders of the departments, units and teams with the highest levels of cultural entropy. The results of a Cultural Values Assessment when disaggregated to the departmental, unit and team levels clearly indicate where these pockets of high entropy are and which leaders need help in lowering their level of personal entropy.

Low-entropy leader

Figure 11.3 shows the LVA values data plot for a low-entropy leader. On the left you find the ten values that the leader picked to describe her leadership style, and on the right you will find the top values picked by her 19 assessors. There are four matching values between the leader's value choices and the assessors' choices— listening, open to new ideas, team builder and vision. The assessors see this leader as an authentic, enthusiastic, caring individual who coaches and mentors her staff. She collaborates with others to make a difference. She is appreciated by her staff because she is open to new ideas, listens to people and operates with integrity.

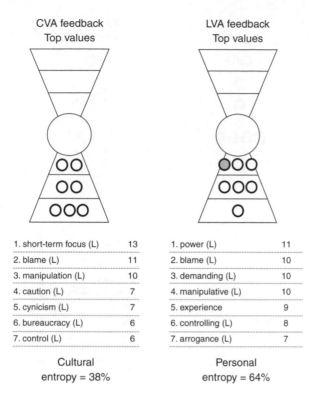

CVA feedback
Top values

LVA feedback
Top values

1. short-term focus (L)	13
2. blame (L)	11
3. manipulation (L)	10
4. caution (L)	7
5. cynicism (L)	7
6. bureaucracy (L)	6
7. control (L)	6

1. power (L)	11
2. blame (L)	10
3. demanding (L)	10
4. manipulative (L)	10
5. experience	9
6. controlling (L)	8
7. arrogance (L)	7

Cultural
entropy = 38%

Personal
entropy = 64%

Figure 11.2 High-entropy organization.

You will immediately notice from the distribution of top values (dots) that the assessors consider this leader's values to be focused at Levels 5 and 6, whereas the leader sees herself operating mainly from Level 4. This underestimation of her own abilities is relatively typical of leaders who are operating from the higher levels of consciousness.

If you look carefully at the values distribution diagram of the assessors in Figure 11.4, you will see that 27 per cent of the leader's values as observed by the assessors are at the level of a self-transforming mind, 43 per cent at the level of a self-authoring mind and 30 per cent at the level of a socialized mind. The overall level of personal entropy is in the healthy range at 4 per cent.

High-entropy leader

My example of a high-entropy leader is one I use a lot. I call it my Darth Vader example. This person is the founder of a small organization. At the time of the assessment, the organization had been running for about five years and was modestly successful. The results of the LVA are shown in Figure 11.5.

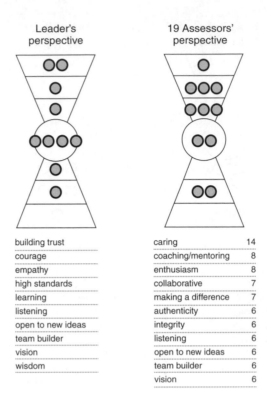

Leader's perspective	19 Assessors' perspective	
building trust	caring	14
courage	coaching/mentoring	8
empathy	enthusiasm	8
high standards	collaborative	7
learning	making a difference	7
listening	authenticity	6
open to new ideas	integrity	6
team builder	listening	6
vision	open to new ideas	6
wisdom	team builder	6
	vision	6

Figure 11.3 LVA: Low personal entropy leader.

The first point to notice is that the leader's perspective and the assessors' perspective are very different. The leader sees himself focused in the upper levels of consciousness and the assessors see him focused in the lower levels of consciousness. When you take a close look at the leader's perspective of his own values, you would have to agree that the values he chose are excellent for getting an organization up and running. The leader brings both his ambition and his passion to bear on his vision. He has courage, he is creative and he is focused on getting results. He builds strategic alliances, operates with integrity and focuses on excellence. An important clue to the way he is viewed by his colleagues is that apart from strategic alliances he has no relationship values in his top ten: He is not a people person.

Whilst the people in his organization recognize many of his strengths, particularly his focus on results and excellence (matching values), he comes across as an authoritarian, demanding, competitive and power seeking.

When you look at the values distribution diagram (Figure 11.6) you will see that this is a person whose behaviours are driven by his fears. He gets his drive from his self-authoring mind (27 per cent of values), but uses the fear-based

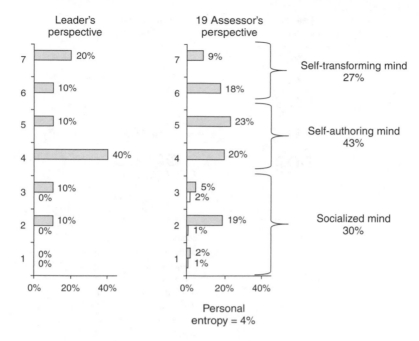

Figure 11.4 LVA: Low personal entropy leader distribution.

values of his socialized mind to bully people into getting what he wants: None of the values chosen by the assessors fall into the self-transforming mind category. The fact that this leader has very little self-awareness is evident from the difference between the leader's perspective on his values and the perspective of his assessors.

My feedback to this person was that he clearly needed to focus his energies, gifts and talents on his external role as a business builder, and hand off his management role to one of his partners who was more suited to caring for the staff of the organization. This feedback did not come as a surprise. He was well aware of his limitations regarding his people management skills, and although a little disappointed, recognized that his talents lay elsewhere.

Individual Values Assessment

The Individual Values Assessment (IVA) is a self-reporting coaching tool that helps people evaluate their level of values alignment and mission alignment and can provide a useful introduction to the use of the Cultural Transformation Tools for prospective clients. The values listed in these plots appear in alphabetical order.

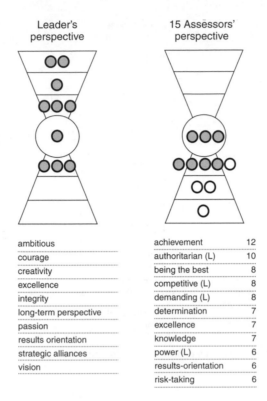

Leader's perspective	15 Assessors' perspective	
ambitious	achievement	12
courage	authoritarian (L)	10
creativity	being the best	8
excellence	competitive (L)	8
integrity	demanding (L)	8
long-term perspective	determination	7
passion	excellence	7
results orientation	knowledge	7
strategic alliances	power (L)	6
vision	results-orientation	6
	risk-taking	6

Figure 11.5 LVA: High personal entropy leader.

Living in a toxic culture

My first example is an ambitious manager with a self-authoring mind who finds himself in a high-entropy organization (see Figure 11.7).

I know this person is relatively ambitious because his personal values of risk-taking, self-discipline and perseverance, combined with his desired culture value of achievement, suggest that he really sets out to get what he wants. Significantly, also, 60 per cent of his personal values are located in Levels 4 and 5—the levels of the self-authoring mind. He is looking for challenges and opportunities to prove himself.

He wants to do well, and he probably will do well because he understands what it takes to create a successful business—his desired culture values are almost full spectrum, with more than 50 per cent of values at Levels 5 and 6, and well distributed across the value types—four individual values, two relationship values and four organizational values. He is also balanced in his personal life: The value of well-being suggests he is focused on balancing his physical, emotional, mental and spiritual needs. He recognizes the importance of customer satisfaction and collaboration and is aware of the need for partnerships.

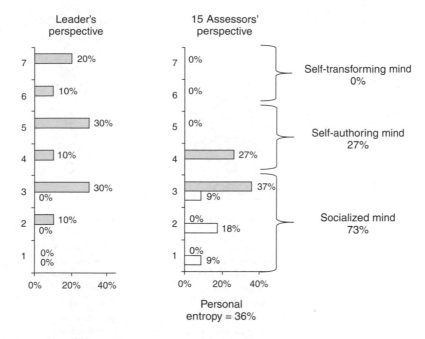

Figure 11.6 LVA: High personal entropy leader distribution.

He sees the current culture of his organization as extremely toxic: Almost anyone would find this culture difficult to work in. The fact that he has self-discipline and control (a potentially limiting relationship value) in his personal values, and has no positive relationship values in his top ten personal values—all the rest are individual values—suggests that he might last longer in this culture than someone who is relationship oriented.

One of the key issues that the coach who is feeding back the results of this IVA needs to ask this individual is to what extent his value of *control* is linked to his value of *self-discipline*. It is highly likely that these two values work together to help this person to weather the toxic culture. In which case, the value of control is more likely to mean self-control to him, and would not therefore be a potentially limiting relationship value, but more of a positive individual value. What makes me suspect that this is the case is we do not normally see *control* juxtaposed with *ease with uncertainty* and *risk-taking* in someone's personal values: *Control* and *risk-taking* are polarities that do not normally sit well together.

Getting grounded in the basics of business

My second example of an IVA, shown below in Figure 11.8, is typical of some of the individual consultants who are drawn to the work of supporting leaders in building values-driven organizations and leadership coaching. They have values

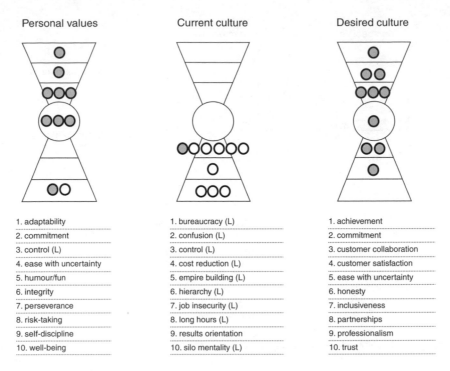

Figure 11.7 IVA: Living in a toxic culture.

in the upper levels of consciousness; they have vision and wisdom and want to cooperate with others to make a difference in the world. What they are sometimes missing are the values associated with the first three levels of organizational consciousness.

This particular individual has three matching personal and current culture values (reasonable values alignment)—cooperation, interdependence and listening; four matching current and desired culture values (reasonable mission alignment)—accountability, excellence, interdependence and making a difference; and two matching personal and desired cultural values (quality and interdependence), one of which—interdependence—is common to all three lists.

The main difference between the current culture and desired culture are the four grounded organizational values that appear in the desired culture—brand image, organizational growth, profit and quality. There are only two organizational values in the current culture—long-term perspective and shared vision.

Intuitively, this person knows that in order to become a full spectrum leader of his own business, he needs to give much more focus to the first three levels of organizational consciousness. This will be difficult for him because it is not where he finds his passion. Taking care of business basics is not what gets his juices flowing.

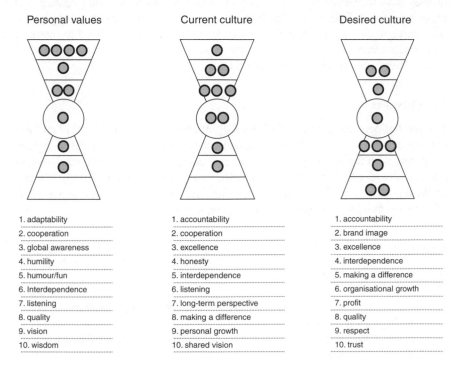

Personal values	Current culture	Desired culture
1. adaptability	1. accountability	1. accountability
2. cooperation	2. cooperation	2. brand image
3. global awareness	3. excellence	3. excellence
4. humility	4. honesty	4. interdependence
5. humour/fun	5. interdependence	5. making a difference
6. Interdependence	6. listening	6. organisational growth
7. listening	7. long-term perspective	7. profit
8. quality	8. making a difference	8. quality
9. vision	9. personal growth	9. respect
10. wisdom	10. shared vision	10. trust

Figure 11.8 IVA: Getting grounded in basic business.

This type of result is also often found in people working in non-governmental organizations (NGOs). The people attracted to such organizations are so intent on living out their passion and making a difference, that they have little interest or energy for running an organization. This causes them problems because it limits their ability to be effective.

Thus, we find that many private sector organizations are lacking the values necessary to inspire people, and many NGOs are lacking the values necessary to be effective. Public sector organizations tend to suffer from both problems.

Those who are drawn to the public sector (health, education, etc.) are usually people who want to care for others, and make a difference in people's lives. They feel blocked and get dispirited by the large amount of time they have to spend on bureaucracy and filling out forms, and have little or no talent or energy for building efficiency, creating order and managing people. Consequently, they do not feel appreciated; they are not able to make as much of a difference as they would like to; and they feel very little sense of engagement with the organization. Their connection is with the people they serve.

The reason why I believe public sector organizations tend to become large bureaucracies is because those who are drawn into the public sector are usually not skilled in managing people and creating efficient systems and processes, nor do they have the passion for it—what they want when they start their careers is to make a personal difference in the lives of their "customers." As they progress in their careers, they get promoted into jobs that they are not equipped to manage, and create layers of bureaucracy (controls) to make up for their lack of people-management and resource-management skills.

Conclusions

The level of personal entropy of a leader significantly impacts the level of cultural entropy of his or her organization, department or team. Low-entropy leaders tend to operate with the majority of their values located in the levels of consciousness associated with a self-transforming or self-authoring mind. High-entropy leaders, on the other hand, tend to operate with values that are mainly located in the levels of consciousness associated with a socialized mind.

Summary

Here are the main points of Chapter 11:

1. Leaders with high personal entropy tend to create organizational cultures with high cultural entropy.
2. Leaders with low personal entropy tend to create organizational cultures with low cultural entropy.

12 The leader as a coach

In order to grow and develop as a leader you must first learn how to lead yourself. Only when you are able to successfully lead yourself will you have the skills to lead a team. And, only when you have mastered how to lead a team, will you have the skills to lead an organization. This progression in leadership development is one of the central themes of *The New Leadership Paradigm* book, website and learning system that I published in 2011.[1]

The first step in leading yourself is to build your personal mastery skills—you must learn how to become your own self-coach if you want to overcome or release your limiting subconscious fear-based beliefs (see Annex 17). The second step in leading yourself is to individuate and self-actualize—you must get in touch with who you really are (your core values and beliefs), and find work that gives your life meaning—work you are passionate about.[2] The third step is to integrate and serve—you must learn how to collaborate with others to make a difference in the world that eventually, as you get older and/or become an elder, leads you into a life of selfless service.

This development process takes you from dependence, to independence, to interdependence. It is a lifelong journey that cannot be rushed. It starts by learning how to minimize the impact of your fear-based beliefs on your life and the people around you. Only when you have done that, found your sense of purpose, and have learned how to make a difference in the world by collaborating with other people, will you be able to successfully manage your team, and only when you truly become a servant leader will you be able to successfully run an organization.[3]

A servant leader is someone who recognizes that their ability to deliver results is a function of building and drawing on the capabilities and motivations of their people. Consequently, they give priority to making sure that the people who report to them are able to meet all their needs—both their deficiency needs and their growth needs. They inspire, coach and mentor their people so they can grow, develop and become all they can become. You cannot do this successfully if you have not been on this journey yourself. This is why learning to lead yourself is so important. Everything you learn about leading yourself will enable you to do a better job at leading and coaching others. As a coach, you cannot lead someone along a path that you have not successfully navigated yourself.

The *Leading Self* workbook/journal that accompanies *The New Leadership Paradigm* provides a step-by-step process, containing 36 exercises, to support you in the journey of moving from dependence, to independence to interdependence.[4]

The *Leading Others* workbook/journal that accompanies *The New Leadership Paradigm* provides a step-by-step process containing 28 exercises for evaluating and managing your team's performance and determining each team member's coaching needs.[5]

The *Leading an Organization* workbook/journal that accompanies *The New Leadership Paradigm* provides a step-by-step process containing 33 exercises for evaluating the performance of your organization and developing a high-performance leadership team.[6]

If you are the leader of a community or nation, then the *Leading in Society* workbook/journal that accompanies *The New Leadership Paradigm* provides a step-by-step process containing 30 exercises for evaluating the performance of your community/nation and developing a high-performance leadership team.[7]

Leading others

If you are wholly focused on attempting to meet your deficiency needs, you will not be sufficiently other-oriented to focus your attention on helping your team members become the best they can become. Successful (low-entropy) leaders are accessible, adaptable, trustworthy team players who coach and support their team members.

As the leader of a team, you will need to be conversant with three forms of coaching:

* *Personal evolution coaching*: Helping your team members to deal with issues that relate to their personal growth, personal mastery, individuation and self-actualization.
* *Professional evolution coaching*: Helping your team members to deal with issues that relate to their professional growth.
* *Performance coaching*: Helping your team members to deal with issues that relate to managing resources so they can achieve their targeted performance outcomes.

Coaching for personal evolution

Your first task as a leader/coach is to find out what levels of consciousness your people are operating from and what type of mind they are principally operating from—a socialized mind, a self-authoring mind or a self-transforming mind. This will tell you what is important to them and what needs they are looking to satisfy through their work. Once you understand their needs, you will know how to create a working environment that optimizes their level of engagement. The tools for making these assessments can be found in *The New Leadership Paradigm* workbook/journal for Leading Others.

Coaching for professional evolution

With inexperienced people who have just started their careers, it will be important to spend a lot of time mentoring them from a professional standpoint. As they become more accomplished they will need less support. Your job as a mentor is not to tell them what to do when a particular issue or problem arises, but to help them work out the answer for themselves.

Coaching for performance

John Whitmore, one of the world's leading authorities on coaching, has been promoting the idea that every manager should be a coach for the past 18 years. In his bestselling book, *Coaching for Performance*, now in its fourth edition, John states:

> Coaching is not merely a technique to be wheeled out and rigidly applied in certain prescribed circumstances. It is a way of managing, a way of treating people, a way of thinking, a way of being. Coaching demands the highest qualities of a manager: empathy, integrity, and detachment, as well as a willingness to adopt a fundamentally different approach to staff.[8]

There are two key concepts to coaching: Creating awareness by helping people to interpret in a more meaningful way what they are hearing, seeing or feeling, and helping people take responsibility for their work, actions and behaviours, thereby increasing their sense of pride in their individual performance and in the team's collective performance.

Ask lots of questions

The first principle of coaching and mentoring is to ask lots of questions. Your job is not to provide answers. In the new leadership paradigm, leaders, managers and supervisors teach their people to think for themselves by increasing their awareness and becoming more responsible for their actions. A starving man will always be starving if you just give him fish. When you can help him figure out the whole process of fishing, so he can do it himself, he will never starve again.

Listen really hard

In addition to asking a lot of questions, a good coach listens really hard; she spends a lot of time getting a clear understanding of what the person she is coaching is thinking; she summarizes frequently by feeding back her understanding of what is being said; she guides people in making their own choices; and she avoids telling people what to do. These are not difficult skills to learn but are essential for leading and managing others in the new leadership paradigm.

To truly listen, you have to get into a mind space where you completely suspend your own needs, and keep your ego-mind quiet. The last thing you want to do is to get fearful or judgmental about what is being said. You have to forget yourself and connect with your staff member's needs. You need to show empathy and compassion.

It cannot be that difficult to listen, can it? Yes, it can, especially if you are coaching a subordinate. A professional coach can more easily separate himself or herself from the content of a coaching session than a manager. As a leader, manager or supervisor it is hard to separate yourself, because you will probably think you know the answers to your team member's problems or dilemmas. You must make sure your ego's desire to get to an outcome (your impatience) does not tempt you to tell your staff member exactly what he or she needs to do. Coaching involves helping people to get to their own answers.

Get a clear understanding

Understanding another person's situation and coaching them through their problems is one of the hardest things to do, especially if you have a self-authoring mind. You will be tempted to see their situation, problems and dilemmas through your own worldview. You have to park your own belief filters and assumptions if you really want to help someone to get to a resolution. Ultimately, it is about helping them find a place of awareness where they can identify their needs and get past their fears. If you can help them get clear on their needs, you will help them understand their motivations. If you can help them get clear on their fears, you will help them see where they are stuck.

Summarize frequently

How do you make sure your coaching is effective? How do you make sure that you are not filtering the situation of the person you are coaching through your beliefs? The answer to this question is by making sure you have clarity. And how do we do that? By summarizing what you think you heard, not just once, but repeatedly. Say things like, "Let me see if I understand you correctly …" or "Is this what you are trying to say …," "You must be feeling …" You know you are on track when you hear them say, "Yes, that is exactly what I am saying/feeling. That is exactly what I need. That is exactly what I want. That is exactly what I fear." Once they have this clarity on their feelings, needs, wants and fears, you can proceed to help them identify the choices they have in front of them.

Guide people to choices

No matter what is happening in our lives, we always have choices. We get stuck when we forget we have choices or don't believe we do. Very often, we have problems, issues and dilemmas because we don't know what choices are available to us. Helping someone to define their choices may involve them facing their fears, challenging their assumptions and connecting with others who can provide the information or support they need. This is what you as a coach have to help the other person to do.

It is always very helpful to get a person to see their current situation from a higher or broader perspective. I always say that the best place to solve problems is from 30,000 feet. Not literally, but metaphorically. You need to find ways to help the person you are coaching to see and understand the larger context. Above all else, your job is to give them hope. When we believe we don't have choices, we are powerless. We become the victims of our ignorance or our fears.

Avoid telling people what to do

"Education" comes from the Latin root "educare," meaning to draw out. That is what you have to do. Your job as a coach is to help the person you are coaching to find their inner wisdom. Deep down, we always know what to do. What prevents us from knowing is our lack of confidence in ourselves. Your job is to uncover what is in the other person's heart; help them isolate and name their fears, ask them, "What is the worst thing that could happen?" and then give them choices on how to set themselves free.

GROW

One of the most well known and frequently used models for coaching is the GROW model: G stands for Goal setting; R stands for Reality checking; O stands for exploring Options; and W stands for What to do.[9]

When you start your coaching session get clear about the topic and scope that the coachee wants to cover, and determine the goals for the session. Determine what the person you are coaching believes is their current level of performance with regard to the topic under discussion—reality checking. Then, identify choices and explore options. Help the coachee to see the different ways he or she can get from their current reality to their goal. Then help the coachee decide what to do— to evaluate the options and make a choice.

I also think it is important, before setting goals, to discuss with the individual what underlying need he or she is trying to satisfy with regard to the issue being covered; what fears they have that may be getting in their way; what needs other people involved may have; and what fears they may be feeling and why.

At the end of the day, you want the person you are coaching to say, "I did it myself" and, if they feel so inspired, "Thanks for your help."

It is important to get across to the person you are coaching that the most successful people display five evolutionary characteristics: They are masters of adaptation; they never stop learning; they are able to bond with team members; they are able to cooperate with non-team members; and they are comfortable about handling complex issues (at ease with uncertainty).[10]

Happiness

Ultimately, if you want to create high levels of employee engagement, you must create an environment where people feel happy and content because they are able to get their needs met. When *their* needs are met they will feel happy. When *your* needs are met you will feel happy.

If you are operating with a socialized mind or a self-authoring mind you may not want the responsibility of managing other people or you may not feel that is where you want to put your energy. There is nothing worse than a half-hearted manager. So many people find themselves thrust into management positions, not because it is what they want to do, but because it is what they feel obliged to do in order to progress in their chosen career. They know they are not cut out for this role, and they know they will not be doing what they love. Being honest with yourself on this matter is vital if you are going to find fulfilment through your work.

If you are someone whose passion involves doing the work rather than supporting, coaching or guiding others in doing their work, then setting your sights on becoming a leader may not be the path for you because you will not be good at it. Ultimately, it all comes down to understanding what you see as your purpose in life, what makes your juices flow and where your creativity lies.

For myself, I know my passion is to understand the evolution of human consciousness and create models and tools to support personal and cultural transformation at the organizational, community and national level. My gifts include writing and speaking. This is who I am. Whenever I am doing this work, I feel vital and alive. Three times in my life, I created and built small organizations, only to realize afterwards that my passion was in doing the work rather than managing others who were doing the work.

That was one of the most pleasing aspects of my many years at the World Bank. I got to pursue my purpose without having to be responsible for others. This is also what is pleasing about my current life. Having spent the past 12 years building a successful organization, I have handed off the day-to-day operations to my colleagues so I can devote my time to pursuing my passion. As an owner, I am still strategically connected to the business, but I am no longer involved in day-to-day operations. What I do each day—my passion and my purpose—contribute directly to the thought leadership of my organization.

So, if supporting and managing others in doing their work is your passion or your default position because you are not sure what else you are supposed to be doing with your life, learning to lead others is most likely what is best for you at this moment in time. In any case, you will find the skills you learn in helping others to become the best they can become will always be useful in your life. If you want to find happiness and lead a fulfilled life you need to follow your passion.

In *The Art of Happiness: A Handbook for Living*, the Dalai Lama makes the following statement:

> In identifying one's mental state as the prime factor in achieving happiness, of course that doesn't deny that our basic physical needs for food, clothing, and shelter must be met. But once these basic needs are met, the message is clear: we don't need more money, we don't need more success or fame,

we don't need the perfect body or the perfect mate—right now, at this very moment, we have a mind, which is all the basic equipment we need for achieving complete happiness.[11]

When asked to define the characteristics of a psychologically healthy or well-adjusted person, he gave the following response:

> Well I would regard a compassionate, kind-hearted person as healthy. If you maintain a feeling of compassion, loving kindness, then something automatically opens your inner door. Through that [door] you can communicate more easily with other people. And that feeling of warmth creates a kind of openness. You'll find that all human beings are just like you, so you will be able to relate to them more easily.[12]

This is why when you do the work of learning to lead yourself—create your own happiness and find your own fulfilment—you will be able to help others do the same. They may have different needs, passions and purposes, but the stages of development they have to pass through are just the same as the stages you passed through. Ultimately, we are all on the same developmental or evolutionary journey. Only when you understand this can you relate to others with empathy and compassion.

Conclusions

In order to be an effective leader you must become an effective coach. You must first learn how to coach yourself. The extent to which you are able to do this will determine the extent to which you are able to coach others. Ultimately, it is all about happiness. When people are able to do the work they enjoy or are passionate about, in an environment where they feel cared for and are able to get their needs met, they will be happy, engaged and committed to their work.

Summary

Here are the main points of Chapter 12:

1. In order to grow and develop as a leader you must first learn how to lead yourself.
2. The first step in leading yourself is to build your personal mastery skills—learn how to become your own self-coach so you can overcome or release your limiting subconscious fear-based beliefs.
3. The second step is to individuate and self-actualize—get in touch with who you really are (your core values and beliefs), and find work that gives your life meaning—work you are passionate about.
4. The third step is to integrate and serve—learn how to collaborate with others to make a difference in the world, which eventually, as you get older and become an elder, leads you into a life of selfless service.

5.   Everything you learn about leading yourself will enable you to do a better job at coaching others.
6.   As the leader of a team, you will need to be conversant with three forms of coaching: Personal evolution coaching, professional evolution coaching and performance coaching.
7.   Your job as a leader/coach is to help people meet their needs and thereby increase their level of commitment and engagement.

Only when you do the work of learning to lead yourself—create your own happiness and find your own fulfilment—will you be able to help others do the same.

Notes

1   In *The New Leadership Paradigm* the Leading Self component is covered in pages 131–219, the Leading Others (a team) component is covered in pages 247–289, the Leading an Organization component is covered in pages 313–381, and the Leading in Society component is covered in pages 405–467.
2   A detailed explanation of this process can be found in *The New Leadership Paradigm* and in *What My Soul Told Me*.
3   Servant leadership is a philosophy and practice of leadership, coined and defined by Robert Greenleaf and supported by many leadership and management writers such as James Autry, Ken Blanchard, Stephen Covey, Peter Block, Peter Sendge, Max DePree, Larry Spears, Margaret Wheatley, Jim Hunter, Kent Keith, Ken Jennings and others. Servant leaders achieve results for their organizations by giving priority attention to the needs of their colleagues and those they serve.
4   www.valuescentre.com/resources/?sec=books__learning_modules (last accessed 29 March 2013).
5   Ibid.
6   Ibid.
7   Ibid.
8   John Whitmore, *Coaching for Performance*, fourth edition (London: Nicholas Brearley Publishing), 2009, pp. 19–20.
9   Ibid., Chapters 6, 7, 8 and 9.
10   Richard Barrett, *The New Leadership Paradigm* (Asheville, NC: Fulfilling Books), 2011, pp. 63–88.
11   Dalai Lama, *The Art of Happiness: A Handbook for Living* (London: Hodder & Stoughton), 1998, p. 25.
12   Ibid., p. 27.

Part IV

Structural alignment

The purpose of Part IV of this book is to provide the reader with a clear understanding of how to create structural alignment in an organization—the alignment of structures, policies, procedures and incentives with the values of the organization and the needs and values of employees.

You will recall from Chapter 4, Figure 4.4 (shown below), that there are four conditions necessary for whole system change. This part of the book focuses on *structural alignment*.

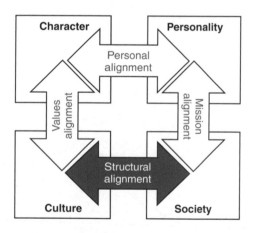

13 Choosing espoused values

The structures, policies, procedures and incentives that an organization embraces are a reflection of the value systems of the organization—the values of the current leaders, and the institutional legacy of past leaders. They dictate what behaviours are acceptable and should be encouraged, and what behaviours are unacceptable and should be discouraged. Together with the values and behaviours of the leaders, the structures, policies, procedures and incentives define the culture of the organization.

We can define the structures, policies, procedures and incentives of an organization in the following way:

- Structures are the way in which parts or components of a system are arranged to create a functioning whole.
- Policies are courses of actions that are adopted and pursued to achieve specific purposes.
- Procedures are sequences of actions or instructions that are followed to accomplish a specific task.
- Incentives are enticements or stimuli provided to motivate people to accomplish a certain task or achieve a specific goal.

In short, the structures, policies, procedures and incentives of an organization, when taken together as a whole, are a codified value system for regulating the behaviours of employees. They represent the "constitution" or "rule book" that the organization plays by.

They send a powerful message to employees from the leadership: The message is: "If you align with the structures, embrace the policies and follow the procedures then you will be rewarded in accordance with the prescribed incentives."

This means that if you want to change the culture of an organization, you must not only analyze, evaluate and help the leaders change their values and behaviours, as discussed in Part III of this book, you must also analyze, evaluate and redesign the structures, policies, procedures and incentives so they align with the espoused values.

Therefore the first task in a carrying out a structural realignment exercise is to choose the espoused values. To this end, the results of a Cultural Values

Assessment together with an espoused values analysis (of the exiting espoused values) will provide you with significant insights into the values that are important to employees at different levels of the organization, and to what extent the existing espoused values are being lived, and to what extent they are desired.

The espoused values you choose should do three things: Meet the needs of employees; meet the needs of the organization; and meet the needs of other stakeholders such as customers, investors, the local communities in which the organization operates and society at large. They should also express the unique character or function of the organization. To this end, it is sometimes useful to designate two types of espoused values: Foundational or core values and operational values.

A foundational or core value is something that everyone regards as vitally important to the running of the organization. For example, in a nuclear power plant or a chemical factory, employee safety and environmental protection should be regarded as foundational values. An operational value, on the other hand, is a value that permits the smooth functioning of the organization. For example, values such as teamwork and trust should be regarded as operational values. The actual blend between foundational values and operational values will depend on the unique function or unique character of the organization.

In Table 13.1, I analyze the values of the motor cycle manufacturer Harley Davidson. You will see from this analysis that their values are strongly focused on the organization's relationships with its stakeholders and its employees. There are no foundational values: They are all operational values. Harley Davidson has one value that focuses on both the organization's needs and the employees' needs—*encouraging intellectual curiosity*. This value is important for innovation and creativity.

Table 13.2 analyzes the values of Google. The majority of Google's values are focused on employees and other stakeholders—mainly customers and society. There are only three values that focus on the organization, and one of them can be regarded as a foundational value—*technology innovation is our lifeblood*. This value expresses the unique character and function of Google. It also speaks to the needs of customers and the contribution that is expected from employees.

Although not explicitly stated in either of these two examples, profit is a foundational value for both corporations (and every other private sector company). What both these organizations implicitly recognize is the way you create profit is

Table 13.1 Values of Harley Davidson

Espoused values	Focus on organization	Focus on employees	Focus on stakeholders
Telling the truth		✓	✓
Keeping our promises		✓	✓
Respecting the individual		✓	✓
Encouraging intellectual curiosity	✓	✓	
Be fair		✓	✓

Table 13.2 Values of Google

Espoused values	Focus on organization	Focus on employees	Focus on stakeholders
We want to work with great people	✓	✓	
Technology innovation is our lifeblood	✓	✓	✓
Working at Google is fun		✓	
Be actively involved		✓	
Don't take success for granted	✓	✓	
Do the right thing		✓	✓
Earn customer and user loyalty and respect		✓	✓
Care about and support the communities where we work and live		✓	✓
We aspire to improve and change the world		✓	✓

by focusing on the needs of employees and the needs of other stakeholders. When you care about your employees and stakeholders, they care about you.

In some situations, where the organization or specific units are experiencing high levels of entropy, you may need to designate some *transitional* values for a period of three to five years. These are values that address specific issues associated with the most embedded potentially limiting values. Once these issues have been rectified or resolved the transitional values can be dropped and full focus given to the core foundational or operational values.

Table 13.3, a repeat of part of Table 5.2, shows the needs of an organization in relation to the seven levels of organizational consciousness. The operational values chosen to be among the espoused values should align with these needs.

For example the Harley Davidson values of *telling the truth*, *keeping our promises* and *being fair* are all about integrity and align with the need to enhance the organization's capacity for collective action. The value of *respecting the individual* aligns with the need to create a sense of loyalty. Employees will not feel a sense of loyalty to the organization if they don't feel respected.

Table 13.4, which is a repeat of part of Table 3.1, shows the needs of employees in relationship to the seven levels of personal consciousness and the three types of mind.

If you work in an organization that depends on the hard work of labourers or craftsmen, such as the mining sector, or operators of machinery that perform manual or low-complexity tasks, then you will want to focus your espoused values on the lower end of the spectrum—the needs associated with a socialized mind. For these people pay and benefits, respect and recognition, and opportunities for professional advancement will be important.

In 2010, two CTT consultants, Judith Mills and Joan Shafer, who have both used the Cultural Transformation Tools to map the values of a variety of public and private sector clients, noticed that employee recognition was showing up frequently in the top ten desired culture values of the organizations they were working with. They decided to investigate. They looked at 106 Cultural Values

Table 13.3 Organizational needs

Levels of consciousness		Organizational needs
7	Service	Creating a long-term sustainable future for the organization by caring for humanity and preserving the Earth's life support systems.
6	Making a difference	Building the resilience of the organization by cooperating with other organizations and the local communities in which the organization operates.
5	Internal cohesion	Enhancing the capacity of the organization for collective action by aligning employee motivations around a shared set of values and an inspiring vision.
4	Transformation	Increasing innovation by giving employees a voice in decision making and making them accountable for their futures and the overall success of the organization.
3	Self-esteem	Establishing structures, policies, procedures and processes that create order, support the performance of the organization and enhance employee pride.
2	Relationship	Resolving conflicts and building harmonious relationships that create a sense of loyalty among employees and strong connection to customers.
1	Survival	Creating financial stability, profitability and caring for the health and safety of all employees.

Table 13.4 Employees' needs

Level of development		Type of mind	Employee needs
7	Service	Self-transforming mind	Opportunities to serve others and/or care for the well-being of the Earth's life support systems.
6	Making a difference		Opportunities to leverage your contribution by collaborating with others who share the same values and have a similar purpose.
5	Internal cohesion	Self-authoring mind	Opportunities for personal growth and development to support you in finding your life purpose and aligning your purpose with your daily work.
4	Transformation		Opportunities to develop your skills by being made accountable for projects or processes of significance to yourself and/or the organization.
3	Self-esteem	Socialized mind	Opportunities to learn and grow professionally with frequent support, feedback and coaching.
2	Relationship		Opportunities to work in a congenial atmosphere where people respect and care about each other.
1	Survival		A safe working environment and pay and benefits that are sufficient to take care of employees' needs and the needs of their families.

Assessments provided to them by the Barrett Values Centre and found that employee recognition was the most common desired culture value: It occurred in 64 per cent of the surveys. The data covered ten countries and 21 business sectors.

As shown by the results of the large low-entropy organization in Chapter 7, and the high-entropy organization in Chapter 8, and corroborated by the findings of the Mills and Shafer study, employee recognition shows up in both low- and high-entropy organizations.

I believe this happens because in almost all medium and large organizations you will always find a significant proportion of the employee population fulfilling low-complexity jobs as clerks, secretaries, operators, supervisors and unit managers. These are people who are mainly operating with socialized minds and are focused on meeting their deficiency needs. They are looking for pay and benefits that meet their survival needs (Level 1), expressions of gratitude and appreciation from their bosses (Level 2) and honours and awards for excellence or achievement that give them a sense of pride in their performance (Level 3). These are the people for whom employee recognition is important.

If, on the other hand, you work in an organization that is trying to change the world for the better, which involves high-complexity tasks, then you will want to focus your espoused values at the higher end of the spectrum of needs—the needs associated with a self-transforming mind. For these people making a difference in the world and serving others or the planet will be important.

If you work in an organization that is building products and selling services to the world, which involve medium-complexity tasks, then you will want some of your espoused values in the mid-range of the spectrum—the needs associated with the self-authoring mind. For these people, challenges that give people the opportunity to use their skills and talents, give meaning to their lives and align with their life purpose will be important.

Based on the above, we can say that most non-labour-intensive organizations (involving knowledge workers doing tasks with medium levels of complexity) should focus their espoused vales on the needs associated with Levels 3, 4 and 5—giving employees opportunities to: (a) grow professionally; (b) use their skills and talents; and (c) align their daily work with their sense of life purpose.

Productivity, innovation and creativity

There are other important reasons why it is important to focus on the organization's espoused values on the mid-spectrum of employee needs—the need to achieve higher levels of productivity, innovation and creativity.

Productivity

The level of productivity achieved when employees find personal fulfilment can be at least twice as high as when they don't. A study of productivity found that for jobs of low, medium and high complexity, highly motivated employees were respectively 52 per cent, 85 per cent and 127 per cent more productive than employees who had average motivation."[1] When the comparison was made between the most highly motivated and the least motivated employees for each category of job complexity, the level of productivity was 300 per cent more for low-complexity jobs, 1,200 per cent more for medium-complexity jobs and so large that it was immeasurable for high-complexity jobs.

What this means is that it is quite possible to get higher levels of productivity from all types of people—from those operating with socialized minds, who are more suited to low-complexity tasks; from those operating with self-authoring minds, who are more suited to medium-complexity tasks; and those operating with self-transforming minds, who are more suited to high-complexity tasks.

Another study involving 14 organizations and 25,000 employees found that approximately 40 per cent of variability in corporate performance could be attributed to the personal satisfaction of employees based on a range of indicators that focused on various aspects of personal fulfilment. The same study found that 60 per cent of the variability in personal satisfaction is attributable to the quality of the employee's relationship with their manager and their manager's empowerment skills.[2] This finding tends to confirm that emotional and social intelligence, which enables us to inspire and motivate others, is significantly more important than intellectual intelligence in building a high-performance work force. Emotional intelligence and social intelligence not only allow us to bring out the best in others, they also allow us to become more productive and creative ourselves.

Innovation and creativity

In *Creative Work*, Willis Harman and John Hormann discuss the relationship between meaning and creativity. They state:

> All of history supports the observation that the desire to create is a fundamental urge in humankind. Fundamentally we work to create, and only incidentally do we work to eat. That creativity may be in relationships, communication, service, art, or useful products. It comes close to being the central meaning of our lives.[3]

The implication of this statement is that work without creativity has no meaning. If work is to be meaningful it must allow us to express our creativity. Without opportunities for expressing our creativity we are unlikely to find personal fulfilment.

The good news is that everyone is creative. It is a gift that we all possess, but many of us lose it because it is socialized out of us at an early age or it is not appreciated by our employers. Dr Calvin Taylor of the University of Utah found that all children are gifted and creative in some form. Some are creative in their speech, some in their body movements and some in drawing and writing. Others are gifted in the way they relate to others or in the way they organize things.[4]

The research work of George Land and Beth Jarman reveals that the vast majority of children are creative geniuses. They gave the same group of 1,600 children a test of divergent creative thinking over a period of 15 years. From age three to five, they found that 98 per cent of the children scored in the genius category. At ages eight to ten, only 32 per cent scored in that category. At ages 13 to 15, it was down to 10 per cent. Two hundred thousand adults over the age of 25 have taken the same tests. Only 2 per cent scored at the genius level.[5] What happened to our natural creativity? The answer is that it was socialized out of us. Our proficiency in expressing our creativity falls off as we accept others' opinions and evaluations of what is good and bad, and right and wrong. Our education systems have much to answer for in this arena. In the words of Jarman and Land, "That five-year-old creative genius is still lurking inside—just waiting to break free. It's not just in some of us, it's in everyone."

The critical issue for business is how to mine that creativity. There are two ways of bringing out this creativity. The first is building a culture of employee participation—giving people a voice—and the second is institutionalizing the search for innovation.

Participation

The pathway to creativity begins with employee participation. There are five stages to participation—invitation, engagement, reflection, listening and implementation. When an organization attempts participation for the first time it should be careful to make sure it completes all the steps. Leave one out and you will have convinced your employees that you are not serious about garnering their inputs. At the beginning, it is important to let *all* employees know that their opinions are important and that they are being invited to share their ideas.

Engagement begins when employees are presented with information about the situation at hand and have the opportunity to ask questions. *Reflection* is necessary to allow them to digest the information and search for creative ideas. When employees come back with their ideas the management should engage in pure *listening*. There should be no attempt to justify or defend past actions. When employees sense defensiveness on the part of those in authority or that they are not being listened to, they will hold back. They will quickly retreat into the "us" (the employees) and "them" (management) syndrome. Everyone's idea should be noted and acknowledged. *Implementation* should include as many employee ideas as possible. The results should be communicated to all employees and those whose ideas have been taken up should be congratulated and rewarded. When this is done on a regular basis employees begin to feel that their ideas matter and that management really cares about what they think. This engages their minds because they see their ideas can make a difference. The workplace becomes a crucible for creativity and a source of meaning. This leads to a growing sense of commitment. Over time, this process should become a normal and natural way of working.

Commitment is enhanced when all those involved in a work unit share a common vision and values. The shared values build trust, and trust gives employees responsible freedom. Responsible freedom unlocks meaning and creativity.

True power lies not in the ability to control, but in the ability to trust. People yearn for supervisors who encourage them to explore their own creativity because in doing so the supervisor gives their life meaning.

In the *Empowered Manager*, Peter Block points out that in every creative act there is a chance that you will fail.

> Every act of creation is an act of faith. The essence of faith is to proceed without any real evidence that our effort will be rewarded. The act of faith in choosing to live out a way of operating that we alone believe in gives real meaning to our work and our lives.[6]

Because creativity involves uncertainty about outcomes, it is easily blocked by fear. Most organizations fail to understand that for creativity to flourish employees must be given responsible freedom (autonomy) to express themselves in their own unique way. They prevent creativity by being over controlling and bureaucratic. In so doing they limit their future survival. Creativity will not blossom in a rigid culture that punishes failure. It requires a culture of trust that encourages risk-taking, where both success and failure are celebrated. Failure must be seen as a learning opportunity if creativity is to be nurtured.

The traditional hierarchical model of management prevents this from happening. In most organizations employees are not paid to think—that is the prerogative of management—they are paid to do. This quote from a worker exemplifies the issue: "For twenty years, you have paid for the work of my hands. If you had asked you could have had my mind and my heart for free."

This attitude of do what you are told to do, which stems from hierarchical management systems, prevents organizations from drawing on the well-spring of knowledge and creativity that exists in the minds of their employees. It can lead to disaster as the following story illustrates.

One of the greatest conundrums for early seafarers was how to measure longitude. Journeys north and south could easily be measured by the position of the sun and stars. Journeys east and west were more difficult to measure. They depended on time and volatile factors such as wind, currents and tides. One night in 1707, returning from naval skirmishes with the French Mediterranean force, Admiral Sir Clowdisley found his fleet trapped in fog. Fearing the ships might founder on coastal rocks he asked his navigators to do their best to estimate where they were. A consensus was reached that they were safely west of Île d'Ouessant off the Brittany peninsula. To their horror they found they had miscalculated their longitude. They found themselves heading straight onto the rocky shores of the Scilly Isles. At least four warships immediately floundered and were lost. Only two men survived. One of them was the Admiral.[7]

The night before this mishap, the captain had been approached by a sailor who claimed to have kept his own reckoning of the fleet's location. It took great courage for the seaman to come forth with this information since subversive navigation by an inferior was forbidden in the Royal Navy. He was so sure of his point, however, that he was ready to risk his neck. And, that is what he did. Sir Clowdisley had him hanged on the spot. If the Admiral had listened, the shipwreck might have been avoided.

Whilst the hanging of subordinates who have different ideas is no longer tolerated, the story has significant relevance to the current state of our organizations. The basis of the hierarchical model is that managers are the corporate mind, and employees are the corporate body. In such a model only managers are allowed to think and be creative.

The implications for traditional managers are significant. They must learn to reinvent themselves. Managers who take on this challenge must display four basic characteristics. The first and hardest part of their transformation is that they must learn to be *authentic*. Authenticity is a prerequisite for building trust. Second, managers must care about *developing their people*. The long-term interests of the company are best served when their employees are encouraged and given the opportunities to become all they can become. The more time that is spent in helping employees grow and develop the more successful the organization will be. Third, managers must see their role as *barrier busters*. They must eliminate road blocks so that their teams can be fully productive and focus on what they do best.[8] Finally, managers must be *mentors and coaches* to the employees that fall under their jurisdiction. Managers must shift their beliefs about their roles from one of control and compliance, to one of building motivation and commitment.

Institutionalizing innovation

In 1973, French economist Georges Anderla of the Organization for Economic Cooperation and Development estimated that humanity was doubling its knowledge every six years. He made this calculation assuming that the known scientific facts in AD 1 represented one unit of collective human knowledge. He calculated that it took until AD 1500 to double this knowledge. It doubled again in 1750, 1900, 1950, 1960, 1967 and 1973.

More recently, Dr Jacques Vallée has estimated that global knowledge is now doubling every 18 months.[9] As far as business is concerned the exponential growth in knowledge provides inestimable opportunities for creating new products and building new businesses.

The main limit to this expansion is the creative capacity of the work force. Increasingly, companies are finding that the creativity of their people is their key asset for growth and expansion. Business guru Peter Drucker states: "Every organization needs one core competence: *innovation*." Richard Gurin, president and CEO of Binney & Smith, Inc. agrees with Drucker: "After a long business career, I have become increasingly concerned that the basic problem gripping the American workplace is the crisis of creativity." Walt Disney considered creativity to be so important that he paid his creative staff more than he paid himself.

To build a truly creative culture, organizations must structurally integrate innovation into their operating processes and set up formal reward systems to celebrate employees' creative ideas. In most high-innovation organizations a formal committee reporting to the management team is tasked with the responsibility of managing the search for innovative ideas. The committee should have sufficient stature and budget to set up cross-departmental project teams to support the exploration of the best ideas through feasibility studies. It should consider both process and product innovations. The committee should also be tasked with carrying out a critical review of the factors influencing their market every year.[10] This is important work, because it can have a direct bearing on strategy.

The committee should include not only internal and external technical specialists but also those who are knowledgeable about social, environmental and economic trends. The committee should be culturally diverse, gender conscious and include representatives from different age groups.

In *Innovation Strategy for the Knowledge Economy*, Debra M. Amidon provides a short questionnaire for determining how well an organization is doing in institutionalizing innovation.[11] It includes questions such as:

- Has one person been chartered with the overall responsibility to manage the corporate-wide innovation process?
- Are there performance measures—both tangible and intangible—to assess the quality of your innovation practices?
- Is there a formal intelligence-gathering strategy to monitor the positioning of both current and potential competitors?
- Do your training/educational programmes have provisions to incubate and spin out new products and businesses?

Making the values pervasive

In the end, no matter which espoused values you choose, to be effective, they must be embedded in the structures, policies, procedures and incentives of the organization. They must become pervasive in how leaders, managers, supervisors and employees think and behave. This involves structural realignment.

To carry out a structural realignment exercise you must first identify the values that are implicit in the *existing* structure, policies, procedures and incentives. Once the implicit structural values have been identified (made explicit), they should be evaluated to see to what extent they align with the proposed espoused values. The best way to do this is to carry out a series of focus group meetings with representatives from all parts of the organization. The job of the focus groups is to reconfigure the structures, policies, procedures and incentives so they align with the espoused values. For example, if an organization espouses the values of teamwork and equality, but calculates bonuses based on position or grade, then it will need to redesign the bonus system so that all employees receive an equal share.

Having carried out this exercise, the next job is to prioritize the changes that need to be made and implement them. The implementation will only be successful if: (a) the proposed changes are explained to the employee population; (b) the leadership group demonstrates the chosen values; (c) the decision-making processes reflect the chosen values; and (d) all human resource processes, procedures and systems (recruitment, rewards, management development, talent management, performance reviews, etc.) are underpinned by the chosen values. The role of the leadership group in demonstrating and living the espoused values cannot be over-emphasized.

The following list provides examples of some of the most important policies, procedures and programmes that will need to reflect the organization's espoused values. Most of these fall under the remit of human resources:

- Decision-making structures/processes.
- Benefits and leave.
- New employee/executive selection.
- New employee/executive orientation programmes.
- Employee/executive performance evaluation.
- Employee/executive promotion criteria.
- Selecting talented performers for fast-track development.
- Leadership development programmes.
- Management training programmes.
- Values awareness programmes.

In large organizations, a structural realignment programme can take up to two years to implement. In small organizations it can usually be completed in six to nine months. The executive responsibility for structural realignment usually falls to the human resource function. This crucial step in the process of whole system change is the one that is most frequently forgotten or poorly executed. When it is well done it helps to safeguard and preserve the integrity of the organizational culture and make it more resilient.

Conclusions

I think it is useful at this point to remind ourselves that the purpose of structural alignment is to increase the level of engagement in the organization so employees are not only willing but want to bring their discretionary and creative energy to their work. The potential loss in revenue of not focusing on structural alignment can be enormous. The Hay Group estimate that top-performing organizations in terms of engagement and enablement achieve revenue growth 4.5 times greater than their industry peers.[12]

Summary

Here are the main points of Chapter 13:

1. The structures, policies, procedures and incentives that an organization embraces are a reflection of the value system of the organization.
2. They send a powerful message to employees from the leadership: "If you align with the structures, embrace the policies and follow the procedures then you will be rewarded in accordance with the prescribed incentives."

3. If you want to change the culture of an organization, you must not only analyze, evaluate and help the leaders change their values and behaviours, you
   must also analyze, evaluate and redesign the structures, policies, procedures
   and incentives of the organization to align with the espoused values.
4. The espoused values you choose should do three things: Meet the needs of
   employees; meet the needs of the organization; and meet the needs of other
   stakeholders such as customers, investors, society, etc.
5. They should also express the unique character or function of the organization.
6. To this end, it is sometimes useful to designate two types of espoused values:
   Foundational or core values and operational values.
7. If work is to be meaningful it must allow us to express our creativity. Without
   opportunities for expressing our creativity we are unlikely to find personal
   fulfilment.
8. There are two ways of bringing out this creativity. The first is building a culture of employee participation—giving people a voice—and the second is
   institutionalizing the search for innovation.
9. No matter which espoused values you choose, to be effective they must
   be embedded in the structures, policies, procedures and incentives of the
   organization.

Notes

1 Michael Cox and Michael E. Rock, *Seven Pillars of Leadership* (Toronto: Dryden),
  1997, pp. 10–13.
2 Study of Business Performance, Employee Satisfaction, and Leadership, Wilson Learning Corporation, http://wilsonlearning.com/wlpc/press_release/press_release_040907/
  (last accessed 4 April 2013).
3 Willis Harman and John Hormann, *Creative Work* (Indianapolis, IN: Institute of Noetic
  Sciences), 1990, p. 26.
4 George Land and Beth Jarman, *Breakpoint and Beyond* (San Francisco, CA:
  HarperBusiness), 1993, p. 153.
5 Ibid., p. 153.
6 Peter Block, *The Empowered Manager* (San Francisco, CA: Jossey-Bass), 1987, p. 195.
7 Dava Sobel, *Longitude: The story of a Lone Genius who Solved the Greatest Scientific
  Problem of his Time* (New York: Penguin Books), 1995, pp. 11–13.
8 For a discussion of the role of managers see *Managing in the High Commitment
  Workplace* by Kim Fisher (New York: Self-Managed Teams, American Management
  Association), 1994, pp. 27–41.
9 Peter Russell, *The White Hole in Time* (San Francisco, CA: Harper), 1992, p. 28.
10 For a discussion on innovation practices see Managerial Practices that Enhance
   Innovation, by André L. Delbecq and Peter K. Mills, *The Creative Edge* (New York:
   American Management Association), 1994, pp. 39–47.
11 Debra M. Amidon, *Innovation Strategy for the Knowledge Economy: The Ken
   Awakening* (Boston, MA: Butterworth-Heinemann), 1997, pp. 62–63.
12 www.haygroup.com/EngagementMatters/research-findings/regional-overview.aspx
   (last accessed 29 March 2013).

14 Organizational democracy

What is clear from my research is that wherever people operate in their daily lives, be it at work, in their home or in their local communities, they want to experience values that align with democratic principles. Let me remind you of the words I used at the start of this book:

> At this point in our collective human history, we are witnessing an unprecedented shift in human values. Millions of people all over the world are demanding their voices be heard, not just in how our nations are governed, but also in how our organizations are run. They want equality, fairness, openness and transparency; they want to be responsible and accountable for their lives; and, they want to trust and be trusted. They also want to work for organizations that are seen to be ethical and do the right thing in the eyes of society. They want to be proud of the organization they work for.

In terms of the history of modern organizations this development is very new. Most organizations in the twentieth century operated with top-down hierarchical power structures that avoided giving employees a voice. Leaders and managers represented the elite. They gave orders. Employees were the workers. They took orders.

Although such organizations still exist in all parts of the world, the most successful organizations in the twenty-first century, as I pointed out in Chapter 3, are those that align their structures, policies, procedures and incentives with employees' needs. Collectively, these are known as the best companies to work for; they practise some degree of conscious capitalism; and they embrace democratic principles. These companies are successful not just because of how they make their employees feel, but because of the impact these feelings have on the productivity and creativity of employees.

In Part Two of my book, *Love, Fear and the Destiny of Nations: The Impact of the Evolution of Human Consciousness on World Affairs*, I speak of the evolution of democracy as a *journey from freedom to trust*. Democracy begins with freedom, and evolves through equality, accountability, fairness, openness and transparency to trust. Each step of this journey, in other words each value, is an essential foundation for the development of the next value, and if you want to reap all the benefits that democracy provides, you cannot miss a step. Without equality, accountability, fairness, openness and transparency there can be no trust, and without freedom (autonomy) people cannot individuate and self-actualize.

In other words, the journey from freedom to trust is not only the journey of the evolution of democracy, it is also the journey of the evolution of human consciousness from the beginning of transformation (Level 4) to the end of internal cohesion (Level 5), and the journey of psychological development from the beginning of individuation to the upper reaches of self-actualization.

In *Love, Fear and the Destiny of Nations*, you will find a full chapter on each of these seven values—freedom, equality, accountability, fairness, openness, transparency and trust.[1] For the purposes of this book, I am providing a one-paragraph description of the importance of each of these values in an organizational setting.

Freedom (autonomy)

People work best when they are given a goal or objective and are then left to get on with it, knowing they have a coach or mentor they can consult if they find themselves getting into difficulty. People with self-authoring minds relish this type of opportunity. However, there is a danger. In an organizational setting you have to be very careful about choosing the people who get this type of opportunity and the level of supervision they get. They have to be well-balanced, responsible individuals. In recent years, there have been several high-profile court cases where relatively young banking professionals have been poorly supervised and have caused the collapse of a bank or created huge losses that have impacted a bank's financial viability. If you are giving people the opportunity to operate with autonomy in an organization, you must start small; let people prove themselves on tasks that do not expose the company to significant financial risk; then as they prove themselves give them more responsibility and accountability. If they make mistakes, celebrate them. Making a mistake is the best way to learn. Viewed from this perspective, our lives are full of learning.

Equality

People work best when they feel they operate on par with others and are treated equally. Equality recognizes that everyone, no matter who they are or what they do, has a contribution to make. There are no privileges in organizations that embrace equality. No one gets a bigger office than someone else, unless there is a functional reason. No one gets a *designated* parking space close to the entrance. Women and men are treated equally. There are no racial or gender divisions related to operational functions. Whilst people may have different salaries based on their years of experience and talents, bonuses from profits are shared equally among all team members. Equality is an essential prerequisite for creating a high-functioning team. Wherever there is inequality there is fear and suspicion and feelings of unfairness.

Accountability

When you give someone autonomy, you must also give them accountability. Autonomy without accountability is a recipe for chaos: People get to do whatever they want without any sense of responsibility to the organization. Furthermore, it is important to make the distinction between accountability and responsibility: They are not synonymous, at least in English. In many languages they are.

Accountability is often confused with responsibility. One can have responsibility without accountability, but in most circumstances you will not have accountability without responsibility. For example, I am responsible for how I lead my life, but as long as my actions and behaviours do not harm others or adversely impact the common good or break the law, I am not accountable (answerable) to anyone, other than myself: I have responsibility without accountability (to another person).

If, however, I am accountable for achieving an outcome or result that someone has entrusted me with, then I have responsibility to deliver that outcome or result for that person. I have accountability for the task with responsibility for delivering the result.

Accountability presumes:

1. There is some level of hierarchical or functional relationship between the person who is accountable and the person or group of people who have delegated the task.
2. There is an agreed outcome or result, in an agreed timeframe, that the person who is accountable is responsible for delivering to the person or group of people to which he or she is accountable.
3. That the person who is accountable is given or has bestowed on them a position of authority (and the resources they require) by the person or group to which he or she is accountable, which is commensurate with the outcome they are expected to achieve (the delegated powers are sufficient to deliver the outcome or result).

When you are a leader, manager or supervisor working within a framework of democratic principles, you are not only accountable for outcomes and results, you are also accountable for ensuring those who report to you have the autonomy they need to do their work.

Responsibility is one of the five principles of how the firm Mars operates. This is how they describe responsibility and accountability:

As individuals, we demand total responsibility from ourselves; as associates, we support the responsibilities of others.

We choose to be different from those corporations where many levels of management dilute personal responsibility. All associates are asked to take direct responsibility for results, to exercise initiative and judgment and to make decisions as required. By recruiting ethical people suited to their jobs and trusting them, we ask associates to be accountable for their own high standards.[2]

Fairness

One could argue that just as the concept of equality only has meaning when you commit to giving people freedom, fairness only has meaning when you commit to treating people equally. Without freedom there is not much point worrying about equality, and without equality there is not much point worrying about fairness. Freedom, equality and fairness naturally follow each other. Equality is therefore a measure of freedom and fairness is a measure of equality.

Fairness also has an important link to justice. John Rawls, one of the most important political philosophers of the twentieth century, successfully argued in *A Theory of Justice* (1971) that "the most reasonable principles of justice are those everyone would accept and agree to from a fair position."[3]

People want to be treated fairly. When they are not, they get bitter and resentful. They disengage. Fairness is critical for creating a high-performing culture. When organizations that practise fairness cut costs, they reduce everyone's salaries rather than fire people. Some will reduce the salaries of higher paid workers more than the lower paid workers.

With increasing pressures to create a sustainable world for future generations, a new issue around fairness has come to the fore: the issue of intergenerational fairness.

The issue of intergenerational fairness, from an ecological perspective, began to attract public attention shortly after the Brundtland Report was published in 1987. This report commissioned by the UN General Assembly provided long-term development strategies for achieving sustainable ecological development. The Brundtland Commission defined sustainable development in the following manner: "Sustainable development is development that meets the needs of the present without compromising the ability of future generations to meet their own needs."

It contained within it two key concepts:

- The concept of "needs," in particular, the essential needs of the world's poor, to which overriding priority should be given.
- The idea of limitations imposed by the state of technology and social organization on the environment's ability to meet present and future needs.

Increasingly, these concepts are being used to evaluate the environmental and social impact of the decisions and actions of organizations. As I explained in the Foreword, business is a wholly owned subsidiary of society and society is a wholly owned subsidiary of the environment. If we cannot sustain our environment then humanity has a very bleak future.

Openness

The definition of openness I like best is, "having the interior immediately accessible." In this regard, openness is one of the key requirements for authenticity, which in turn is a key requirement for trust.

Openness, in terms of "having the interior immediately accessible," requires an absence of fear. People will not be open with each other if they have fears—if they have fears that what they say might be used against them, if they are afraid of repercussions or punishment, or find it difficult to handle personal conflict. Openness requires us to master these fears. We are supported in alleviating our fears at the *societal* level by a commitment to democratic principles. We are supported in alleviating our fears at the *individual* level by a commitment to personal growth.

If we feel we have something to hide—something that we feel guilty about, or something that we feel covers us in shame—we will not be open. Owning your guilt and shame, and being willing to be open about it, requires great courage and great honesty—the hallmarks of true authenticity.

Openness facilitates the value of fairness because it requires those in authority to fully disclose their motivations when making decisions. Only when motivations are disclosed can suspicions be lifted and fairness established.

Transparency

There is much confusion between openness and transparency. Let me try to abate some of this confusion by defining these two terms. Openness is "having the interior immediately accessible," whereas transparency is "the degree to which you are able to see through something." Openness is relational and deals with motivations. Transparency is factual and deals with processes and information.

Clearly, in an organizational setting, complete transparency could put a company at risk, particularly when it comes to sharing details of innovations to products or services that are being considered or declaring expansion plans prematurely. In some companies, full transparency can also raise issues regarding the disclosure of salaries and bonus payments. However, there is much that can be done to increase transparency that is not being done: For example, the practice of open book management, where monthly financial information is provided to employees to let them know how well the company is doing. This lets employees know they can be trusted with such information, and it allows them to see how the results of their efforts are showing up in the bottom line. It also helps them understand during hard times why cost reductions may be necessary.

The problem with transparency, like openness, is that when it is missing it creates suspicion. Organizations should keep their policies with regard to transparency under review and disclose as much information as they possibly can to employees.

Trust

Finally we come to trust. Trust is an "end" value. All the other values listed above are the "means" to that end. Without them, trust is impossible. Without trust there is no internal cohesion. The idea that internal cohesion based on strong bonds (trust) builds successful human group structures is not new. The fourteenth-century philosopher Ibn Khaldun noticed that the most successful tribes in North Africa operated with *asabiya*, which can be translated as "a capacity for collective action." He further noticed that, in the most resilient groups, the level of *asabiya* was strongest at the highest levels of leadership. They operated with a high level of trust and internal cohesion.[4]

In *Trust: The Social Virtues and the Creation of Prosperity*, Francis Fukuyama states: "As a general rule, trust arises in such a way as to create expectations of regular and honest behaviour. To some extent, the particular character of those values is less important than the fact they are shared."[5]

In *The New Leadership Paradigm* I write:

> Trust is the glue that holds people together and the lubricant that allows energy and passion to flow. The ability to display and engender trust corresponds to the fifth level of personal consciousness. Trust increases the speed at which the group is able to accomplish tasks and takes the bureaucracy out of communication.[6]

In *The Speed of Trust*, Stephen Covey states that trust means confidence, and the opposite of trust (distrust) means suspicion. In other words, trust breeds connectedness. When we trust someone, we know he or she will have our interests at heart. Suspicion, on the other hand, breeds separation. When we are suspicious of someone, we will not disclose our innermost thoughts. Openness disappears. We keep things back. We avoid connecting with someone we do not trust. "Trust always affects outcomes—speed and cost. When trust goes up, speed will also go up, and costs will go down. When trust goes down, speed will also go down, and costs go up."[7]

Conclusions

To prosper in the twenty-first century, the leaders of our organizations will need to embrace democratic principles. They will need to give their employees a voice; listen to what they say, treat them fairly and give them autonomy. They will need to create a culture of trust based on equality, fairness, openness and transparency. They will need to do this, because this is the only way they will be able to attract the most talented people—those who want to be accountable for their own futures and the future of the organization.

Summary

Here are the main points of Chapter 14:

1. Wherever people operate in their daily lives they want to experience values that align with democratic principles.
2. Democracy begins with freedom, and evolves through equality, accountability, fairness, openness and transparency to trust.

3. Each value in this journey forms an essential foundation for the development of the next value.
4. If you want to reap all the benefits that democracy provides you cannot miss a step.
5. Without equality, accountability, fairness, openness and transparency there can be no trust, and without freedom (autonomy) people cannot individuate and self-actualize.
6. People work best when they are given a goal or objective and then left to get on with it, knowing they have a coach or mentor they can consult if they find themselves getting into difficulty.
7. When you give someone autonomy, you must also give them accountability.
8. Accountability is often confused with responsibility. One can have responsibility without accountability, but in most circumstances you will not have accountability without responsibility.
9. Without freedom there is not much point worrying about equality, and without equality there is not much point worrying about fairness. Freedom, equality and fairness naturally follow each other.
10. Openness is "having the interior immediately accessible." In this regard, openness is one of the key requirements for authenticity, which in turn is a key requirement for trust.
11. Openness, in terms of "having the interior immediately accessible," requires an absence of fear.
12. Transparency is "the degree to which you are able to see through something." Openness is relational and deals with motivations. Transparency is factual and deals with processes and information.
13. Trust is an "end" value. All the other values—freedom, equality, accountability, fairness, openness and transparency—are "means" to that end. Without them, trust is impossible.
14. Trust always affects outcomes. When trust goes up, speed will also go up, and costs will go down. When trust goes down, speed will also go down, and costs go up.

Notes

1 Richard Barrett, *Love, Fear and the Destiny of Nations: The Impact of the Evolution of Human Consciousness on World Affairs* (Bath: Fulfilling Books), 2012, pp. 195–302.
2 See www.mars.com/uk/en/the-five-principles.aspx (last accessed 2 April 2013).
3 John Rawls, *A Theory of Justice* (Cambridge, MA: Harvard University Press), 1971.
4 Peter Turchin, *Historical Dynamics: Why States Rise and Fall* (Princeton, NJ: Princeton University Press), 2003.
5 Francis Fukuyama, *Trust: The Social Virtues and the Creation of Prosperity* (New York: Free Press), 2005, p. 53.
6 Richard Barrett, *The New Leadership Paradigm* (Asheville, NC: Fulfilling Books), 2011, p. 73.
7 Stephen M.R. Covey, *The Speed of Trust: The One Thing That Changes Everything* (New York: Free Press), 2006, p. 13.

15 Embedding the culture

One of the best ways to create internal cohesion in an organizational setting, and at the same time safeguard and promote the culture of an organization, is to develop a cadre of internal cultural ambassadors—internal change agents and values champions—who live the organization's values and deeply believe in the purpose of the organization. Over the past 15 years, we have come across many organizations that have developed an internal capacity for sustainable cultural maintenance and renewal. Some examples of the practices they have used for embedding the culture of their organizations are described briefly below.

ANZ

The first example I want to highlight is ANZ. ANZ is a large multinational bank based in Melbourne, Australia. In 2000, a centralized group referred to as "Breakout" was established to support the organization on its cultural journey.

The head of the Breakout Group, Sonia Stojanovic, reported directly to the CEO of ANZ, and they jointly led ANZ's cultural journey. The "Breakout Team," as they became known, was initially established as a project group to partner with Mckinsey and Company (consultants) in an organizational renewal programme. As implementation got underway, it soon became obvious that the bank would need to set up a permanent capacity for sustainable cultural renewal. This role was given to the Breakout Team.

For a short period of time the Breakout Team was centrally financed. Very quickly, however, it was turned into an internal profit centre generating AU$10 million in revenues from the services it offered to the business units and departments across the 31,000-person bank. The Breakout Team's remit was to develop a high-performance culture and establish ANZ as the Bank with a Human Face.

From an initial seed group of three people, the Breakout Group developed into an operating unit with a Consulting and Project Management Team, an Internal Communications Team, a People Capital Team, a Media Relations Team, a Marketing and Brand Team and an Investor Relations and Corporate Affairs Team. A series of internally run transformational workshops were designed aimed at shifting mindsets and developing interpersonal skills in line with the new culture. An internal coaching academy was also established.

Led by the Breakout Team, ANZ developed several cultural initiatives including partnerships with other ANZ units to ensure total values alignment: Units and functions such as people capital, group communications, media relations, marketing and brand, investor relations and corporate affairs. One of the most important innovations was the establishment of breakout champions, communication champions and values champions. The people designated as "champions" were volunteers drawn from all levels of the organization. Every one of them held a passionate belief in the purpose of the organization and were aligned with its vision. The key idea was to spread accountability for the new culture to as many people as possible throughout the organization, thus bringing it alive and making it more resilient and sustainable.

Tracking and measurement of progress was critical for the Breakout Team. A number of different diagnostics were used, including Barrett Value Centre's Cultural Transformation Tools.

Volvo IT

The second example I want to highlight is Volvo IT. Volvo IT is a global company of 6,000 employees based in Gothenburg in Sweden. Its primary role is to provide IT services and support teams to the global network of Volvo industries.

The approach used by Volvo was developed by Tor Eneroth, formerly culture manager at Volvo IT and now network director of Barrett Values Centre. Over a ten-year period Tor developed a company-wide Cultural Ambassador Programme that was charged with protecting, safeguarding and supporting the Volvo IT culture.

Tor's principal role as culture manager was to build a critical mass of cultural ambassadors to support the cultural evolution of Volvo IT. Before describing the cultural ambassador network, I think it is important to be clear about the role of the culture manager.

The primary role of the culture manager is to be the "guardian" of the culture; not the designer of the culture, nor the primary promoter of the culture, but the person who keeps track of what is happening in the culture, and develops organization-wide programmes and specific interventions that enable the culture to grow and develop in line with the changing needs of the organization, employees and external stakeholders. The culture manager should report directly to the leader of the organization and be involved in the meetings of the leadership team.

In Volvo IT the culture manager and the head of human resources (HR) work closely together to protect, sustain and grow the culture. The HR manager focuses mainly on the structural alignment and the culture manager focuses mainly on the personal alignment of the leaders, managers and supervisors and the values alignment of the staff. The HR manager and culture manager collaborate with each other to build mission alignment.

The task of *designing* the culture should fall to the leader and the leadership team. The task of *promoting* the culture should be the responsibility of everyone in the organization. In this respect, every employee and every leader is an ambassador of the culture regardless of whether they are conscious of it or not. In Volvo IT every leader has been trained as a cultural ambassador.

One of the most important duties of the culture manager is to coach and support the leaders of the organization in their roles as cultural ambassadors. In addition, the culture manager needs to be a role model for the values of the organization, and a supporter, coach and teacher of the cultural ambassadors. The culture manager in Volvo IT is supported by a group of cultural navigators.

Cultural navigators are essentially internal change agents (organization and development practitioners). Their main tasks are to facilitate the personal alignment of the leaders, managers and supervisors; improve the values alignment and mission alignment of the employees, and train and support the cultural ambassadors by providing them with practical tools, methodologies and instruments for protecting, safeguarding and supporting the culture of the organization. The cultural navigators also need to be role models for the values of the organization and support the culture manager in his or her duties.

Another important role of the cultural navigators is to facilitate the feedback of the Cultural Values Assessments to the leadership teams of the departments and divisions of the organization. They should also be skilled in delivering feedback from Leadership Values Assessments and Leadership Development Reports.

Whereas the culture manager and the cultural navigators are devoted full-time to their roles, cultural ambassadors are regular staff members who have volunteered to take special training that will enable them to intervene in situations where the values of the organization are not being lived by leaders of the organization. Cultural ambassadors are the guardians of the culture and the eyes and ears of the culture manager. They too, along with the culture manager and cultural navigators, should be role models for the values of the organization. The principal role of the cultural ambassadors is to make the culture tangible and visible by keeping the vision, mission and espoused values and behaviours front and centre in all the daily operations of the organization. Starting a culture initiative is relatively easy compared with maintaining it. This is the work of the cultural ambassadors and they are supported in this work through the process of structural alignment that is usually the responsibility of the human resource or people management function.

How many ambassadors?

As a general rule, in large organizations with more than 2,000 employees, there should be one cultural ambassador for every 50 to 75 employees—about 13 to 20 cultural ambassadors for every 1,000 employees. You will also need approximately one cultural navigator for every 500 employees. Based on these numbers an organization of 20,000 employees would need one culture manager, 30 to 40 cultural navigators and 300 to 400 cultural ambassadors.

In medium-sized organizations (500 to 2,000 employees) the culture manager may need to double up as a cultural navigator. In addition, you may need one, two or three more cultural navigators and ten to 40 cultural ambassadors.

Training

The initial training for cultural ambassadors should be of two-to-three days' duration. The training begins with each participant discovering their most important values and understanding how these values influence their behaviours. To this end, the Personal Values Assessment discussed in Chapter 1 could be used along with the Values, Beliefs and Behaviours exercise presented in Annex 3 as a starting point for this discussion. At the same time, the participants learn about the history of the organization, its commitment to values and its major challenges. They also learn the language of consciousness and transformation, and how it applies in their organizational setting. If the organization is using the Cultural Transformation Tools, then it will be important for participants to learn about the Seven Levels of Consciousness Model and receive a brief overview of the Cultural Transformation Tools.

The second day of the training focuses on more practical matters: How people learn; moving from the results of a values assessment to actions, at an individual and collective level; and deepening participants' understanding of the concept of values alignment and mission alignment through working with the results of their own Individual Values Assessment (IVA). Once they understand how they as individuals see the culture, they should then be presented with a group plot (CVA) of the organization or of the group of participants undergoing the cultural ambassador training.

On day three of the training, participants apply what they have learned in the previous two days to the situations of the groups they work in, and design specific interventions that they will undertake in the following six to 12 months. They design these interventions to support the four conditions necessary for whole system change—personal alignment, values alignment, mission alignment and structural alignment.

Part of the role of the cultural ambassadors is to hold frequent dialogues with employees about the values and behaviours that are necessary to support shifts in the organization's strategy. For this purpose the cultural ambassadors will require a set of tools that the culture manager and the cultural navigators should develop, provide and train the cultural ambassadors to use.

Many of the tools used for these purposes can be found in the journals/workbooks for Leading Self, Leading Others and Leading an Organization, which form part of the learning materials associated with the *New Leadership Paradigm*[1] book and website. Another source of tools for facilitation of cultural transformation is the book "Get Connected," which can be freely downloaded from www. valuescentre.com/getconnected.

Old Mutual Group

The third example I want to highlight is the Old Mutual Group.

Old Mutual is a leading international long-term savings, investment and protection group. Three of Old Mutual's well-known brands at the time of writing are Nedbank, Old Mutual and Skandia, all users of the Cultural Transformation Tools.

Transforming the culture across all of the Old Mutual businesses started with Nedbank in 2005, and became group-wide when the aspiration of becoming "our customers' most trusted partner" was articulated as part of the group vision in 2010. Work was done with the executive leadership teams to increase self-awareness, build trust in relationships and cascade a practice of strategic story-telling. Organizational structures and processes continue to be aligned to support the development of the desired culture from the top-down, including the group operating model, performance management, selection assessment, leadership development and, most recently, the incorporation of cultural entropy levels into the long-term incentive plan for executives. Staff have been left with no doubt that the organization is taking its values and culture seriously.

Recognizing that working with the top would not be enough to catalyze and sustain the change in all teams everywhere, Old Mutual began to embed a capacity for culture change into the business via the introduction of Culture Leads, firstly in their UK-based Wealth business and later in the South African-based Emerging Markets businesses. The role of the Culture Leads, which in the main are senior managers, is to actively sponsor the transformation in their business units and to stimulate deeper dialogues around living the values. Culture Leads are equipped with a deeper set of skills to support transformation in their teams. Synnova, a boutique consultancy firm based in the Netherlands, supported Old Mutual in the work of building this internal transformation capacity—working with the top teams, training the Culture Leads and co-designing a toolkit for supporting transformation.

The Old Mutual Cultural Transformation Toolkit[2] includes sections on: Building mindsets and capabilities; transforming your leadership; holding meaningful team meetings; debriefing the annual Barrett assessment results; working with organizational assessment results; and working with leadership assessments.

The Culture Leads are skilled in making change happen "on the ground" in their part of the business. An important aspect of the role is to both support and challenge the Executive Committee members to drive the change agenda and to carry this agenda, or change story, further into the organization. Thus, the culture change is embedded throughout multiple levels in the business. Here are some comments from senior members of the Old Mutual Group about their experiences.

A senior executive at Old Mutual speaking about the work of the Culture Leads: "My Culture Leads are extremely helpful to have around. They offer advice and a lot of support. Most importantly, they are a very good conduit for gauging the mood on the floor and soliciting staff feedback."

One of the Culture Leads described his experience as follows: "My biggest learning has been to take time, to pause, to consider what we're finding out. I think we tend to rush to deadlines and action plans: actually sitting back and taking time to deepen our understanding of the issues is really important. I found it a personal challenge."

Pleuntje van Meer, from Synnova, who has helped facilitate the organizational transformation in the Old Mutual Group and many other organizations over the past decade, has this to say about the process of culture change:

> Firstly, the lived commitment of the leaders is vital. A leader-led intervention is necessary to shift the mind sets of the organization. Secondly, the Human Resource Department and those responsible for strategy need to fully partner with the leadership in co-creating the culture change story. Thirdly, transformation takes time. Fourth, there's a bit of magic required for a transformation to take place. This does not happen through a project with deadlines and deliverables. It is more of an inspired, emergent learning process. Lastly, success requires clarity of direction and healthy connections, based on trust. Only when this happens will people in the organization feel they can fully bring themselves to work.

Julian Roberts, CEO of Old Mutual PLC, puts it this way:

> When I think about Old Mutual and what will continue to make us successful in this new world, two factors are paramount:
>
> Firstly, we understand our customers, meet their needs and exceed their expectations in the markets we choose to be in; and, secondly, our behaviours are responsible and transparent to earn the trust of all our stakeholders.
>
> In 2010, we made customer focus explicit in our vision, and since then we have been investing in programmes to drive the development of customer focused products and services; and we're adopting externally recognised metrics to monitor progress and identify areas where we still need to improve.
>
> In terms of behaviour, we are absolutely clear about what behaviours are acceptable, and are not acceptable in our business. We have a strong set of values and behaviours which we have communicated across the organization. I believe that the culture of our business is critical to its success.
>
> We monitor our culture using an annual process of engagement with all our people—the Barrett Cultural Values Assessment. Managers all around the organization are tasked to address issues raised; and the results affect management remuneration. Nedbank first implemented this methodology in 2005 as part of its recovery programme, and I believe firmly that it has played a major part in the bank's turnaround. Indeed, statistics show that companies that have the right culture outperform the market on shareholder returns.
>
> We understand and believe in the importance of putting our customers at the heart of our business, and creating the right culture and behaviours to support our vision of becoming our customers' most trusted partner. This will continue to be critical to our success as we head into the future.

Conclusions

Ultimately, you want everyone who works in your organization to be an ambassador for the organization, particularly those who have outward-facing roles that connect them with customers, the general public and other primary stakeholders. There can be no better advertisement for your organization than having employees who are not only respected by their co-workers, but are also respected by the people they interact with outside the organization.

Summary

Here are the main points of Chapter 15:

1. One of the best ways to safeguard and promote the culture of an organization is to develop a cadre of internal cultural ambassadors—internal change agents and value champions—who live the values of the organization and are passionate about the purpose and vision of the organization.
2. The principal role of a cultural ambassador is to make the culture tangible and visible by keeping the vision, mission and espoused values and behaviours front and centre of the organization's daily operations.
3. Everyone who works in an organization needs to be an ambassador for the organization, not just those with outward-facing roles that connect them with customers, the general public and other primary stakeholders, but also those with inward-facing roles particularly those who work in the Human Resources arena.
4. If you are using the Barrett Cultural Values Assessments to manage the values of your organization, it will be important to create a cadre of cultural navigators—internal change agents—who are trained in the Seven Levels of Consciousness Model and the Cultural Transformation Tools.

Notes

1 Go to www.valuescentre.com/resources/?sec=books__learning_modules (last accessed 2 April 2013).
2 The Tool Kit can be downloaded from www.synnova.com/files/OMG%20Toolkit.pdf (last accessed 2 April 2013).

16 The twenty-first-century organization

In the Preface to this book, I indicated that there were two central questions that I wanted to address: "What is the source of our commitment?" and "How do leaders create the conditions that engender high levels of commitment from their employees?"

If you have read the whole of this book up to this point, I believe you will have found the answers to these questions. Let me summarize what I believe you will have learned.

1. Commitment to a person, organization or a cause arises when the person, organization or cause provides you with opportunities to satisfy your needs. When a person, organization or cause does not support you in satisfying your needs, you do not feel a sense of commitment.
2. Commitment is the key to employee engagement. Employees feel committed when the organization provides them with opportunities to satisfy their personal needs.
3. The key to employee engagement is *values alignment*—feeling a sense of personal alignment with the lived values of the organization, and *mission alignment*—finding a sense of meaning through your work by understanding how what you do makes a difference to the success of the organization, and believing in the organization and what it is attempting to do.
4. Commitment to the organization is enhanced when the leaders, managers and supervisors embrace democratic principles, treat you as an equal, listen to what you have to say, deal with you fairly, and give you opportunities and challenges to grow and develop both professionally and personally.
5. Your commitment to the organization is further enhanced when you believe the leaders, managers and supervisors care about you, care about the organization, and care about the local community and society in which you live.
6. Your sense of commitment to the organization continues to heighten when you feel you can trust the organization, its leaders, managers and supervisors to always do the right thing.

The bottom line on commitment is this: Whatever person, organization or cause you feel a sense of commitment towards, you identify with; and whatever you identify with you care about. However, you will only feel a sense of commitment to the person, organization or cause if you feel supported in meeting your needs.

How does commitment show up?

You can recognize commitment in an organization in the following ways.

At the first level of consciousness (survival), commitment shows up as willingness to do what is necessary to secure the financial stability and health of the organization, and the health and safety of its employees.

At the second level of consciousness (relationship), commitment shows up as a deeply engrained loyalty—a steadfastness of belief in the organization and its leaders and what they are attempting to do—and as heartfelt connection and camaraderie among employees.

At the third level of consciousness (self-esteem), commitment shows up as a willingness on the part of employees to go the extra mile whenever it is necessary. When employees are committed, they bring their discretionary energy to their work.

At the fourth level of consciousness (transformation), commitment shows up as a willingness to adapt and change—let go of old habits and change who you are, change how you operate, and change *how* you do what you do for the benefit of yourself, your subordinates and the organization. Commitment also shows up at this level of consciousness as a willingness to try new ideas, take risks and innovate.

At the fifth level of consciousness (internal cohesion) commitment shows up as passion for your work and enhanced creativity.

At the sixth level of consciousness commitment shows up as a deeply held desire to make a difference in the world.

At the seventh level of consciousness commitment shows up as devotion to selfless service—a profound sense of interconnectedness, a focus on the common good, and the desire to leave a legacy.

Conclusions

Whilst all these aspects of commitment are important, the most important is the ability and willingness to adapt—continuous transformation. The most successful organisms and species have always been those that learned how to adapt to their changing environments. Evolution has never been an exercise in long-term, strategic planning; it has always been an exercise in emergent learning.[1] Emergent learning along with a predilection and facility for adaptation lies at the core of all successful evolution and cultural transformation.[2,3]

Successful organisms have always evolved by making continuous real-time adjustments to their way of being based on feedback from their internal and external environments. This is why organizations that display a high level of internal cohesion are able to survive and prosper more easily than those that do not. The interpersonal connectedness that arises from internal cohesion enables an organization to act as a single organism, thereby facilitating emergent learning, adaptation and agility. The key factor in creating internal cohesion is interpersonal trust. Trust is built on six values: autonomy, equality, accountability, fairness, openness and transparency—each one of them a strategic component of universal democratic principles.[4]

This means that the most successful organizations in the twenty-first century will be those that not only understand how to build internal cohesion through values and mission alignment, but are structurally agile enough to adapt to the changing needs of society and the changing needs of the market place. They will be working with free-form, flexible organizational structures that create high levels of employee engagement and empower people to focus their energies on innovation and continuous renewal.

The role of the leaders, managers and supervisors will be to create a values-driven culture based on democratic principles and create working conditions that support employees in meeting their deficiency and growth needs—thereby engendering high levels of employee engagement. When the culture and working conditions are right, employees will bring their hearts and souls to their work and release their creative and discretionary energies.

In addition to caring about the needs of employees, the successful twenty-first-century organization will also care about the needs of the organization's external stakeholders—customers, suppliers, investors and the local communities and societies in which they operate.

To achieve all these objectives, the leader of the organization will need to: (a) build an inspiring vision and a purposeful mission for the organization that goes beyond making money; (b) manage the values of the organization by getting regular feedback from employees, customers, suppliers and society at large about how the organization can meet their needs; (c) manage his/her way of being/operating by getting regular feedback from colleagues and direct reports about how they can change their way of being/operating to enhance the performance of the organization; and (d) require that the directors, managers and supervisors in the organization do the same.

In summary, in order to be successful in the twenty-first century, the leaders of our organizations will need to embrace a new leadership paradigm—a shift in focus from "I" to "we"; from "*what's in it for me*" to "*what's best for the common good*"; and from "*being the best* in *the world*" to "*being the best* for *the world*."[5]

Notes

1 Marilyn Taylor, *Emergent Learning for Wisdom* (New York: Palgrave Macmillan), 2010.
2 See George E. Vaillant, *Adaptation to Life* (Cambridge, MA: Harvard University Press), 1977, which traces the history of 100 Harvard graduates to determine the key factors that led to their success or failure in life.

3 See also Richard Barrett, *The New Leadership Paradigm* (Asheville, NC: Fulfilling Books), 2011, p. 21 for the results of the study of Harvard graduates cited in the previous reference.
4 See Richard Barrett, *Love, Fear and the Destiny of Nations: The Impact of the Evolution of Consciousness on World Affairs* (Bath: Fulfilling Books), 2012, pp. 195–302.
5 Richard Barrett, *The New Leadership Paradigm* (Asheville, NC: Fulfilling Books), 2011, pp. 13–22.

Annex 1

The seven stages of psychological development

The seven stages of psychological development occur in consecutive order over the full period of our lives. We begin the journey by learning to survive, and we complete the journey by learning to serve. We begin our adult lives in ego consciousness; and if we complete the course, we end our adult lives in soul consciousness.

Surviving

The quest for survival starts as soon as a human baby is born. The infant child instinctively knows it must establish itself as a viable entity if it is to remain in the physical world. At this stage, the infant is totally dependent on others to meet its needs. During the first stage of psychological development the child has to establish its own separate sense of identity and learn how to exercise control over its environment so that it can get its survival needs met.

If, for whatever reason, the child is unable to accomplish these tasks, because its parents are not vigilant enough to its needs, or the child is left alone or abandoned for long periods of time, the child's nascent ego will very likely form subconscious fear-based beliefs (early maladaptive schema) that the world is an unsafe place and that other people cannot be trusted.

If, on the other hand, the child's parents are attentive to its needs, and are watchful for signs of distress, then the child will grow up with a sense of security and the feeling that others can be trusted. Feeling safe and secure is the first and most important need of the ego-mind.

Conforming

During the next stage of psychological development, the conforming or self-protective stage, young children learn that life is more pleasant and less threatening if they live in harmony with others. The task at this stage of development is to learn how to feel loved and safe in your family group. Adherence to rules and rituals (conforming) becomes important, because they consolidate your sense of belonging, and enhance your sense of safety.

At this stage, children also learn beliefs and behaviours that allow them to maximize pleasure and minimize pain. If punishment is used to assure conformity, then the child may adopt a strategy of blaming others to avoid reprimands. If the child believes the rules or reprimands are unjust or unfair, he or she may develop a rebellious streak.

If, for any reason (usually because of poor parenting), you grow up feeling unloved or you don't belong, your ego may develop subconscious fear-based beliefs that you are not lovable. Later on in life you may find yourself constantly seeking affection and wanting to find a group or community that accepts you for the way you are. Feeling loved and a sense of belonging to a group or community is the second most important need of the ego-mind.

Differentiating

During the next stage of psychological development, the differentiation stage, the child seeks to become special—recognized by his or her parents for excelling or doing well. The task at this stage is to develop a healthy sense of pride in your accomplishments and a feeling of self-worth. You want to feel good about who you are and you want to feel respected by your peers.

Your parents are instrumental at this stage of your development for giving you the positive feedback you need. If you fail to get this feedback, you will grow up with the subconscious fear-based belief that you are not good enough. You will feel driven to prove your self-worth. You may become highly competitive, attempting to seek power, authority or status so that you can be acknowledged by your peers or those in authority as someone who is important or someone to be feared. If your ego-mind does not get the reinforcement that it needs, you could grow up with a feeling that no matter how hard you try, recognition escapes you: The successes you achieve never seem to be enough. Feeling a sense of self-worth or pride in your accomplishments is the third most important need of the ego-mind.

If you were able to successfully transition through these first three stages of your psychological development without significant trauma and without developing too many subconscious fear-based beliefs, then you will find it relatively easy to establish yourself as a viable independent adult providing you can find the opportunities you need to earn a living that meets your survival needs. You will begin to move from a state of dependence to a state of independence.

Individuating

During the next stage of psychological development—the individuation stage—which usually occurs after we have become adults, we begin to transcend our physical and emotional dependence on our parents and the family, or the cultural group in which we were raised, by releasing the fear-based beliefs we developed about satisfying our survival, relationship and self-esteem needs.

Learning to reduce the impact of the fear-based beliefs you learned during the first three stages of your development may require a long-term commitment to personal mastery—understanding and releasing the subconscious fear-based beliefs (early maladaptive schemas) you learned during the surviving, conforming and differentiation stages of your psychological development. Embracing *your own* values and beliefs requires you to establish your independence and seek your own path in the world.

This can be especially challenging if you grew up in a kinship or tribal culture, where people are dependent on each other for survival, and where the pressures to conform are large. There are billions of people on the planet who live in conditions that make it difficult for them to individuate: they either live in poverty, a conforming culture or they are dependent on others to meet their needs.

If, on the other hand, you grew up in a rich country with self-actualized parents, who took care of your basic needs and always treated you like a young adult, by teaching you to be responsible and accountable for your life and your emotions, then you will find the process of individuation relatively easy.

Once you have learned how to master your basic needs, and have established yourself as viable independent individual, you may, after a certain amount of time, feel a natural pull towards the next stage of your psychological development—self-actualization.

Self-actualizing

The self-actualization stage of psychological development involves learning to align with and satisfy the needs of your soul—learning how to lead a values-driven life, and learning how to live a purpose-driven life.

Leading a values-driven life means letting go of the decision-making modalities of the ego (beliefs) and embracing the decision-making modalities of the soul (values). The progress you make in this regard will dictate how well you are able to manifest your soul's purpose. You will need to learn to live with trust, empathy and compassion if you are going to fully actualize your soul's purpose.

Finding your soul's purpose—your calling or vocation—usually begins with a feeling of unease or boredom with the work on which you depend for your livelihood. You may find your work no longer challenging. You may feel blocked in your progress, unable to grow and develop.

As you begin to discover your soul's purpose, you will feel a pull towards a new activity or a lifetime interest—something more meaningful to you personally. Uncovering your soul's purpose and your sense of mission will bring passion and creativity back into to your life, and give you a deep sense of meaning. Finding your vocation and embarking on living a values-driven life represent the first level of soul activation.

Integrating

Integrating involves cooperating with others who share a similar purpose or mission to leverage your impact in the world. The people you collaborate with will be people with whom you empathize and resonate: People who share your values and your sense of purpose or mission—people who are operating from a similar level of consciousness.

The task at this stage of development is to find ways to actualize your sense of purpose by making a difference in the world. You realize that by joining forces with others in collective endeavours, you can achieve far more than you could on your own. To make this shift you will have to move from independence to interdependence. You begin to realize that the contribution you can make and your level of fulfilment is leveraged by the quality of the connection you have with the group you are working with. Integrating with others to make a difference in the world represents the second level of soul activation.

Serving

The final stage of psychological development involves recognizing the unity and interdependence of all things; modifying your behaviours to alleviate the suffering of humanity and preserve the world's life support systems for future generations—embodying compassion and living sustainably in everything you do.

The task at this stage of development is to lead a life of selfless service in alignment with your soul's purpose. You may find that your job and your workplace have become too small for you to fulfil your calling. You may need to find a new and larger role for yourself in society: You may become an elder in your community; you may become a mentor to those who are facing life's challenges; you may care for the sick or dying; or you may find ways to support young children or teenagers in dealing with the difficulties of growing up. It does not matter what you do, your purpose is to support the well-being of your community or the society in which you live. Deep down, you will begin to understand that we are all connected, and that by serving others you are serving yourself. Selfless service represents the third level of soul activation.

For a more detailed account of the process of psychological development read *What My Soul Told Me: A Practical Guide to Soul Activation* by Richard Barrett.

Annex 2

The six modes of decision making

There are six modes of decision making available to human beings—instincts, subconscious beliefs, conscious beliefs, values, intuition and inspiration. Your primary mode of decision making—the one you most frequently use—depends on your level of psychological development and the level of consciousness that you are operating from. The six modes of decision making are shown in Table A2.1, along with the levels of consciousness at which they principally operate.

Instinct-based decision making

Instinct-based decision making takes place at the atomic/cellular level because the actions that arise are based on learned DNA responses, principally associated with issues of survival. For example, babies instinctively know how to suckle, how to cry when their needs are not being met, and how to smile so they can get the attention they need. No one taught them how to do this. It is encoded in their DNA.

In adult life, instinct-based decision making kicks in to help you survive and avoid dangerous situations. It is also at the root of the fight-or-flight response common to all animals. In certain situations, our instincts may cause us to put our life at risk in order to save the life of another. Instinct is the principal mode of decision making by which all creatures operate. (In higher order creatures, such as mammals, we can also find subconscious and conscious beliefs guiding decision making.) The main features of instinct-based decision making are:

- Actions always precede thought. There is no pause for reflection between making meaning of a situation and decision making that precipitates an action.
- The decisions that are made are always based on past experiences—what our species history has taught us about how to survive and keep safe.
- You have no opportunity to reflect on your decision before you act—your reaction is automatic.
- When you are involved in instinct-based decision making, you are not consciously in control of your words, actions and behaviours. They are in control of you.

Table A2.1 Modes of decision making and levels of consciousness

Levels of consciousness		Mode of decision making
7	Service	Inspiration
6	Making a difference	Intuition
5	Internal cohesion	Values
4	Transformation	Conscious beliefs
3	Self-esteem	Subconscious beliefs
2	Relationship	
1	Survival	Instincts

Subconscious belief-based decision making

In subconscious belief-based decision making, you also react to what is happening in your world without reflection, but on the basis of personal memories rather than the species memories encapsulated in your DNA. In this mode of decision making, action also precedes thought. The release of an emotional charge often accompanies the action.

You know when subconscious fear-based beliefs are dominating your decision making if you feel resistance, impatience, frustration, upset, anger or rage. Whenever you experience such feelings, you are dealing with an unmet deficiency need that has not been resolved. Your reactions and emotions are being triggered by a present moment situation that is making you recall a memory about a situation from the past when you failed to get your emotional needs met.

When a positively charged emotion is triggered, such as happiness, you are subconsciously recalling memories from your past that supported you in meeting your needs. For example, a picture of someone you have not seen in a long while or the sound of their voice may unleash tears of happiness. Your reactions and emotions are being triggered by a present moment situation that is making you recall a positive memory with positive emotional content from the past. The main features of subconscious belief-based decision making are:

- Actions always precede thought. There is no gap for reflection between making meaning of a situation and decision making that precipitates an action.
- The decisions that are made are always based on past experiences, what your personal history has taught you about maximizing pleasure and minimizing pain in the framework of existence of your childhood. This history is stored in your personal memory.
- You are not in control of your actions.
- You have no opportunity to reflect on your decision before you act—your reaction is automatic.
- When you are involved in subconscious belief-based decision making you are not in control of your actions and behaviours. They are in control of you.

In this mode of decision making, the only way you can get back into conscious control of your actions is either to release or bottle up your emotions. Releasing helps you to return to rationality; bottling up builds up emotional pressure that will need to be released at some time in the future, usually in the form of anger or in extreme cases in the form of rage.

Subconscious fear-based decision making is the source of your personal entropy and is always related to meeting your unmet deficiency needs.

Conscious belief-based decision making

If you want to make rational decisions, you have to leave behind subconscious belief-based decision making and shift to conscious belief-based decision making. You have to insert a pause between the event that triggers your subconscious belief and your response to it. The pause allows you time for reflection so you can use logic to understand what is happening and then make a choice about how to respond. By inserting a pause, you also have time to discuss the situation with others and get advice about the best way to meet your needs. The main features of conscious belief-based decision making are:

- Thought precedes action. You insert a pause between an event and your response to it so you can use logic and get advice in order to determine the best way of meeting your needs.
- The decisions that are made are based on past experiences and what your personal history has taught you about maintaining internal stability and external equilibrium in your childhood and adulthood. You make decisions based on what you believe you know.
- You are in control of your actions and behaviours.
- You can consult with others to support and enhance your decision making.

Conscious belief-based decision making has one thing in common with subconscious belief-based decision making and instinct-based decision making: It uses information from the past—personal or species beliefs—to make decisions about the future. Because you are using beliefs or assumptions from the past, the future you create through conscious belief-based decision making is usually only an incremental improvement on decisions you have reached in the past.

Values-based decision making

The shift from conscious belief-based decision making to values-based decision making is not easy. You have to individuate (become viable and independent, physically and emotionally, in your framework of existence) before values-based decision making is fully and naturally available to you.

The reason why the shift from belief-based decision making to values-based decision making requires individuation is because, prior to individuation, we make meaning of our world through our learned beliefs. Most of these beliefs are associated with our personal and cultural upbringing. Beliefs are assumptions we hold to be true. They may not be true, but we assume they are. The process of individuation involves examining these beliefs and letting go of those that don't serve you and those you consider, based on new information, to be no longer true. The process of reflecting on your beliefs opens you up to a new and more powerful guidance system—your deeply held values. Values are the universal guidance system of the soul, whereas beliefs are the context-related guidance system of the ego. When you shift to values-based decision making, you can effectively throw away the rulebooks. Every decision you make is sourced from what you consider to be "right action"—what is deeply meaningful to you which supports connection rather than separation.

Values-based decision making allows you to create a future that resonates deeply with who you really are. It creates the conditions that allow authenticity and integrity to flourish. That is not to say there is no place for conscious belief-based decision making based on logic or rational thinking. There is. However, you will quickly realize that all the critical decisions you need to make in your life should pass the values test. If a decision seems logical, but it goes against your values, you will not want to proceed.

The main features of values-based decision making are:

- Thought precedes action. You reflect on the values that you believe will allow you to get your needs met and make decisions accordingly.
- The decisions that are made are not based on past history. They are based on the future you want to experience. They are a direct reflection of your needs.
- You are in control of your actions and behaviours.
- You can consult with others to support and enhance your decision making.

You make values-based decisions so you can consciously create the future you want to experience. For example, if you value trust, then you make decisions that allow you to display trust. If you value accountability, then you make decisions that allow you to display accountability. The quality of the energy you put out into the world through your decision making is the quality of the energy you receive back. If you put out love and trust, you get back love and trust.

Intuition-based decision making

The shift from values-based decision making to intuition-based decision making develops over time as the centre of gravity of your psychological development moves from satisfying your deficiency needs to satisfying your growth needs. Although intuition can arise at all stages of development, it is not until you begin to focus on satisfying your growth needs that it captures your attention and begins to flourish. You reach this level of psychological development after you have made progress on your internal cohesion and have become a self-actualized individual.

Intuition allows you to access your own deeper intelligence and the collective intelligence of a wider group. The principal characteristics of intuition-based decision making are as follows:

- Awareness is expanded through a shift in your sense of identity/ consciousness.
- Judgment is suspended. No meaning making takes place, either subconsciously or consciously.
- The mind is empty. Thoughts, beliefs and agendas are suspended.
- The mind is free to make a deep dive into the mind space of the collective unconscious and emerge with a deep sense of knowing.
- The thoughts that arise reflect wisdom and align with your most deeply held values.

In intuition-based decision making, there is no conscious or subconscious attempt at making meaning of a situation, and there is no focus on the past or the future. You accept what is without judgment. The intuitive decision arises out of your presence in the current moment—the non-judgmental mind space you have created. Even though intuition-based decision making may appear to be illogical, it is the principal source of our most important breakthrough ideas. When we work with others to create a collective, non-judgmental mind space, intuition can become even more powerful. This is the basis of *Theory U*, used for collective decision making, described by Otto Scharmer in his book of the same name.[1] When we are totally present to a situation without thought, belief or judgment, we create the conditions that allow our minds to intuitively recognize what wants to emerge.

Inspiration-based decision making

Inspiration is the term I use to describe the soul-based promptings that enter into our minds. Inspiration is always very personal and directive. It is a persistent thought that will not go away, or it is the next step you have to take in a soul-centred activity. It will keep prompting you to take action until you do something about it. It is about what *you* need to do. The purpose of inspiration is to support you in fulfilling your soul's purpose.[2]

Inspiration is different to intuition. Intuition is nondirective. Intuition is an idea or insight that arises from nowhere at an undetermined moment that provides a solution or a clue to resolving a problem that is on your mind. Intuition can best be described as a *Eureka moment*, whereas inspiration is best described as *guidance for staying in a state of flow*.

When you keep receiving a soul-driven thought about an action or direction you need to take, and you do not follow this directive, you will eventually have to deal with the emotional consequences. For example, when you continually allow your ego's fears about satisfying your deficiency needs to take precedence over fulfilling your soul's growth needs you may find yourself getting more and more depressed. You will feel stifled and out of alignment.

The principal characteristics of inspiration-based decision making are as follows:

• Thought appears to arise from nowhere.
• The thought is persistent.
• The thought is linked to actions that you need to take.
• There are consequences for not following your inspiration.

In the preface of *The New Leadership Paradigm*, I spoke about my calling to write a book on leadership. For me, that was inspiration in action. When I began to write the book, I often found myself in a state of flow. Ideas and insights just kept flooding my mind. Whenever I was stuck with my writing, I would seek assistance from my higher self. Very soon thereafter I would find words streaming into my conscious awareness without need of editing. At those moments, I was experiencing a state of flow.

Notes

1 Otto Scharmer, *Theory U: Leading from the Future as it Emerges* (San Francisco: Berrett-Koehler), 2009.
2 For a full account of inspiration-based decision making consult Richard Barrett, *What My Soul Told Me: A Practical Guide for Soul Activation* (Bath: Fulfilling Books), 2012.

Annex 3
Values, beliefs and behaviours exercise

The following exercise helps you to explore and clarify your values and, at the same time, helps you understand the difference between values, beliefs and behaviours. This exercise is very powerful when done with family members or with people who work with you in the same team.

Take a pen or pencil and create a three-by-three matrix (three rows and three columns) on a piece of paper. In the first column, write down three values that are important to you. They should be single words, such as "family," "education" and "respect." In the second column, write down a statement that describes why the values in the first column are important. These represent the beliefs you hold about your values. In the last column, write down the behaviours you exhibit when you are living the values you have listed in first column. Table A3.1 provides an example of this exercise that I carried out for myself.

Clarity is important to me because I believe it brings focus to my decision making. In order to find clarity, I seek out as many data points as I can, look for patterns and explore what is common and what is different. Friendship is important to me because it gives me a feeling of belonging and helps me to

Table A3.1 The values, beliefs and behaviours exercise

My top three values	My beliefs about these values	The behaviours I exhibit
Clarity	Clarity brings focus to my decision making.	I seek out many data points, look for patterns and explore what is common and what is different.
Friendship	Friendship gives me a feeling of belonging, so I feel connected to people.	I seek out people that I resonate with; people with whom I can have meaningful conversations about matters that I consider important.
Creativity	My creativity helps me to bring my gifts to the world.	I organize my life and prioritize my work so that I can devote as much time as possible to thinking and writing.

feel connected to people. In order to establish friendships, I seek out people that I resonate with; people with whom I can have meaningful conversations about matters that I consider important. Creativity is important to me because it helps me to bring my gifts to the world. In order to experience creativity, I organize my life and prioritize my work so that I can devote as much time as possible to thinking and writing.

Annex 4

The top 40 publicly traded best companies to work for in North America

Adobe Systems Inc.
Aflac Inc.
Amazon.com Inc.
American Express Co.
Autodesk Inc.
Build-A-Bear Workshop
 Inc.
Capital Trust Inc. Class A.
Chesapeake Energy Corp.
Devon Energy Corp.
Dreamworks Animation
 SKG Inc.
EOG Resources
FactSet Research
 Systems Inc.
General Mills Inc.
Goldman Sachs Group
 Inc.

Google Inc. Class A.
Hasbro, Inc.
Intel Corp.
Intuit Inc.
Marriott International
 Inc. Class A
Mattel Inc.
Medical Properties Trust
 Inc.
Men's Wearhouse
Microsoft Corp.
National Instruments
 Corp.
NetApp Inc.
Nordstrom Inc.
Novo Nordisk,
 A/S ADR
Nustar Energy, L.P.

Publix Super Mkts,
 Inc.
Qualcomm Inc.
Rackspace Hosting
 Inc.
Salesforce.com Inc.
Southern Michigan
 Bankcorp.
St Jude Medical, Inc.
Starbucks Corporation
Stryker Corporation
SVB Financial Group
Ultimate Software
 Group, Inc.
Umpqua Holdings
 Corporation
Whole Food Markets,
 Inc.

Annex 5

Firms of Endearment

*Amazon.com Inc.
*Best Buy Co Inc.
BMW
*CarMax Inc.
*Caterpillar Inc.
*Commerce Bankshares Inc.
Container Store
*Costco Wholesale Corporation
*eBay Inc.

*Google Inc. Class A.
*Harley-Davidson Inc.
*Honda Motor Co.
IDEO
IKEA
*Jet Blue
*Johnson & Johnson
Jordan's Furniture
L.L. Bean
New Balance
Patagonia

Progressive Insurance
REI
*Southwest Airlines Co.
*Starbucks Corporation
*Timberland Inc.
*Toyota Motor Corp.
Trader Joe's
*UPS Inc.
Wegmans
*Whole Foods Markets, Inc.

* *Firms of Endearment* for which financial data were readily available for their North America operations.

Annex 6

Good to Great companies

Abbott Laboratories	Kimberly-Clark	Pitney Bowes Inc.
*Circuit City	Kroger Co.	Walgreen Company
**Fannie Mae	Nucor Corp.	*** Wells Fargo & Co.
Gillette Company	Philip Morris International Inc.	

* No longer trading.
** Involved in a home mortgage scandal.
*** Received $25 billion bailout from the Troubled Asset Relief Program (TARP) as part of the United States government's response to the subprime mortgage crisis of 2008.

Annex 7

The energy available to an organization

We can estimate the amount energy that is available to an organization for value-added or useful work from the following formula:

$$E_o = E_i + E_d - E_n - CE$$

E_o is the energy available to an organization for doing value-added work (output energy).

E_i is the normal amount of energy employees bring to their work (input energy).

E_d is the amount of discretionary energy employees bring to their work when they are feeling highly motivated and committed.

E_n is the normal amount of employee energy needed to keep the organization functioning when everything is going well (overhead energy that is not devoted to value-added activities).

CE is the amount of cultural entropy (energy required to overcome the dysfunction, disorder, frictions and inefficiencies in an organization).

Thus the amount of energy that is available to an organization—the energy that makes a positive contribution to the development and delivery of products and services (value-added energy)—is equal to the amount of energy employees bring to their work (E_i plus E_d) minus the amount of energy needed to keep the organization functioning (E_n) and the energy needed to overcome the internal dysfunction, disorder, frictions and inefficiencies (CE). The amount of energy needed to keep the organization functioning in normal conditions (E_n) is the energy required for overhead functions, such as accounts, legal, human resources and so forth—energy that does not add significant value to the delivery of the product or service.

When the degree of dysfunction, disorder, friction or inefficiency (cultural entropy) in an organization is high, due to factors such as excessive control, caution, confusion, bureaucracy, hierarchy, internal competition, blame, silo mentality, short-term thinking and so forth, the amount of energy employees have for value-added activities decreases. This makes it difficult for employees to do their work. It leads to employee disengagement and decreases the level of discretionary energy that people bring to their work.

On the other hand, when the degree of dysfunction, disorder, friction and inefficiency (cultural entropy) is low, due to factors such as autonomy, trust, integrity, honesty, openness and cooperation, the amount of energy employees have for value-added activities increases. This makes it easy for employees to do their work. It leads to employee engagement and increases the level of discretionary energy that people bring to their work.

Annex 8
The Four Why's Process

The Four Why's Process is a methodological construct for creating mission and vision statements. The process differs from other methods in that: (a) it differentiates between the internal and external motivations of an organization; and (b) it addresses the needs of employees, customers and society. The objective of the process is to create four statements that represent the internal mission and vision and the external mission and vision (see Table A8.1). The internal mission goes in Box 1, the internal vision goes in Box 2, the external mission goes in Box 3 and the external vision goes in Box 4.

The statement that goes in Box 1 describes the key ideas that will guide the internal development of the organization. The statement that goes in Box 2 describes what the organization will look like in the future if it pursues the ideas contained in Box 1. The statement that goes in Box 3 describes the key ideas about what the organization wants to do for its customers. The statement that goes in Box 4 describes what the impact will be on society if the organization pursues the ideas contained in Box 3.

Mission statement

A mission statement does two things. It keeps the energies of employees focused on the core business and it tells the external stakeholders what the organization is about.

Mission statements should be concise, inclusive and easily memorized and allow room for the organization to expand into associated areas of its core business. For example, Steelcase, a provider of office furniture has the following mission— *helping people work more effectively*. It is concise, easily memorized and it leaves room for expansion into different lines of office products and services.

Vision statement

A vision statement declares the organization's intention about the future it wants to create. Vision statements make a compelling assertion about what the organization wants to achieve. The mission statement is the "means" and the vision statement is the "end." In other words, the mission statement tells you how you are going to create the future you want to experience (the vision).

Table A8.2 provides an example of the four statements that were developed for the Barrett Values Centre when it was first created in 1997.

Table A8.1 Four Why's overview

	Internal motivation	*External motivation*
Vision	**(2) Internal vision** Organizational fulfilment	**(4) External vision** Impact on society
Mission	**(1) Internal mission** Organizational development	**(3) External mission** Impact on customers

The process usually begins by building a statement of internal mission. Two important questions must be asked to arrive at this first statement: (1) *What is our core business?* and (2) *What do we need to do to grow and develop the organization?* Both these questions are internally focused. The answer to the first question tells us what we are about—the primary focus of our work. The answer to the second question gives direction to our growth and development. We are in the business of *cultural transformation*—that is our core business, and we will grow and develop by *building a worldwide network of change agents*. The statement, "To build a worldwide network of change agents committed to cultural transformation," provides a clear statement for our employees about what business we are in and our intention with regard to how we are going to grow the company.

The next step is to build a statement of internal vision. We formulate this statement by asking "Why?" in front of the internal mission. The answer represents the vision—a deeper level of motivation. When we asked, "Why do we want *to build a worldwide network of change agents committed to cultural transformation?*" we came up with the answer, "*To be a global resource for the evolution of human consciousness.*" That is the future we want to create for the organization—*to be a global resource*. If we now ask "*How?*" in front of the internal vision, we should be able to arrive back at the statement of internal mission. How are we going *to become a global resource for the evolution of human consciousness?* The answer is "*by building a world-wide network of change agents committed to cultural transformation.*" If these statements align and resonate with the senior management, and inspire employees, then we have completed the internal mission and vision.

Now we move to the external mission. This is a statement that describes the service we provide to our clients. If we ask "*Why?*" again in front of the internal mission, thinking in terms of our customers, "Why do we want *to build a worldwide network of change agents committed to cultural transformation?*" we get the

Table A8.2 Barrett Values Centre mission and vision statements

	Internal motivation	*External motivation*
Vision	**(2) Internal vision** To be a global resource for the evolution of human consciousness	**(4) External vision** To create a values-driven society
Mission	**(1) Internal mission** To build a worldwide network of change agents committed to cultural transformation	**(3) External mission** To support leaders in building values-driven organizations

answer, "*To support leaders in building values-driven organizations.*" Again, if we now ask "*How?*" in front of the external mission, we should be able to arrive back at the statement of internal mission, "How are we going *to support leaders in building values-driven organizations?*" The answer is "*by building a world-wide network of change agents committed to cultural transformation.*"

Finally, we tackle the external vision. This is a statement that describes the impact we want to have on society. If we ask "*Why?*" in front of the external mission, thinking in terms of society, "Why do we want to *support leaders in building values-driven organizations?*" we get the answer, "*To create a values-driven society.*" Again, if we now ask "*How?*" in front of the external vision, we should be able to arrive back at the statement of external mission, "How are we going *to create a values-driven society?*" The answer is "*by supporting leaders in building values-driven organizations.*" If these statements align and resonate with the senior management, and inspire employees, then we have completed the external mission and vision.

We can now do another check to see if the statements align by thinking about the external vision and asking "*Why?*" in front of the internal vision. We should be able to find an answer in the external vision. When we ask the question, "Why do we want *to be a global resource for the evolution of human consciousness?*" we get the answer "*to create a values-driven society.*" These statements align, and we can now be sure that the mission and vision statements have integrity.

The four steps in the process are shown in the following diagrams.

Table A8.3 The first "Why?"

	Internal motivation	External motivation
Vision	**Internal vision** To be a global resource for the evolution of human consciousness	**External vision**
Mission	**Why?** … build a worldwide network of change agents committed to cultural transformation	**External mission**

Table A8.4 The second "Why?"

	Internal motivation	External motivation
Vision	**Internal vision** To be a global resource for the evolution of human consciousness	**External vision**
Mission	**Why?** … build a worldwide network of change agents committed to cultural transformation	**External mission** To support leaders in building values-driven organizations

Table A8.5 The third "Why?"

	Internal motivation	External motivation
Vision	**Internal vision** To be a global resource for the evolution of human consciousness	**External vision** To create a values-driven society ⬆
Mission	**Internal mission** To build a worldwide network of change agents committed to cultural transformation	**Why?** … support leaders in building values-driven organizations

Table A8.6 The fourth "Why?"

	Internal motivation	External motivation
Vision	**Why?** … be a global resource for the evolution of human consciousness ⟹	**External vision** To create a values-driven society
Mission	**Internal mission** To build a worldwide network of change agents committed to cultural transformation	**External mission** To support leaders in building values-driven organizations

Here are some of the questions I am often asked about the Four Why's and mission and vision statements in general:

- Why do we need an internal mission and vision? Won't an external mission and vision do?
- Who should be involved in the creation of the mission and vision statements?
- How do you know when you have finished the Four Why's Process?
- Do you have to start the process with the internal mission?

Why is it important to have an internal and external vision and mission?

Clearly you want to have a mission and vision statement that tells your clients or customers what your intention is with regard to the services or products you will provide for them: The question therefore is *why do you also need an internal mission and vision?*

If you have a medium- or large-sized organization you will have a significant number of people who are not involved in the production and delivery of products or services. These are the "back office" inward-facing human resource professionals, accountants, secretaries and clerks whose main focus is on the efficient internal working of the organization. These people need a sense of mission and vision for their work just as much as the outward facing employees. They need to know how the organization is going to grow and develop and what the long-term intention is—in what direction the organization is heading. Whilst it may not be as necessary to have an internal mission and vision in a small organization, the process of thinking about what the organization will look like in the future, and how it is going to grow and develop, is extremely useful.

Who should be involved in the creation of the mission and vision statements?

It is important that the mission and vision of an organization provides inspiration to the people who: (a) are most invested in the long-term success of the organization; (b) represent the key intellectual capital; and (c) have the broadest understanding and view of the business.

For these reasons, I believe the vision and mission should be crafted by the senior group of leaders with inputs from the upper echelons of managers.

Choosing the espoused values of the organization, on the other hand, should involve as many employees as possible.

How do you know when you have finished the Four Why's Process?

If you are facilitating the Four Why's Process, you will know you are finished when the energy in the room shifts to a higher gear—when resonance occurs. It can sometimes take up to two days to craft mission and vision statements. The process is extremely iterative involving back and forth discussions asking the Why's and How's. When you notice people in the room getting more and more excited, that is when you know you are getting close to closure. The excitement of resonance is an energetic reaction that arises from an alignment of the inner purpose of the people in the room with the statements that have been crafted.

Do you have to start with the internal mission?

No, you do not have to start with the internal mission. You can start in any of the four boxes. If for example we had started with our external vision, we would ask "*How are we going to create a values-driven society?*" and then work back to the external mission. The answer is "*by supporting leaders in building values-driven organizations.*" We would then do the same again, asking "*How are we going to support leaders in building values-driven organizations?*" The answer is: "*In order to find our internal mission.*" And so on. The "*Why?*" takes you around the four boxes in one direction and the "*How?*" takes you in the reverse direction.

Annex 9

Guidelines for choosing values and developing mission and vision statements

There are two key factors in getting the "right" values, and mission and vision statements for your organization: The first is "resonance," and the second is "context."

Resonance

Resonance is a term that applies to energy. Resonance occurs when two energy systems that have similar frequencies of vibration meet or come together. The coming together causes an increase in the amplitude of vibration of the energy frequency. This felt increase in vibration energy is known as resonance.

Many people are familiar with the fact that an opera singer can shatter a glass by singing a note that has the same frequency as the resonant frequency of the glass. The glass shatters because of the increase in the amplitude of vibration.

Everything that has physical mass is comprised of vibrating energy, including human beings. The resonant frequency of human beings depends on the level of consciousness they are operating at; which in turn reflects their level of psychological development.

When you grow and evolve in consciousness you will find yourself letting go of some of your friends and connecting with new friends. This is all due to resonance. You let go of the friends you no longer resonate with, and form new friendships with people you do resonate with—people with similar frequencies of vibration as you, people who are operating at a similar level of consciousness. These are people with similar values and similar interests in the world.

Words and phrases (values, and mission and vision statements) also have resonant frequencies. When, for example, you are asked to pick the values that are most important to you, as in the exercise described in Annex 3, or when you are choosing ten personal values as part of a Cultural Values Assessment, the values you pick have a resonant frequency that is the same or very similar to the level of consciousness you are operating at. This is why you pick the values you pick rather than other values. And this is why, in Chapter 7, the values alignment of the small company was at a different level of consciousness than the values alignment of the large company. The average resonant frequency of vibration of the employees was different.

This has significant implications for choosing espoused values and crafting mission and vision statements. When you choose a set of espoused values for an organization, you should involve all employees. You want to choose values that a majority of employees resonate with.

Because in a large organization you will have people at different levels of consciousness—usually a relatively large proportion that are operating with socialized minds in the first three levels of consciousness, a smaller proportion operating with self-authoring minds at Levels 4 and 5 and an even smaller proportion operating with self-transforming minds at Levels 6 and 7, you will need to choose a set of values that are spread over several levels of consciousness, preferably Levels 2, 3, 4 and 5.

If the organization is focused on making a difference in the world and has a greater proportion of "higher consciousness" individuals operating with self-transforming minds, the spread of values should also include values at Levels 6 and 7. For example, a higher consciousness organization would choose *employee fulfilment* as an espoused value, whereas a lower consciousness organization would choose *employee recognition*.

There is nothing right or wrong or better or worse about these choices. The point I am making is that to achieve the highest level of employee engagement, which unlocks the most discretionary energy, you need to choose values that resonate with the levels of consciousness at which your employees operate.

The same principles apply to mission and vision statements. However, as I explained in Annex 8, these statements are best prepared by the higher echelons of management, who have a global overview of the business. This means such statements will normally, but not always, reflect what is important to people who are operating at Levels 4 through 7—those with self-authoring or self-transforming minds.

A typical Level 1 internal mission statement would be: *Profitable growth is our primary purpose.*

A typical Level 2 internal mission statement would be: *To foster a strong sense of loyalty to the company.*

A typical Level 3 internal vision statement would be: *To be the number one provider of [description of services or products] in the world.* This type of statement is about being the *best in the world*. Hence, it is all about self-esteem.

A typical Level 4 internal vision statement would be: *Respect for individual initiative and personal growth.*

A typical Level 5 internal vision statement would be: *Respect and encourage each individual's passion and creativity.*

A typical higher consciousness organization, say Level 6, would have an external vision statement along the lines of: *To develop the finest or best adapted [description of services or products] for the advancement of the welfare of humanity.*

A typical Level 7 external vision statement would be: *We are in the business of preserving the planet's ecology and improving human life.*

Context

The second consideration in choosing the "right" values, and mission and vision statements for your organization is context. The values you choose to guide your decision making depend on what business you are in, where your organization is in its lifecycle, and where the communities and societies you work in are in their evolutionary development—what levels of consciousness they are operating from.

If you are in the petro-chemical, nuclear power or any other industry where if things go wrong people's health could be seriously affected, then *environmental awareness*, *safety* and *employee health* should be high on your agenda as corner-foundational values. In the media world, *creativity* would be an important value to focus on. In consulting, law and police enforcement, *honesty* and *integrity* should be given prominence. In health services, *patient care* should be paramount. If you work in a profession that requires you to do short-term projects for clients, then *teamwork* and *collaboration* will be important values to consider. In banking, where there is little room for product differentiation, *customer service* and *community involvement* are important values. And so on.

Where your organization is in its lifecycle could also influence which values you choose to espouse. Young start-up companies will necessarily want to focus on *innovation* and *creativity*. As companies grow and begin to employ more people, *financial stability* and *employee recognition* will become important. Mature companies that have established themselves in the market place will want to focus on *teamwork* and *collaboration.*

Finally, you need to consider the basic needs of the communities and societies you work in—where they are in the evolution of their consciousness. People who live in poor societies, where survival is difficult, are strongly motivated by the affordability of your products and services. For them, *cost* and *reliability* are important. In such situations, businesses that contribute to the local community by supporting people's basic needs, such as education facilities and health clinics, will find favour with customers. In economically more advanced societies, *quality*, *aftercare services* and *environmental sustainability* will find more favour with customers than low costs and community support.

No matter which stakeholders you consider—employees, customers, partners or investors—the values you choose should support them in meeting their needs. As far as society is concerned, the values you choose should contribute to building a safe, resilient society that takes care of the needs of the present-day population without compromising the needs of future generations. Basically, the values that you espouse should improve the well-being of people and contribute to making the world a better place to live.

When you think this way, and have a larger purpose than just making money, you will engender higher levels of commitment from your employees, customers, partners, investors and the communities and societies in which you operate. In business, like every other domain of life, the golden rule always applies—when you care about the well-being of others, they will care about your well-being.

Because we all have the potential to grow and evolve, individually and collectively, we should be willing to re-examine our values from time to time. As we evolve in consciousness, not only does our way of thinking change, our value priorities change too. Therefore, do not be afraid to change your values and the values of your organization from time to time. As you master satisfying your needs—as you become competent at meeting a particular need—you no longer focus on that value. In such circumstances, you may want to replace that value with a value that reflects your new, more pressing needs. Our values—what we consider important—tend to reflect what we are lacking or what we consider to be fundamentally important to our lives.

Annex 10

The Trust Matrix exercise

To build a strong team there has to be a high level of trust. Trust is the glue that holds people together and the lubricant that allows energy and passion to flow.[1] Trust builds internal cohesion. The ability to display and engender trust corresponds to the fifth level of personal consciousness. Trust increases the speed at which the group is able to accomplish tasks and takes the bureaucracy out of communication. The principal components of trust are character and competence. See Figure A10.1.[2]

Character is a reflection of how you are on the inside, your *intent*, and the level of *integrity* you display in your relationship to others. These depend primarily on the level of development of your emotional intelligence and social intelligence. Intent is demonstrated by caring, transparency and openness; integrity is demonstrated by honesty, fairness and authenticity.

Competence is a reflection of how you are on the outside, your *capability*, and the *results* you achieve in your role. These depend primarily on the level of development of your mental intelligence, your education and what you have learned during your professional career. Capability is demonstrated by skills, knowledge and experience. Results are demonstrated by reputation, credibility and performance.

Even though the focus on competence (capability and results) is important, these are skills that can be learned and accumulate over time. I believe the focus on character (intent and integrity) is more important because these qualities are required for bonding and are much more difficult to develop. Competence is about achieving results; character is about how you achieve them.

In *The Speed of Trust*, Stephen Covey states that trust means confidence and the opposite of trust (distrust) means suspicion. In other words, trust breeds connectedness. When we trust someone, we know he or she will have our interest at heart. Suspicion, on the other hand, breeds separation. When we are suspicious of someone, we will not disclose our innermost thoughts. We keep things back. We avoid connecting with someone we do not trust.

Trust reduces cultural entropy: Suspicion increases cultural entropy. Covey puts it this way: "Trust always affects outcomes—speed and cost. When trust goes up, speed will also go up, and costs will go down. When trust goes down,

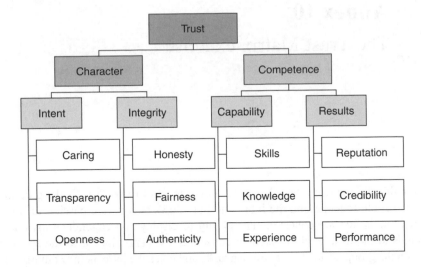

Figure A10.1 The Trust Matrix.

speed will also go down, and costs go up."[3] A 2002 study by Watson Wyatt shows that total return to shareholders in high-trust organizations is almost three times higher than the return in low-trust organizations.[4]

Bestselling author Francis Fukuyama says, "Widespread mistrust in a society ... imposes a kind of tax on all forms of economic activity, a tax that high-trust societies do not have to pay."[5] This tax is a reflection of cultural entropy. Table A10.1 describes each element of the Trust Matrix in more detail.

If you want to evaluate the level of trust in your leadership team or any other working team, hold a workshop and ask each member of the team to identify which elements of the Trust Matrix they believe are the strongest and which are the weakest in the way the team operates.

Give every person five points to allocate to the strengths and five points to allocate to the weaknesses—you can use green and red dots for this purpose (green for strengths and red for weaknesses). They can allocate the points in any combination to each of the 12 components of the Trust Matrix. Give them a few moments to think about how to allocate their dots. In a large team, people can work in pairs. As each person or pair declares their allocation of points, they have to explain to the rest of the group why they chose to allocate their points in that particular way. When everyone has placed their dots on the chart, add up the results for the whole team. You will see immediately which elements of the Trust Matrix are most lacking and which elements are most present.

Based on these findings, begin an open dialogue on how to build on the strengths and minimize the weaknesses that the team has identified. At the end of this discussion, ask each member of the team to state which elements of

Table A10.1 The components of trust in an organizational setting

The components of trust			
Character		Competence	
Intent	Integrity	Capability	Results
Caring To look out for the well-being of the organization and all its employees	Honesty To be truthful and frank in all interpersonal communications	Skills To accomplish professional tasks with ease, speed and proficiency	Reputation To be held in favourable esteem by bosses, peers, subordinates and customers
Transparency To be clear about the motivations that lie behind all decision making	Fairness To act without bias, discrimination, or injustice towards all employees	Knowledge To be very familiar and conversant in a specific topic or subject matter	Credibility To consistently articulate ideas in a convincing and believable manner
Openness To make what is going on in our minds clearly visible to those whom we work with	Authenticity To be consistent and sincere in thought, word and action in all situations	Experience To accumulate practical knowledge through personal observation and experiences	Performance To discharge personal responsibilities with accomplishment and excellence

the Trust Matrix he or she is least competent in and what he or she proposes to do to improve. This exercise makes the whole team accountable for improving the level of trust.

Notes

1 Stephen M.R. Covey, *The Speed of Trust: The One Thing That Changes Everything* (New York: Free Press), 2006.
2 The Trust Matrix was developed by Richard Barrett and inspired by the work of Stephen M.R. Covey.
3 Stephen M.R. Covey, *The Speed of Trust: The One Thing That Changes Everything* (New York: Free Press), 2006, p. 13.
4 Ibid., p. 21.
5 Francis Fukuyama, *Trust: The Social Virtues and the Creation of Prosperity* (New York: Free Press), 2005.

Annex 11

A brief overview of the origins of the Seven Levels of Consciousness Model

I created the Seven Levels of Consciousness Model to give greater definition and understanding of human motivations. The model is based on Abraham Maslow's hierarchy of needs. It was clear to me that Maslow's research and thinking was ahead of his time. Abraham Maslow died in 1970 at age 62, well before the consciousness movement had taken root. I saw that, with some minor changes, his hierarchy could be transposed into a framework of consciousness. In 1996, I set about making these changes by shifting the hierarchy of needs into a model of consciousness. The Seven Levels of Consciousness Model and the changes I made are summarized in Table A11.1 and Figure A11.1.

Changing from needs to consciousness

The first change I made to Maslow's model was to shift the focus from needs to consciousness. It was evident to me that when people have underlying anxieties or subconscious fears about being able to meet their deficiency needs—survival, relationship and self-esteem, their subconscious or conscious minds remain focused on finding ways to satisfy that need. They are focused at the level of consciousness that represents the need they are experiencing.

For example, when a person has a fear-based belief at the survival level of consciousness, no matter how much money he or she earns they will always be left wanting more. For them enough is never enough. Such people can remain focused at the survival level of consciousness all their lives, even though they may have mastered some of their other needs—for example, they may be in a loving relationship and have all their needs met at that level.

Those who have underlying anxieties or subconscious fears about belonging, being accepted or being loved, subconsciously operate from the relationship level of consciousness. They have a strong need to experience affection or affiliation that was not accorded to them in their childhood. As adults they may compromise their own integrity to get these needs met. They want to be liked or they want to be loved. They find it hard to deal with conflicts and may use humour to reduce tensions and bring harmony to a situation. They are afraid of not being loved or accepted. They are dependent on others for the love they crave.

Table A11.1 From Maslow to Barrett

Maslow	Barrett	
Hierarchy of needs	*Levels of consciousness*	
	7	Service
Self-actualization	6	Making a difference
	5	Internal cohesion
Know and understand	4	Transformation
Self-esteem	3	Self-esteem
Belonging	2	Relationship
Safety	1	Survival
Physiological needs		

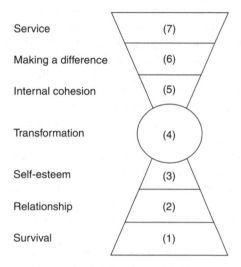

Service (7)

Making a difference (6)

Internal cohesion (5)

Transformation (4)

Self-esteem (3)

Relationship (2)

Survival (1)

Figure A11.1 The Seven Levels of Consciousness Model.

Those who have underlying anxieties or fears about their performance or ranking in relation to their peers subconsciously operate from the level of self-esteem consciousness. They have a strong need for recognition or acknowledgement that they failed to receive in their childhood. As adults they seek power, authority or status to get these needs met. They can never get enough praise or acknowledgement. Consequently, they become perfectionists, workaholics and overachievers. Despite all the accolades they may get, they are always left wanting more.

These considerations led me to recognize that our early maladaptive schema (subconscious fear-based beliefs) directly influence the levels of consciousness we operate from and can block or undermine our ability to shift to the transformation (individuate) and internal cohesion (self-actualize) levels of consciousness.

They show up in our lives as negative (potentially limiting) values such as greed, control, blame, status-seeking, etc.

Expanding the concept of self-actualization

The second change I made was to expand Maslow's concept of self-actualization. I wanted to give more definition to our soul's needs (sometimes referred to as our spiritual needs). I achieved this goal by integrating the concepts associated with the states of consciousness described in Vedic philosophy—soul consciousness, cosmic consciousness, God consciousness and unity consciousness—into the Seven Levels of Consciousness Model.

According to Vedic philosophy our multi-dimensional minds have the ability to experience seven states of consciousness. The first three—waking, dreaming and deep sleep—are part of everyone's daily experience.

In the fourth state of consciousness (soul consciousness) you begin to recognize that you are more than your ego and your physical body. You start to identify with the values and purpose of your soul and its energetic reality. You can experience this state of consciousness through meditation. During meditation the body and its neurological systems become fully relaxed. At the same time your mind basks in the peace that lies beyond space and time.

Beyond soul consciousness is a fifth state of consciousness, known as cosmic consciousness. In this state of consciousness you remain totally identified with your soul at all times, not just when you meditate. You live in a fear-free state of mental and physiological functioning. In this state, you effortlessly fulfil your desires while simultaneously supporting the interests of others. You are able to live your life to its fullest without ever feeling dependent on others for approval. You are the master of your destiny because you have become the servant of your soul.

At the sixth state of consciousness, known as God consciousness, you become aware of the deep level of connection between your soul and all other souls—there remains only the finest sense of separation between you and others. You begin to realize that beyond the soul level of consciousness there are no "others"—we are all individuated aspects of the same universal energy field. When I give to you, I am giving to another aspect of myself. When I criticize you, I am criticizing another aspect of myself.

At the seventh state of consciousness, known as unity consciousness, you become one with all there is. The self fuses with the self-aspect of every other form of creation in total oneness. There is no separation between the knower and the object of knowing. As far as I am aware, this represents the highest state of consciousness that humans can attain.

As you progress through these different stages of consciousness, you experience an increasingly higher and more inclusive sense of identity.

Whereas we all experience the first three states of consciousness—waking, dreaming and sleeping—almost every day of our lives, the frequency of our experiences of the higher states depends on the level of our psychological development and the evolution of our personal consciousness in the waking state—the degree to which we have learned how to release our conscious and subconscious fears and live a values-driven and purpose-driven life.

As we make progress on mastering our basic physical and emotional needs, letting go of our subconscious fear-based beliefs and liberating our souls, we gain more frequent access to the higher states of consciousness. You will recognize these moments quite easily because you will be overcome by feelings of love, joy or bliss. You may feel energy surging or tingling through your body in moments of resonance, or you may feel a profound sense of connection to another person or to the world in general. Sometimes these experiences will last for a short moment, sometimes for several seconds, and if you are lucky, for several days.

Transformation

The first realization I had from studying the states of consciousness described in Vedic philosophy was that the onset of soul consciousness corresponds closely to Maslow's need to "know and understand" and Carl Jung's concept of "individuation." This is the fourth level of consciousness. I called this level "*transformation*." It is an essential precursor to self-actualization. Transformation is the level of consciousness where we begin to inquire into the true nature of who we are, independently of the culture and environment in which we were raised. At this level of consciousness, we are able to step back far enough from the social environment and our parents that have conditioned our beliefs to make our own choices so we can become the author of our own lives and develop our own voice.

The first level of self-actualization

I believe cosmic consciousness corresponds to the first level of self-actualization. I refer to this level of consciousness as "*internal cohesion*," the fifth of the seven levels of consciousness. At this level of consciousness, your ego and your soul blend together in unison. This is the meaning of internal cohesion. At this level of consciousness, you find your personal transcendent purpose (soul's purpose). Your ego and soul become energetically aligned. You become a soul-infused personality wanting to lead a values-driven and purpose-driven life.

The second level of self-actualization

I believe God consciousness corresponds to the second level of self-actualization. I refer to this level of consciousness as "*making a difference*," the sixth of the seven levels of consciousness. At this level, you begin to uncover the deeper attributes of your soul. You develop a sense of knowing that goes beyond logic and reasoning, and your intuition plays a larger role in your decision making. At this level of consciousness, you fully activate your soul's purpose by making a difference in the world. You quickly learn that the degree of difference you make can be significantly enhanced by your ability to collaborate with others who share the same values and a similar mission, vision or purpose.

The third level of self-actualization

I believe unity consciousness corresponds to the third level of self-actualization. I refer to this level of consciousness as "*service*," the seventh of the seven levels of consciousness. We arrive at this level of consciousness when the pursuit of making a difference becomes a way of life. At this level of consciousness, we embark on a life of selfless service. We are at ease with uncertainty and can tap into the deepest sources of wisdom. We learn to operate with humility and compassion. We become one with our soul and we base many of our decisions on our soul's inspiration.

Whilst I fully realize the correlations I have made between the Vedic philosophy and the seven levels of human consciousness may not be exact, they are sufficiently close to warrant our attention and provide insights into the motivations and underlying spiritual significance of the process of self-actualization.

Re-labelling the lower levels of consciousness

The last change I made to Maslow's hierarchy of needs was to combine the physiological survival level with the safety level into a single category. I felt justified in doing this because it is our cells and organs (our body-mind) that essentially care for the physiological needs of our body, not our personal consciousness. Only in times of distress or dysfunction does our personal consciousness intervene in the functioning of the body. For example, our body sends signals to our personal consciousness when it needs food and water or needs to eliminate waste. Our personal consciousness is not in control of these natural functions. I named this combined level "*survival consciousness*" because it focuses on issues of physical survival, physical safety and physical health.

I also renamed the level of love/belonging: I gave it the name "*relationship consciousness*." I felt justified in doing this because our ability to experience a sense of belonging and love depends on the quality of our relationships. I did not rename the self-esteem level. The self-esteem level together with the relationship level represent our emotional needs.

I thus created three levels of human consciousness from the first four levels of Maslow's hierarchy of basic needs: Survival consciousness (survival and safety combined), relationship consciousness (replacing love/belonging) and self-esteem consciousness. Together, these three levels of consciousness represent the emergence and development of the ego—the first three stages of psychological development.

With these three changes to Abraham Maslow's model (needs to consciousness, expanding self-actualization and relabelling the basic needs), I was able to construct a model of consciousness that corresponds to the evolution of the human ego and the activation of the human soul. Every level of the model represents an evolutionary need that is inherent to the human condition.

The needs we have generate motivations that in turn determine our behaviours. If you are unable to meet a particular need, your consciousness will remain focused at that level until you are able to satisfy that need. When we have learned to master the needs of a particular level, we automatically shift the focus of our consciousness and our motivations to satisfying our next most important need—usually a need that exists at the next higher level of consciousness.

Annex 12
Defining consciousness

Philosophers and scientists tend to write about consciousness as if it were a mystery. For me, consciousness is something very practical. I define consciousness as: *Awareness with a purpose*. Whether you are an individual human being, or part of a human group structure, such as an organization, a community or a nation, the purpose that is associated with our awareness is always the same: *To attain, maintain or enhance internal stability and external equilibrium*.

If you as an individual or the group structure you belong to cannot maintain internal stability and external equilibrium in the framework of your existence then you will perish. If you can attain, and maintain, internal stability and external equilibrium, you will continue to survive. If you can enhance your internal stability and external equilibrium, you will thrive. The same is true of all living creatures and the cells, molecules and atoms of which they are made.

Every year thousands of companies go bankrupt, because: (a) they are unable to maintain internal stability due to low levels of employee engagement and high levels of cultural entropy—excessive bureaucracy, political infighting, blame, short-term focus and a lack of clear direction, or (b) they are unable to maintain external equilibrium, because of poor relationships with their customers, partners, workers' unions, shareholders or society.

In order to survive and prosper (maintain internal stability and external equilibrium) as an individual or an organization you need to be able to meet your physical, emotional, mental and spiritual needs (see Figure A12.1).

Individuals maintain internal stability and external equilibrium by first learning how to satisfy their physical needs—gaining sufficient income to cover their needs, as well as creating a safe and secure environment to live in; then learning how to satisfy their emotional needs—building friendships and strong family ties, as well as developing a sense of pride in who they are and the work they do; then learning how to satisfy their mental needs—having the courage to express themselves and explore who they really are; and finally by learning how to satisfy their spiritual needs—finding meaning in their lives, making a difference in the world and serving others.

Organizations maintain their internal stability and external equilibrium in a similar manner: First by learning how to satisfy their physical needs—sufficient income to cover costs and invest in the growth of the company; then by learning

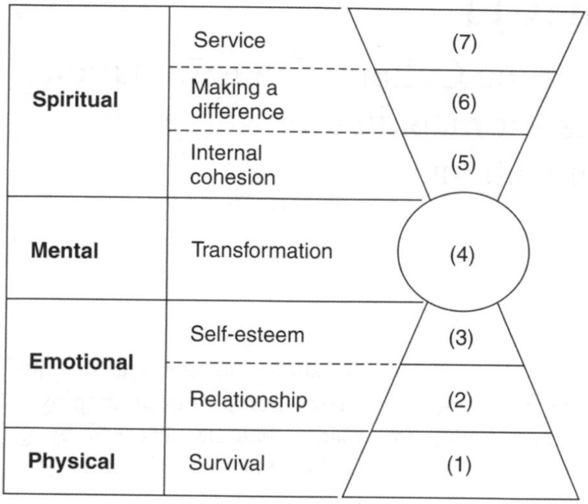

Figure A12.1 The Seven Levels of Consciousness Model.

how to satisfy their emotional needs—building strong relationships with their employees and customers, as well as embracing excellence and quality so that employees feel a sense of pride in performance; then by learning how to satisfy their mental needs—empowering employees by giving them a voice and encouraging them to innovate; and finally by learning how to satisfy their spiritual needs—creating a sense of internal cohesion that maximizes employee creativity, making a bigger difference in the world by collaborating with partners and serving the communities and societies in which they operate.

Based on this approach we can define seven stages in the development of personal and group consciousness. Each stage focuses on a particular existential need that is inherent to the human condition corresponding to the stages of our psychological development. The seven existential needs are the principal motivating forces in all human affairs.

Individuals develop by learning to master the satisfaction of their needs. Individuals (and organizations) that learn how to master all seven needs, without harming or hurting others, operate from full spectrum consciousness. They have the ability to respond appropriately to all life's (and the market place's) challenges.

Annex 13

List of the Cultural Transformation Tools for mapping the values of organizations

Table A13.1 provides a list of the survey instruments that are available for mapping the values of organizational cultures from an employee and customer perspective. More detailed information can be accessed by going to www. valuescentre.com/products__services/ (last accessed 2 April 2013).

Table A13.1 CTT survey instruments for mapping and managing the values of organizations

Name of instrument	Purpose
CVA Cultural Values Assessment	Used to create a comprehensive diagnostic of the culture of an organization or any group of people with a shared purpose. Contains value plots and full written analysis. Measures values alignment, mission alignment and degree of cultural entropy.
CDR Cultural Data Report	Same as a CVA but without the full written analysis. A cost-effective way of mapping the values of a large number of demographics for people who are experienced CTT users. Provides only the essential data.
CER Cultural Evolution Report	Uses successive CVAs to analyze the detailed changes that have taken place in the time period between two Cultural Values Assessments.
SGA Small Group Assessment	Same as a CVA without the full written analysis. A cost-effective way of mapping the values of a group of 15 people or less. Uses standard values templates.
SOA Small Organization Assessment	Same as a CVA without the full written analysis. A cost-effective way of mapping the values of an organization whose entire staff consists of 25 people or less. Uses standard values templates.
Comparison Report	Compares the CVA results of two groups to highlight the key differences. Uses the same values templates for both groups.
Merger/Compatibility Assessment	Uses CVAs of different groups to highlight cultural differences and support cultural integration. Also used for cultural due diligence.
Customer Values Assessment	Same as a CVA using customer feedback to assess the performance of an organization.
EVA Espoused Values Analysis	Provides a quantifiable measure of the degree to which employees feel aligned with the core values of an organization.

Annex 14

Using the BNS to develop a balanced set of strategy indicators

This annex focuses on using the Business Needs Scorecard (BNS) to create a balanced business strategy.

The power of the BNS to improve the performance of an organization increases significantly when the organization's strategic goals and objectives are driven by its mission and vision. The process of developing the indicators for a Business Needs Scorecard that is driven by mission and vision consists of three stages.

Stage 1: Develop the organization's internal and external mission and vision using the "Four Why's" process. Identify the values that support the internal and external motivations.

Stage 2: Identify goals for each category of the scorecard that are in alignment with the organization's missions and visions. Develop corresponding objectives and stretch targets for each goal. Identify for each objective a set of indicators that can be updated on a monthly or quarterly basis.

Stage 3: Identify the values that are necessary to achieve the objectives in each category of the scorecard. Compare these values with the espoused values of the organization. Adjust the organization's or department's values accordingly.

This three-stage approach ensures the close alignment of the goals and objectives of the Business Needs Scorecard with the strategic intent of the mission, vision and values of the organization. The six categories of the Business Needs Scorecard and the key indicators in each category are described below.

Finance

Performance in this category of the BNS is measured by financial indicators. The indicators chosen should reflect the financial goals. These are usually lag indicators. A start-up company, for example, would have indicators related to raising capital. A well-established company would want to measure profit, return on assets and cash reserves, and a publicly traded company would want to measure its stock market price. Over time, as the goals of financial strategy change, the preferred indicators also change. Key lead indicators include brand loyalty and market share.

Fitness

Performance in this category of the BNS is measured by indicators related to continuous improvement of speed, cycle time, quality, productivity and efficiency. The indicators chosen should reflect the organization's goals with regard to improving operating processes. The most important of these processes are those that impact on customers and finances. Thus, the order taking to delivery of product cycle, and the order taking to receiving payment cycle, are often the main targets for corporate fitness. Other important processes for improvement include: the idea generation to product development cycle, and the order taking to completed service cycle. Improvements in processes are often achieved through re-engineering or total quality management. Performance indicators in this category tend to focus on scientific measurement of times and quantities. They are mostly lead indicators—they improve inputs. The improved inputs should show up as outcomes that improve customer satisfaction and retention, improved cash-flow—lag indicators.

External stakeholder relations

Performance in this category of the BNS is measured by indicators that relate to how well the organization is doing in creating strategic alliances with customers, suppliers and partners. The indicators should relate to the organization's strategic alliance and partnership-building goals. Lead indicators in this category should measure the quality of relationships, degree of collaboration and shared values with external partners, suppliers and customers. A modified form of the Cultural Values Assessment can be used to get feedback from customers, suppliers and partners on the quality of the organization's external relationships. Key lag indicators for customers include brand loyalty, customer retention and customer satisfaction. Key lag indicators for suppliers include supplier generated cost efficiency and product innovation improvements.

Evolution

Performance in this category of the BNS is measured by indicators related to how well the organization is doing in product and process innovation—identifying new markets, keeping track of competitors, creating new products and services, adapting its existing products and services to changes in market trends and generating ideas that improve internal processes. The indicators chosen should reflect the organization's research, learning and innovation goals. Performance indicators in this category tend to be qualitative. Key lead indicators will be those that improve creativity—employee development, professional training, information and knowledge sharing and the frequency and quality of external feedback mechanisms. Key lag indicators will be those that measure product innovation and process innovation.

The Cultural Values Assessment together with targeted questionnaires can be used to measure improvements in this category. Values that promote evolution should be showing up in the organization's top ten values. There should also be a strong concentration of values at the transformation level of corporate consciousness. One of the big advantages of the Cultural Values Assessment is that it is able to provide both qualitative and quantitative information that can be compared over time.

Culture

Performance in this category of the BNS is measured by three sets of indicators: Trust/engagement—indicators that reflect intellectual and emotional engagement; direction and communication—indicators that reflect internal cohesion; and supportive environment—indicators that reflect care for employees.

Traditionally, performance indicators in this category have been qualitative. The Cultural Values Assessment changes this situation. It provides both qualitative and quantitative measures of corporate culture. The Cultural Values Assessment makes it very easy to measure changes in the indices, the distribution of consciousness and order of the values. Frequent sample surveys enable an organization to keep in close touch with the evolution of the corporate culture.

Lead indicators in this category should focus on leadership and employee training and improvements that help employees find fulfilment at work. Lag indicators include alignment of culture with espoused values, degree of trust, and employee innovation and creativity.

Societal contribution

Performance in this category of the BNS is measured by indicators that relate to how well the company is doing in becoming a respected member of the community and a good global citizen. The indicators chosen should relate to the organization's environmental and social responsibility goals. Lead indicators in this category could measure funding and volunteer hours. Lag indicators could measure societal goodwill and the impact the organization is having on target groups in the local community and in society at large in quantitative and qualitative terms.

Annex 15
CVA data plots and tables

Table A15.1 provides a list of the data plots and data tables that form part of the output from a CVA.

Table A15.1 Diagrams and tables included in a CVA report

CVA plots and tables	*Description*
Summary page	Highlights the results of the key indicators—personal alignment, cultural alignment and level of cultural entropy, with a brief description of what these mean.
Values plot diagram	Maps the top ten personal values, current culture values and desired culture values to the Seven Levels of Consciousness Model. It reveals the personal motivations of the employees (personal values); the values they experience in the organization (current culture); and the values they believe are necessary to become a high-performance organization (desired culture). Other cultural indicators include: • Number of matching personal and current, current and desired, and personal and desired values—values and mission alignment. • Ratio of values types (IROS)—individual, relationship, organizational and societal. High-performing cultures have no potentially limiting values in the top ten current culture values; three or more matching personal and current culture values; and six or more current culture and desired culture values.
Entropy report table	Breaks down the cultural entropy by level of consciousness and shows how many votes each potentially limiting value received.
Value jumps table	Lists the values that have the largest jump in votes between the current culture and desired culture. These are the values that participants are asking to see more of in the organization.

(Continued)

CVA plots and tables	Description
Positive values distribution diagram	Shows the distribution of all positive personal, current culture and desired culture values, selected by participants, across the Seven Levels of Consciousness Model. It highlights the levels of consciousness where there are significant gaps between the distribution of personal, current and desired culture values. High-performing cultures have a roughly equal distribution of personal, current culture and desired culture values at each level of consciousness.
Business Needs Scorecard (BNS) diagram and table	Provides a business lens on the top current and desired culture values. It maps the top ten current and desired culture values in the values plot to a six-part scorecard including finance, fitness, external stakeholder relations, culture, evolution and societal contribution. The culture area has three subsections: trust/ engagement, direction/communication, supportive environment. High-performing cultures show an even distribution of values across all six categories of the scorecard in the current culture.
Business Needs Scorecard (BNS) values distribution	Shows the percentage distribution of the positive and potentially limiting current culture values across the BNS areas and highlights the areas where there are significant gaps with the positive desired values selected by participants.
Espoused values analysis table	Provides a quantifiable measure of the degree to which participants feel aligned with the core values of an organization and the extent to which they think these values are necessary or desirable. This is an optional table.

Annex 16

Brief description of principal maladaptive schema

Early maladaptive schema lie at the core of the ego's fear-based beliefs, and are the source of most of the emotional trauma and personal dysfunction that we experience in our lives. If the trauma associated with a particular schema is significant, you will need to consult a psychotherapist. If the trauma is "normal" (we all have them to some degree), then you may be able to deal with them through learning personal mastery techniques involving mindfulness, meditation and self-coaching (see Annex 17).

Young and Klosko[1] identify 11 common life traps (negative schema or limiting beliefs), which are listed below under three subheadings—the first three levels of human consciousness.

Safety and security (not safe enough)

Abandonment

If you suffer from the *abandonment* life trap, you feel that the people you love will leave you, and you will end up emotionally isolated forever. This causes you to cling to people.

Mistrust and abuse

The *mistrust and abuse* life trap is the expectation that people will hurt or abuse you in some way—that they will cheat or lie to manipulate, humiliate, physically harm or otherwise take advantage of you. You hide behind a wall of mistrust in order to protect yourself.

Dependence

If you are caught up in the *dependence* life trap, you feel unable to handle everyday life in a competent manner. You use others as a crutch. You need constant support.

Vulnerability

If you are suffering from the *vulnerability* life trap, you live in fear that disaster is about to strike—natural, criminal, medical or financial. You do not feel safe in your world.

Relationships and belonging (not loved enough)

Emotional deprivation

If you are caught up in the *emotional deprivation* life trap you believe that your need for love will never be met adequately by other people. You feel no one truly cares for you.

Social exclusion

If you suffer from the *social exclusion* life trap, you feel separate, isolated and different. You feel excluded and not welcome.

Subjugation

If you are caught up in the *subjugation* life trap, you sacrifice your own needs and desires for the sake of pleasing others or meeting their needs. You do this either through feeling guilty that you hurt other people by putting your own needs first, or feeling fear that you will be punished or abandoned if you disobey.

Self-esteem (not good enough)

Defectiveness

If you suffer from the *defectiveness* life trap, you feel inwardly flawed or "broken." You believe you are fundamentally unlovable or you are not worthy of being respected.

Failure

If you suffer from the *failure* life trap, you feel inadequate in areas of achievement, such as school, work and sports. You believe you have failed relative to your peers.

Unrelenting standards

If you are in the *unrelenting standards* life trap, you continually strive to meet extremely high expectations of yourself. You place excessive emphasis on status, money, achievement, beauty, order or recognition at the expense of happiness, pleasure, health, a sense of accomplishment and satisfying relationships.

Entitlement

Entitlement is associated with the inability to accept realistic limits in life. People in this life trap feel special in that they expect to be able to do, say or have their needs met immediately. They disregard what others consider reasonable.

Note

1 Jeffrey E. Young and Janet S. Klosko, *Reinventing Your Life: How to Break Free From Negative Life Patterns and Feel Good Again* (New York: A Plume Book), 1994, pp. 18–24.

Annex 17

The personal mastery self-coaching process

In *The New Leadership Paradigm* and *What My Soul Told Me* I have put forward an eight-step self-coaching process for managing or mastering your conscious or subconscious fears. An overview of the process is presented in Table A17.1.

You know you have some conscious or subconscious fears when you experience an upset. There are many different levels of upset. They all involve emotions. In all cases, you are dealing with an energetic imbalance that is compromising your internal stability and, therefore, your ability to be happy. You are allowing fear, rather than love, to dominate your motivations. The different levels of upset you can experience include resistance, anxiety, impatience, frustration, anger and rage.

Resistance

You experience *resistance* when someone wants you to do something you don't want to do, or someone has an idea that affects you in some way that is not in alignment with your idea. As soon as you experience resistance, you feel out of alignment. Sometimes, it is difficult to understand why you are feeling resistance. The challenge you face after feeling resistance is to express what is on your mind without fear, without feeling you are compromising your relationship with the person who you are resisting. Say something along the lines of: "I need to tell you that for some reason I am feeling a certain level of resistance to this idea. I am not sure why." The truth of the matter is that you will be compromising your relationship if you do not express what you are feeling. If you don't say anything, it is almost certain that the other person will sense your resistance, so it is best to get it out into the open and be transparent.

Anxiety

You experience *anxiety* when you are holding on to fear-based beliefs about not being able to meet or cope with the stresses involved in meeting your deficiency needs. People with severe subconscious fear-based beliefs live in a constant state of anxiety. Anxiety is an underlying background state of upset that continues until you are able to master your subconscious fears. All other upsets (resistance,

Table A17.1 Steps in managing your conscious and subconscious fears

Step	Action	Explanation
Step 1	Release your emotions	If you are noticing any pent-up emotional energy or hurt, first allow it to dissipate.
Step 2	Engage your self-witness	Employ mindfulness to move into the balcony and observe what is happening to you on the dance floor of your life.
Step 3	Identify your feelings	Name your feelings, describe them to yourself in detail and write them down.
Step 4	Identify your thoughts	Notice what you are thinking about: Write down your thoughts, assumptions and judgments.
Step 5	Identify your fears	What are the fears that lie behind your thoughts? What do you fear may happen? Write down your fears.
Step 6	Identify your needs	What needs do you have that are not being met? These unmet needs are the source of your fears. Write down your needs.
Step 7	Identify your beliefs	Develop belief statements about: (a) what you think you are lacking; and (b) what you think you need.
Step 8	Question your thoughts/beliefs	Differentiate between your perception of what is happening and your reality. Ask yourself, are these beliefs really true? You may want to get a reality check by asking your close friends for their opinions. After you have finished reflecting, reshape your thoughts and beliefs, and re-evaluate your needs.

impatience, frustration, anger and rage) occur in the moment and are situational. Again, if you are able, it is always best to declare how you are feeling; something along the lines of: "I am not sure why, but I have been feeling anxious about this situation for some time."

Impatience

You experience *impatience* when you are not able to get what you want, when you want it; you are unable to live with not getting your needs met immediately. Impatience is a sign that you think your needs are more important than other people's needs or you do not have compassion or understanding for the person who is trying to satisfy your needs.

Frustration

If you can't resolve a situation—get what you need, when you want it—your impatience transforms into *frustration*. You experience frustration (intense dissatisfaction) when, for whatever reason, you are finding it impossible to get your needs met. You begin to take the situation personally. You think to yourself, "Why don't these people recognize how important my needs are?" Your fear that you won't get your needs met begins to mount.

Anger

Continual frustration can lead to *anger*. You experience anger when you feel a sense of injustice or lack of fairness in the way you are being treated by others, or in a situation that thwarts you in some way—when you feel unable to satisfy your unmet needs. Whereas your fear-based emotions were bubbling up in frustration, now, with anger, they get unleashed. When anger is ongoing, it leads to belligerence. When you hold back your anger over a long period, it may eventually surface as *rage*.

Rage

Rage is uncontrollable anger that has possessed your mind and your body. When you are in rage, you are out of control. The rage, like the anger you feel, is never about the situation or event you are experiencing. The situation or event is just the trigger that releases the unexpressed emotions you have been storing in your mind for many years about not getting your needs met. Rage erupts when your fears become visceral.

Wherever you are on the spectrum of upset (from resistance to rage), if you want to improve the situation, you should follow the process of personal mastery shown in Table A17.1. Normally, the amount of time spent in releasing the energy of resistance will be much less than the amount of time spent in releasing the energy of rage—the fear-based beliefs associated with rage usually go back many years and are deeply engrained.

Let us now examine in detail each of the steps involved in learning how to manage your ego's conscious and subconscious fears.

The self-coaching process

Step 1: Release your emotions

The moment you recognize you are upset, say and do as little as possible. This is not the moment for action. It is the moment to stop, pause and release the energy associated with the hurt or pain you are experiencing. It has taken possession of you. Your rational mind is no longer in control. There is no way you can get your needs met while you are in this place.

For your own good, minimize the damage you can do by saying and doing nothing. Pause and take a deep breath, excuse yourself and find a way to release your emotions. Go for a long walk. Go for a workout. Talk to a friend. Shout out loud. Beat the hell out of a cushion. If you are driving, find a place where you can stop and take a break. Get the energy out and I repeat, don't do anything while you are in a state of upset that you might later regret.

Step 2: Engage your self-witness

As soon as you have calmed down, step into the space of the self-witness, and remind yourself that whatever you just felt, you created subconsciously through your beliefs. The other person did not create your feelings. You created them. Nobody has that amount of power or control over you. He or she triggered your emotional upset, anger or resistance. They did not cause it; they just triggered it unknowingly. As soon as you can, ask yourself the following questions:

- What is my body feeling right now? Do I have physical sensations, such as tightness in my throat, a knot in my stomach or an acute sense of alarm?
- What is my ego thinking or feeling right now? Do I feel frightened, scared, inadequate, ignored, put down, not considered, unloved or abandoned?
- You can use the list of feelings in Table A17.2 to help you with this.

The best time to develop your self-witness consciousness is when your life is going well. Practise asking yourself the following question: "*What is alive within me today?*" Observe what comes up for you. What was the first thing that came to your mind? Was it something you are excited about that will happen soon? Was it something that has been worrying you for days? Whatever it was, it is where your consciousness is focused. Observe it for a few minutes. If you need to, find a way to soothe yourself.

Even when you understand the process of personal mastery and know how to move into your self-witness, there may be nothing you can do to stop your emotions and feelings rampaging through your body and mind.

Most people do not realize they can observe their feelings. The thoughts circulating in their minds totally mesmerize them. They spend their lives judging themselves and others. If they have a real or imagined conflict with someone, their minds constantly rehearse what they are going to say to this person when they next meet or get in touch with them on the phone.

When you are operating in this way, you will feel and behave like a victim of your circumstances. You will use words and phrases that suggest to others that you are not responsible for the misfortunes in your life. You will probably be looking for someone or something to blame. This is a sure sign that you are not taking ownership of your thoughts, feelings and emotions. You are not being responsible for the reality you are creating. You are probably not even aware that you created your upset.

Step 3: Identify your feelings

To become adept at using your self-witness, you must learn how to become aware of the ebb and flow of the subtle and not-so-subtle feelings (energies) that are generated by your emotions and the thoughts that go with them. To do this, you need to develop your feeling vocabulary.

The following table provides a brief lexicon of the feelings that your body, ego and soul experience. The feelings that create lightness are driven by alignment (love, connection or life-enhancing energy). The feelings that create heaviness are driven by misalignment (fear, separation or life-depleting energy).

Some of the body's feelings or sensations are driven by the state of your ego-mind, and some may be driven by your soul-mind. For example, when I feel

Table A17.2 Examples of feelings generated by the body-mind, ego-mind and soul-mind

	Body-mind feelings	*Ego-mind feelings*	*Soul-mind feelings*
Lightness and alignment	Energetic	Eager	Bliss
	Enlivened	Friendly	Centred
	Rejuvenated	Happy	Compassionate
	Renewed	Proud	Fulfilled
	Rested	Satisfied	Joyful
	Revived	Secure	Trusting
Heaviness and misalignment	Exhausted	Afraid	Bereaved
	Lethargic	Anxious	Depressed
	Listless	Annoyed	Detached
	Sleepy	Impatient	Grief
	Tired	Jealous	Troubled
	Weary	Stressed	Withdrawn

a deep sense of soul connection to a person or a thought or idea, I will feel energy flowing through my body—a sort of tingling. When this happens, I know my soul is in a state of resonance with that person, thought or idea.

Step 4: Identify your thoughts

Notice the thoughts that are going through your mind. They are usually thoughts of judgment, blame, shame or guilt. Write down your thoughts as soon as you can. Don't hold back. Get them all down. Your ego creates these thoughts to justify and protect itself. They are the clues you need to identify your fears.

Step 5: Identify your fears

In order to work with your fears, you have to not only identify them; you also have to name them. You have to bring them from the darkness of your subconscious into the light of your conscious awareness. Only when they reach your conscious awareness are they malleable to reason and logic. When you experience a negative thought, feeling or emotion, ask yourself: "[Insert your name as if your soul is talking to you], I am noticing that you are angry/upset/impatient/frustrated/sad/ jealous [choose a negative feeling word that describes what is going on inside you]. [Insert your name], what is the fear you are holding on to that caused you to have this negative thought, feeling, or emotion?"

One of the things you can do to help with this process is to carry out an inventory of your fears. Ask yourself the following three questions about your home life and then your work life:

- What fears do I have regarding security/safety/money/protection/survival at home/work?
- What fears do I have regarding friendship/acceptance/connection/love/ belonging/respect at home/work?

- What fears do I have regarding acknowledgement/recognition/encouragement/authority/power/status at home/work?

When you have finished your inventory, make a list of your fears.

Step 6: Identify your needs

Ultimately, every energetic misalignment you experience can be traced back to one of your unmet needs. If you have identified your fears using the three questions above, you will be close to identifying your unmet needs. Ask yourself:

- What unmet needs lie at the source of my fears regarding security/safety/money/protection/survival at home/work?
- What unmet needs lie at the source of my fears regarding friendship/acceptance/connection/love/belonging/respect at home/work?
- What unmet needs lie at the source of my fears regarding acknowledgement/recognition/encouragement/authority/power/status at home/work?

When you have finished your inventory, make a list of your unmet needs.

Step 7: Identify your beliefs

Almost all your fears are based on your subconscious or conscious beliefs about meeting your deficiency needs. There are three types of fear-based beliefs that correspond to your deficiency needs:

- I don't have enough security/safety/money/protection to satisfy my need for survival and safety.
- I don't have enough attention/connection/friendship/physical touch to satisfy my need for love and belonging.
- I don't have enough acknowledgement/encouragement/positive attributes/power/authority/status to satisfy my need for respect and recognition.

If you experienced a lack of protection in your childhood and were unable to resolve the situation by expressing your needs, you will have stored away the anxiety and emotion you felt at that time about feeling vulnerable or abandoned. This subconscious fear-based belief will manifest in your adult life as a lack of trust towards others and possibly a predisposition to wanting to control what is happening around you, or perhaps wanting to hide away from the world. It may cause you to constantly seek reassurance.

If you experienced a lack of love in your childhood and were unable to resolve the situation by expressing your needs, you will have stored away the anxiety and emotion you felt at that time about not feeling accepted or not belonging. This subconscious fear-based belief will manifest in your adult relationships as a neediness for affection or need to be liked.

If you experienced a lack of attention in your childhood and were unable to resolve the situation by expressing your needs, you will have stored away the anxiety and emotion you felt at that time about feeling unworthy. This subconscious fear-based belief will manifest later in your adult life as a need for recognition or acknowledgement and a predisposition for status seeking or overachieving.

At this point you may wish to remind yourself of the early maladaptive schema I listed in Annex 16. Read through the list I provided and identify which of the schema you most experience in your life. If you are earnest in your inquiry, you may want to ask your spouse or friends which of these schema they see in your life.

Now, take the list of your fears created in Step 5 and the list of needs created in Step 6, and put words around them to make them into a belief statement.

- I do not have enough *control* to satisfy my need for safety.
- I do not get enough *love* to satisfy my need for belonging.
- I do not get enough *recognition* to satisfy my need for self-esteem.

Fill in the words in italics that most represent your needs. The belief statement you come up with should state what you are not getting enough of, and what need you have that is not being met.

If your fear-based thought is, "Nobody likes me," turn it into a belief statement by saying, "I do not get enough attention to satisfy my need for acceptance." The following table provides some typical examples of thoughts that have been turned into belief statements.

Table A17.3 Belief statements

Thought	Belief statement
Nobody loves me.	I do not have enough close connections to satisfy my need for love.
I am not liked.	I do not get enough attention to satisfy my need for belonging.
I am not good enough.	I am not recognized enough by others to satisfy my need for self-esteem.
I am ignored.	I am not listened to enough to satisfy my need for respect.
I am a failure.	I do not get enough recognition to satisfy my self-esteem needs.
Nobody listens to me.	I can't get enough attention to satisfy my need for recognition.

Step 8: Question your thoughts/beliefs

The best technique for questioning the reality of your thoughts/beliefs I have come across is known as "the work" invented by Byron Katie Reid.[1] Byron Katie, as she is known, discovered, after much personal suffering, that, when she believed her thoughts, she suffered, but when she didn't believe them, she didn't suffer. This is true for every human being. In other words, suffering is optional. By changing your attitude towards your beliefs, you can find freedom. She learned how to separate herself from her thoughts and become her own self-witness.

Byron Katie's method of self-inquiry is based on four questions and a process called a "turnaround." You begin by identifying a thought or belief related to a topic that causes anxiety or unhappiness. The four questions are:

1. Is this thought/belief true?
2. Can you absolutely know that this thought/belief is true?
3. How do you react? What happens when you believe this thought/belief is true?
4. Who would you be without the thought/belief?

You can use this method on yourself or with another person. Either write your answers down if you are on your own or speak the answers if you are with someone.

So, if you have the thought, "I am a failure," ask yourself, "Is this thought true?" Can you absolutely know this thought is true? When you realize that failure is an artificial construct of the mind with no other reality than the reality you give it, you are free to call it something else that is less emotive and judgmental. For example, you could replace the "failure" thought with, "I am someone who gladly accepts challenges and never gives up."

The turnaround involves taking the thought and turning it around. For example, if your thought was, "My boss doesn't like me," turn it around so it becomes, "My boss does like me." Or make it into a statement about yourself, such as, "I don't like myself" or "I don't like my boss." The purpose of the turnaround is to see if you can also see if any of these new thoughts are true. If they are, then you immediately have a perspective that you had not previously considered that makes the original thought less believable.

When you explore "My boss does like me," think of all the times when your boss has connected with you or helped you. When you explore "I don't like myself," think of the ways that you criticize yourself or the ways in which you deny yourself. See if this relates in any way to the thought you are projecting onto your boss. When you explore "I don't like my boss," examine what you do not like about your boss. See if this relates in any way to what you believe your boss doesn't like about you.

The turnaround really helps you to identify your projections, the judgments your ego is unwilling to accept about itself, that are placed on another person so the ego can feel good. Whatever upsets you in the outer world is very often related in some way to what upsets you about yourself.

I am suggesting you use this methodology because it works. It is an excellent self-coaching tool. It works because you can use it to question your thoughts, assumptions and beliefs, and it helps you to realize that you may have an old belief that is no longer serving you, and you may find that it is no longer true.

Note

1 Byron Katie, *Loving What Is: Four Questions That Can Change Your Life* (New York: Three Rivers Press), 2002.

Annex 18

Tools for mapping the values of individuals and leaders

Table A18.1 provides a list of the survey instruments that are available for mapping the values of individuals, leaders, managers and supervisors. More detailed information can be accessed by going to www.valuescentre.com/products__services/ (last accessed 2 April 2013).

Table A18.1 CTT survey instruments for mapping and managing the values of individuals and leaders

Name of instrument	Purpose
LVA Leadership Values Assessment	Used to provide detailed insights into how the leader's values/ behaviours support or hinder the performance of his or her organization, department or team. Contains value plots and full written analysis. Measures the level of personal entropy and the degree to which the leader's perception of his or her operating style aligns with the perception of his or her superiors, peers and subordinates. Outlines the leader's strengths and areas for development.
LDR Leadership Development Report	A more automated version of the LVA. Instead of allowing the assessors to write free-form responses about the leader's strengths and areas for improvement, the LDR asks assessors to rate the leader against a prescribed set of 26 behaviours that our research has shown to be significant. The LDR delivers a fully automated report, whereas the LVA provides a hand-written report crafted by one of the BVC Assessment Consultants. The LDR uses a standard template of values, whereas the LVA uses a customized template to reflect the cultural attributes of the organization. The LDR is a more cost-effective way of carrying out a large number of leadership feedback assessments.
IVA Individual Values Assessment	Used to assess the degree to which an individual is aligned with the culture of his or her organization (values alignment and mission alignment). This is the same assessment instrument that is used in the preparation of a CVA.
PVA Personal Values Assessment	A simple, free, online survey to give people a deeper understanding of their values. Also provides exercises.

Annex 19

IVA, LVA and LDR data plots and tables

Table A19.1 provides a list of the data plots that form part of the output from an IVA, an LVA and an LDR.

Table A19.1 Diagrams and tables included in an IVA, an LVA and an LDR report

IVA data plots	*Description*
Values plot diagram	Maps the top ten personal values, current culture values and desired culture values to the Seven Levels of Consciousness Model. It reveals the personal motivations of the individual (personal values); the values he or she experiences in the organization (current culture); and the values he or she believes are necessary for his or her organization to achieve its highest performance (desired culture). Other cultural indicators include: • Number of matching personal and current, current and desired, and personal and desired values—values and mission alignment. • Ratio of values types (IROS)—individual, relationship, organizational and societal. If the individual has a strong alignment with the culture there will be no potentially limiting values in the top ten current culture values; three or more matching personal and current culture values; and six or more current culture and desired culture values.
Business Needs Scorecard (BNS) diagram and table	Provides a business lens on the top current and desired culture values chosen by the individual. It maps the top ten current and desired culture values in the values plot to a six-part scorecard including: Finance, fitness, client/supplier relations, culture, evolution and societal contribution. The culture area has three subsections: Trust/engagement, direction/communication, supportive environment.

(*Continued*)

Table A19.1 Continued

LVA data plots	Description
Values plot diagram	Maps the leader's perception of his or her top ten values/behaviours, and the assessors' perception of the leader's top values/behaviours.
Values distribution diagram	Maps the leader's perception of his or her values across the Seven Levels of Consciousness Model (same as values plot diagram), and the distribution of the values/behaviours that represent the perception by the assessors of the leader's values across the Seven Levels of Consciousness Model. Also calculates the level of personal entropy of the leader based on the values/behaviours chosen by the assessors.

LDR data plots	Description
Values plot diagram	Maps the leader's perception of his or her values/behaviours, the assessors' perception of the leader's values/behaviours, and the requested values/behaviours that the assessors would like to see demonstrated by the leader.
Values distribution diagram	Shows the distribution of the leader's perception of his or her values/behaviours, the distribution of the assessors' perception of the leader's values/behaviours, and the distribution of the requested values/behaviours, as well as the level of personal entropy perceived by the leader and the assessors.
Value jumps table	Shows the values that have the greatest increase in the number of votes between the observed value/behaviours and the requested value/behaviours.
Positive values diagram/table	Shows the percentage of positive values/behaviours at each level chosen by the leader, and the percentage of observed and requested values/behaviours at each level chosen by the assessors.
Entropy table	Shows by level, the number of votes for potentially limiting values chosen by the assessors.
Analysis by level	Shows by level, the assessors' perception of the leader's strengths and areas for improvement. The standard list of 26 values/behaviours are rated as either an existing strength, needing some development, needing significant development and not relevant to role.

Index

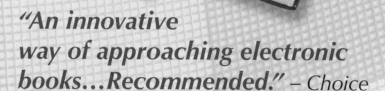

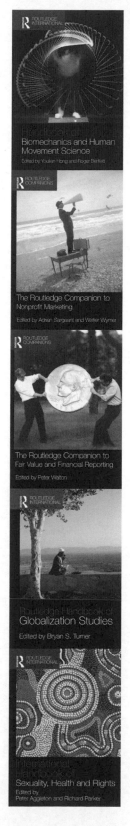